27.12.07

Kwani? is published by KWANI TRUST
P.O Box 2895, 00100
Nairobi,
KENYA
Tel : +254 (0) 20 4451383

First Published 2008
First Impression
ISBN 9966-7182-1-4

Creative Direction / Design Layout: BLACK BUTTERFLY LTD
Art Director: WANGARI NYANJUI
Designers: MAZA LENJO & HAFIZ SHERIFF
Illustrator: MIKE ARAKA

Printed in Mumbai, India by Print House

Kwani Trust is a FORD FOUNDATION GRANTEE
www.kwani.org

For the Concerned Kenyan Writers Group (CKW)

CONTENTS

editorial

THE FIRE NEXT TIME
OR
A HALF-MADE PLACE: BETWEEN TETRA PAKS AND PLASTIC BAGS
In Kenya, democracy is the growth in popularity of bad manners. Anonymous

About six months ago in August I wrote an editorial to appear in the twin issues of *Kwani 5, Part 1* and *2* (this issue). However, that editorial only ran in *Part 1*; I yanked it from this issue- *Part 2*, because what I had to say back then today feels jaded, naïve and foolish as is any attempt to capture public life in this country beyond the span of a few weeks.. The certainties, ideas and chest-thumping of August 2008 are dust motes and vapours. I wake up to the Kenyan morning and look around, and the new day seems to forgive the recent past, and mostly because the public life is one of amnesiac collusion, a physical fact without regret or hope. So I start again.

The two parts of *Kwani? 5* are dedicated to our 'troubles'. And it is exactly 11 months since the two principals of these "troubles,", PNU and ODM, signed a peace accord through President Hon Mwai Kibaki and Hon Raila Odinga and "decided to work together". In just a year there has been a speedy re-make of the initial buddy

movie that was Kenya Part 1- 2002: *On The Road To Democracy*. In quick
succession we have produced Kenya Part 2 – 2007: *The Disaster Movie*, then
Kenya Part 2 ½ – 2009: *The Epic Government Movie*. Two buddies fall out
in the first, have a showdown in the second and are now uneasy "comrades"
in an epic fight for peace against larger and more evil forces like justice. We
await Kenya Part 3 – 2012: *Apocalypse Now*. If we are to believe rumour and
innuendo, we are in trouble in 2012.

Democracy, the wags say, is not so much the practice of the people's
will but the successful political practice of the best players in a marketplace
we call elections. It has been a Kenyan fact for awhile that there is a huge
chasm between the will and call for change that leads people to the polls
every five years and our political realities, the practice of those players who
are successful in the political game – our elected officials. But 2007 was
something special. And yet the will of the masses of new voters in the ill-fated
elections—if recent big issues like the Waki Commission, MPs' salaries (to
tax or not to tax), the Media Bill and that blast from the past, famine, coming
right after the skyrocketing of the price of *unga* and a maize "scandal" are
anything to go by—will not have been realized The people's will – if there
is anything like it, apart from the less sanguine loot, slash and burn or, as
someone aptly put it, "democracy is the growth in popularity of bad manners"
– if we are to gauge from clamour and soundbyte, is that the Waki Report
should be fully implemented, MPs' salaries should be reduced and taxed
and that the media should be left alone. And that corruption has once again
reared its ugly hydra head.

The above issues seem counter to the interests of the successful players in
the game of politics, our elected officials, if their reaction is anything to follow.
Even after the first 100 days of 2008, nothing has really changed. We are in
Naipaul's "half-made State" - a "rhetorical commodity" at best, consistently
engaging in "fairy tales, fantasies, vapors and motes of dust, imported magic
and borrowed images, metaphors, fantasies and applauded lies," fairy tales
that come together in prescriptive spaces such as *The Kenya We Want*.
The Kenya We Live In is something that is never broached in public spaces.
We are great masters at sleight of brain and idea. The politicians sell, and
we, the saps, buy it. We get played by what I see as the smartest people in
Kenya – the un-tourists, the uber- Realists, the clown kings and princes in what
Cameroonian political theorist and academic, Achille Mbembe, has described
as a "strange carnival in which a pervasive atmosphere of macabre conviviality
binds the potentate and the dominated in a drawn out orgy of violence and

death". We buy the idea of a prescriptive leadership rather than a descriptive one; talk about what we want as we skirt the real.

Rewind to April 2006. Day of National Prayer. A building collapses in Kenya, most likely because of the defective nature of building materials and bribes given out by the owners for the law to look the other way. Also, famine rocks North Eastern province, and floods once again wash over Western and Nyanza provinces – all this takes place not because of acts of God but poor planning and a lack of proper management in national food distribution. North Eastern province starves for weeks, ignored by the soundbytes and the politicians' speeches. A building collapses on River Road, and almost the entire Parliament heads there in an afternoon.

Fast forward to 2008 – and not to take away anything from the sad losses of life in the Nakumatt and Molo oil tanker fires, but these incidents overshadow famine in Ukambani. And yet again the same soundbytes. Selective choices.

An anecdote might be appropriate here.

Before we took to prayer back in 2005, one of the biggest worries in this country was the ubiquitous plastic bag. Described as the national flower, it sprouted everywhere. This seems hysterically laughable now in light of the negative ethnicity, crime and insecurity, famine and fire of the last couple of years. And so I went into Mathare, the second biggest slum in Nairobi, a space in which plastic bags sprouted everywhere like flowers, to observe this scourge for an environmental magazine.

My guide took me to a kiosk. We ordered some tea, and the proprietor asked whether I wanted *garatathi*—a plastic bag. The guide reacted to my puzzlement with a grin; in Mathare milk, he explained, comes in plastic bags and is so diluted with water that tea with very little milk was called *garatathi*. So I nodded, yes, tea with very little milk, like the English drink it, would suffice, and the proprietor walked outside whistled and shouted Njoki. She appeared carrying two clear plastic bags with very watery milk. The proprietor handed over some money.

I could not get over that image of milk in see-through plastic bags. These were the same bags that my environmental research told me took five million years to decompose. During my childhood, the milk truck, *lorry ya maziwa,* and the sound of crates spelled Order. Those morning sounds came with family breakfast, school uniforms, early morning traffic – a normal Kenyan morning. Order. Predicatibility. And of course, the milk packs came with a stamp of reassurance – fine print that stated that the milk had been pasteurised.

Seeing milk in clear plastic bags felt to me like the loss of all those things. The plastic bag milk had no licensed stamp, had clearly not been tested with a lactometer. When I thought of the years between milk in packets and plastic-bag milk, the years of predictability and order and the years of informality and chaos,

I felt the sudden breakdown of things. I did not realize how lucky we had been even then, for places like Mathare that were so locked out of regular systems had not let their general anger show. But of course, watered down milk in clear plastic bags is just a beginning; sooner or later such parallel universes, parallel economies, parallel lives, futures and realities and many other things trigger the actualisation of a people's will—the fire this time. Diluted milk in clear plastic bags, open sewers, shit in plastic bags (flying toilets), all these give rise to a people's will, or as others would have it, bad manners democracy the Kenyan way. And at some point, the breakdown since the calm and peace of Nyayo milk and a call for justice took over. And the rest is history.

Nairobi controls at least 45 per cent of our GDP, has roughly 3 million people, 2.1 million of whom live in Nairobi's slums and so-called low income neighbourhoods. Kibera, Mathare and Korogocho, three of the largest slums in Nairobi. It is no coincidence that the greatest violence in the first 100 days of 2008 was witnessed in these three areas. Watching conflagrations in Mathare over the last few years, I suddenly recognized some of the places I'd been back in 2005 and realized another thing was lost: the idea that this country is calm and peaceful. In a week, I now realize that we continue to irrevocably reach a place that is incomparably more disorderly than watery milk. But the scary thing is that public life continues, as if the first 100 days of 2008 had never happened. And so we wait for the fire next time. Enter the writer.

This issue, *Kwani 5 Part 2: Revelation and Conversation* continues where *Part 1* left off trying to explain how the fire began. And in it are expressions about what, why, where, when, who and how it happened. But two events, one purely literary, the other literary but bigger than that, leave me less than elated, or at least with mixed feelings. The first is that I have been lucky enough to have been selected a co-judge of the Commonwealth Regional Prize for Africa. I have over the last four months read a huge part (at least 70 books) of what has been published on the continent. There were only two entries from this region, even as I ask where are the defining texts that preceded what I am calling *The Fire This Time*, and even as a letter from Marjorie Oludhe McGoye (in these pages) sets me straight on what has come before, I am not sure what is currently being attempted at the moment. But maybe the candidates for the Commonwealth Writers Prize are not an indicator of the non-production in this region. Perhaps only Nigerian and South African writers are interested in it; that in a single year South Africa can produce secondary books by Zukiswa Wanner, Mandla Langa and Sindiwe Magona that are eligible for the prize, and Nigeria can produce works by Ifeanyi Ajaegbo, Sefi Atta, Toni Kani. Someone might say that I should consider the literary economies of scale; Nigeria and South Africa have different dynamics. Simple comparisons cannot be made.

I would say that even if this region were allowed a special dispensation to enter books published within the last five years, we would be found wanting. Or they might say, of course, books are being published – look at the Jomo Kenyatta Prize for Literature. Look at the entries for the last five years. My question is why these do not seem as incisive and full of expression, as defining as the the candidates for the Commonwealth Prize are of their respective spaces. Are there even any defining texts for the present or for the future, let alone from the past? I am yet to read a work of which I can say: yes, this is a Nairobi,in all its plastic bag glory, these are the Nakuru, Kisumu and Mombasa that I recognise. The Commonwealth Writers Prize is full of such examples. And yes, not to be wholly dismissive, I would throw Ken Kamoche's *A Fragile Hope*, John Sibi Okumu's *Role Play*, Stanley Gazemba's *The Stone Hills of Maragoli*, Kinyanjui Kombani's *The Villains of Molo*, all in there, as good as anything I've seen as a candidate for this year's prize. But … I know writers who have lots of promise, whom I've known for more than five years, and I want to see things from them.

The other event is the publication of the wonderful, wonderful book by Michela Wrong, *It's Our Turn To Eat*, her take on the contextual social and political space in which John Githongo found himself when he decided to bail. This is a work that reminds anyone who calls themselves a Kenyan writer what their business is and should be. To quote a writer friend's reaction when she looked through it: "Many writers I know are carrying full dossiers, but they are too busy talking rather than writing." More power to Ms Wrong for the book she's written, but where are the other books? Hers takes Kenya on its own terms, and its sings. It encounters, analyses and concludes within a real framework that I recognise, goes beyond the "rhetorical commodity" – and of course, we will be "talking" about this book for years to come. That is its power, that it will create a whole slew of rhetorical commodities of and by itself. Another writer friend told me all during the three years she was writing her book, Kenyan writers were talking. I have no problem with talking. That's what writers do; they need space to vent as they go back and forth from the word processors. I have no problem with prescriptive ideas, playing sap to the politician, imposing theories that might not have much to do with realities on the ground. But who is to say what is reality or what isn't. All I might ask, starting with myself, is that my rhetoric, my theories, my musings--at least even I call myself a writer--can be seen between the pages of a book. That I am part of the defining texts of the here and now, and that they are written down and and not just talked about. Because we really need them, as much as we need many other things, if we are to avoid, faint hope, the fire next time. And if we can't avoid it – the moment has been defined for all to see.

BILLY KAHORA
Kwani Editor

editor's note

Kwani Trust thanks Books First, the Nakumatt Superstore bookseller, for responding graciously instead of angrily to the diatribe against them we published in *Kwani? 4*. Friends have disagreements, and we take it as a mark of our friendship that we can put this one behind us and move forward as partners in the business of putting African writing into African homes.

*

We would also like to take this opportunity to apologise to Shalini Gidoomal for copy errors concerning her story, 'Life of Brian', published in *Kwani? 4*. Further to this, we regret the improper use of the photographs provided by the writer.

We are currently reviewing the above errors and plan to re-publish 'Life of Brian' as part of our Kwani-ni? Series. We regret any inconvenience these errors might have caused.

*

Kwani Trust would also like to thank the African Centre For Open Governance (Africog) who underwrote travel expenses for the creative non-fiction and testimonial sections of both issues of the *Kwani? 5* Twin Edition: Part 1 - 'Maps and Journeys' and Part 2 - 'Revelations and Conversations'.

ACKNOWLEDGEMENTS

Our deepest and most unforgettable thanks go to all the people and organizations that stepped up to confront the beast of Kenya's election crisis. Among many other things, you made this book possible:

Our partners, Wangari Nyanjui of Black Butterfly, illustrator Maza Lenjo, and the intrepid copyeditors who answered our last minute distress call – Keguro Macharia, Lisa Nesbitt, Phyllis Muthoni, Andia Kisia and especially Susan Linee.

Much much love to Professor Wambui Mwangi and GenerationKenya for the endless patience in meeting in person and over e-mail, all the essay writers, poring over pages and pages of huge thoughts and dangerous arguments to come up with the groundbreaking analyses provided in these pages.

We are indebted to the Kenya National Commission on Human Rights (in particular Victor Bwire) and the Kenya Human Rights Commission(Njoki Wamai), who let us to pilfer their database of sinister sms messages, emails and posters that spread across the country before and after the election, as did George Gachara, the National Youth Leader who set up a call centre in January to which people in distress could send text messages for help; the crew at GenerationKenya (Wambui Mwangi again, Jerry Riley and Melissa Wainaina) for all their collaborative support and bright ideas; Judy Ogana and the Godown Arts Centre, for having the audacity to hold an exhibit like 'Kenya Burning' and then letting *Kwani?* reproduce a portion of it; Yasuyoshi Chiba, Boniface Mwangi, and Tom Otieno, the bold photographers who practically gave away the photographs that decorate this volume; Patrick Gathara and Benjamin Luta, the cartoonists who did the same; our testimonial writers: Josh Muraya, Brian Walumbe, Joyce Omondi, Isabella Mugo, Samuel Munene, Mwas Mahugu, Dancurf Obwogi, and Daniel Oballa, who put in many long hours on the road and heard out many hard stories; the Concerned Citizens for Peace coalition, an umbrella group of outstanding Kenyans whose contributions to the post-election dialogue and healing go far beyond their invaluable leads and suggestions to *Kwani?*; the Concerned Kenyan Writers group, who permanently raised the level of discourse and analysis in Kenya, and the Serena hotel for hosting many of their meetings; Daudi Were, *Kwani's* web designer extraordinaire and the man who provided online support to CKW; the British Council, for providing free workshop space to many of our contributors; the Kwani Litfest team, led by Shalini Gidoomal; Dipesh Pabari, for always having a suggestion ready; and the Goethe Institut, for partnering with us and hosting many of our events, not to mention hooking us up with good people like George Gathara.

As well, the following groups and individuals offered their time and assistance in various invaluable ways:

Trust Africa; the Pan African Literary Festival; the African Centre for Open Governance; Oxfam; *Granta* magazine; *Kass* magazine; Carolina for Kibera; Ukoo Flani Mau Mau; Storymoja; Sunday Salon founders Nita Novena and Caroline Berger; the ASPEN writers group; Nation Media Group; Club Soundd, and Kengeles in Lavington Green; Heron Court; Café 64; Jacques Vroom, Yvonne Owuor, Alhaji Burhandi Kyakuhairwe, Dickson Irumba, Ono Muto pa Lajur, Dr. Godfrey Asiimwe, Mwambutsya Ndebeesa, Henry Ford Mirima, Daniel Otieno, John Oyuwa, Riaga Ogallo, David Odira, David Ohingo, John Mwai, Philip Ochieng, Duncan Okello, Aluoka Otieno, Yvonne Owuor, Stella "Steezo" Adams, Elizabeth Mwangi, Afande Malavi, Jane Onyango, and Father Healey.

A big shout out to Books First, the Nakumatt Supermarket bookseller, who suffered the wrath of an angry editor's rant in *Kwani? 04*; rather than pull all our books from their shelves in retaliation, they have graciously agreed to stock *Kwani?* and other African publications in greater numbers than before – they'll even deliver them for free if you order through www.booksfirst.co.ke. Go African writing!

Other bookstores and outfits to whom we are grateful for carrying our books: Book Stop (Yaya Centre), Nu Metro Junction and Westgate, Text Book Centre, Simply Books, Book Point, Prestige Bookshop, Chania Bookshop, Kenya Museum society, Uchumi Supermarket, Suba Books, African Books Collective, Town Center Booksellers, Legacy Books, Nairobi University bookshop, Daystar University Bookshop, and Kenyatta University Bookshop. A special thanks as well to Camerapix for distributing our books at the airport.

Thanks to the advertisers who believe in us: Safaricom (who have been with us since *Kwani? 01*), Resolution Health, Alliance Francaise, British Council, Kenya Film Commission, Lake Nakuru Lodge, and Crater Lake Lodge.

Hey Kwani trustees, Tom Maliti and Malla Muno – we love ya.

And last but most definitely not least, underpinning every last word *Kwani?* ever printed is the incredible support we receive from the Ford Foundation. Asante sana.

Middle Ground

Binyavanga Wainaina

What we will become, after the machete line in the sand was drawn early this year, will only reveal itself in the fullness of time. We are, though, the designers of that future.

To me the large choices are stark: we will either use this as a measure of a thing we never want again, and become a more purposeful whole; or we will continue to stumble and splinter and hide our truths from ourselves.

The source of the biggest shame for me was our middle classes. Not once during those months did we take to the streets in huge numbers to say no; to be seen by the world and ourselves to stand for one reasonable Kenya. Instead we resorted to general sneakiness, snide sms', ethnic paranoia, raising money for arms; flapping our arms about haplessly. When the state said we should stay at home, we did, and hoped the wananchi would stop wananchi-ing about.

In this great test of our tensile strength, we failed to hold ourselves together and separate our reasonableness from the unreason and power games of a cynical political class.

I do not think there is a place outside of this continent so endowed with human skills, able to compete anywhere. But unlike a Ghanaian middle class; or a Nigerian one, our commitment to Kenya is self-serving and cynical. We do not really want to 'be involved'. We do not want to be a part of a country of ideas – we see politics are a network for corporate advancement, for feudal connection; for protections and deals.

Most of all, we have refused to grow up.

For the whole of January, I was calling my father every day, and without really realizing it, I was berating him for not doing enough. My father is retired, and worked day and night for 40 years for this country. It dawned on me that it is not just the wazees who are refusing to let go; the vijanas, some of them now 50 years old, refuse to create a vision for a future, and take charge. Civil Kenya is somebody else's job.

So we all sat, glued to the television, and saying Kofi Annan, Kibaki, Raila, pleeease meet. Somehow this all would boil down to them, and then life would go on, because the safcom share issue was being delayed. So when Condoleezas and Ramophosas, and Gracas were threatening, and cajoling – we remained at home.

What we were doing was passing on the responsibility of our country to others.

Already outrage is being forgotten. It is being suggested everywhere that the Post election madness was a sort of anomaly, let us go back to where we were and it will be alright.

As writers, we have said no to this. We have to look at what happened in the full-face. If there is any single reason this all happened, it is because we have refused to see, hear or listen. We are still consuming ethnic stereotypes created by the British when they first allocated work and power based on their ignorant and simplistic ideas. If we have not yet thought our way past 1910, maybe it is time for us to start to consume ideas more. Our media is obsessed with the soap opera of political characters. So Kenya is really just a theatre-screen where we watch a few people play drama games on stage, and clap, or cry or laugh.

All the many many amazing writers and intellectuals who have given their lives and time to think and help us to think are still knocking on the door of our national television screen, while news programs spend endless time talking about why Martha and Uhuru did what.

We have produced two Kwani's this year. More than ever, we feel a sense o purpose to look hard at ourselves. Yes, we can still laugh at our own foibles; but to stop looking is to make our country as a place as base and crude as our politicians tell us it is.

Let me take a small moment here to say to Philip Ochieng that he has my Nobel. More than anybody, he spoke the truth of his heart and mind, and rose about the general pettiness and melodrama. It seemed almost like he has been waiting his whole life to put all he has gathered together for us now. When I was floundering, it seemed like somebody out there believed in Kenya, was properly outraged.

Binyavanga Wainaina is the founding editor of Kwani?. He holds a Caine Prize for African Writing (2002) for his story 'How To Write About Africa,' and is a contributor to such international publications as National Geographic, Vanity Fair, Granta and many more.

We have refused to grow up

Dear Kwani?

In his introduction to *After the Vote*, Billy Kahora asks 'Where are the texts to explain why, what, where and how' what we blandly call *Mzozo wa baada ya uchaguzi* came about?

Of course it is too soon to answer these questions in depth. But we do not have the equivalent of the Viva supplement that so tellingly encapsulated the events of August 1082. I take it that you refer to literary texts, since there is abundant material for an academic assessment of the situation. One of the most illuminating is Tabitha Kanjo's *Squatters and the rise of Mau Mau*. These are not available, through price and erratic distribution, to the majority of readers, but remember that in normal Kenyan parlance 'novel' does not mean a work of fiction but any volume read for pleasure rather than for passing examinations of the secular or spiritual variety, and the outstanding bestseller of its day in the home-grown Kenya market was *The Kenyatta Succession,* by Philip Ochieng and Joseph Karimi, published by Transafrica in 1980. I do not have figures to compare sales with the other trade phenomenon, Charles Mbugua's *Son of Woman* (EAPH 1971). I am sure if the NCCK report, *The Crooked Arrow,* on the land clashes of the 1990s had been presented to the public it would have had similar sales. Well, Philip is still active and exemplary prose stylist; I don't know whether anyone has asked him what he has up his sleeve.

In fact the consciousness of violence is present in most Kenyan novels and drama, even where it is not the main theme, but we have often shirked the communal aspects of conflict. After all what happened in January was neither unprecedented nor unanticipated. What shocked us was the scale of it.

The novel closest to resolving the topic is *The Last Villains of Molo,* by Kinyanjui Kombani (Acacia 2004), because it depicts a way both perpetrators and victims can go on living after the clashes of the 1990s and effect a partial reconciliation. Though one character is hard to believe in, the writing is not sentimental or evasive. *A Friend of the Court,* by Murioki Ndung'u (Focus 2004), is not easily readable but it depicts a situation in which a political party masterminds communal violence in order to justify a self-fulfilling prophecy and so stay in power. Much of it strikes the reader as credible. Anthony Waweru

Mwangi's poems reflect his experiences of 1992, since repeated; they remain unpublished, but a few pieces have been accepted for the forthcoming *Kwani?* poetry anthology.

Kithaka Mberia's play *Maua Kwenye Jua La Asubuhi*, performed at the Goethe Institut in 2007 and published by Marimba in 2004, is precisely a reflection of communal violence. The staging of non-Kenyan plays can also be used to highlight local situations.

In fact when the West African play *Muntu* was set for Form Four about 1980, the authorities stopped performance because it was said to be too violent. The panel had not observed the violence from the printed page. John Sibi Okumu's *Role Play* (Mvule 2005), first performed in 2004, includes an account of violence against Asians in the 1982 abortive coup. His 2007 play *Minister Karibu* is not yet published. Thomas Akare's *Twilight Women* also attempted to deal with the 1982 situation. I am not sure how much it was edited before eventual publication (Heinemann 1988).

In generalizing, critics must be aware of the amount of unpublished material circulating privately and of pressures to self-censorship.

Akare's earlier book, *The Slums* (Heinemann 1981), which received acclaim in *African Writers' Series*, can represent the many novels which observe ethnic diversity in ordinary Nairobi life without emphasizing it. The same is true of Meja Mwangi's stunning trilogy, *Kill Me Quick* (Heinemann 1970 and AWS), *Going Down River Road* (Heinemann 1975 and AWS) and the award-winning *The Cockroach Dance* (Longman 1979). Keeping a low profile, this author is not always given the pre-eminence he deserves. Even his 'foreign' novels centre on themes relevant to Kenyan experience. Wahome Mutahi's *Three Days on the Cross* (Heinemann 1991) exemplifies those novels which avoid giving identifiable local names to characters and yet clearly describe political realities. Charles Githae's *A Worm in the Head* (Heinemann 1987) draws attention to the difficulties of being a policeman in Kenya.

I had almost forgotten, till taking books from the shelf for reference, Casper Odegi Owuondo's 1992 pamphlet, *The Rise of the 'Cheering Crowd': Fiction and Kenya's Political History*. Not at all of us would agree with him, but it is evidence that the topic was under debate.

Yours Sincerely

Marjorie Oludhe Macgoye

Marjorie Oludhe Macgoye is the author of several poetry collections, children's stories, and novels, including Coming To Birth, winner of the 1986 Sinclair Prize for fiction, and Homing In, runner up for the Jomo Kenyatta Prize for Literature in 1985.

Give War A Chance

Tony Mochama

'O you, o yoo, X 3' (the 'oooos' must be blood curdling)
Abasacha Abagusii, Arise,
Amachuma, aye, bring your chumas,
The vigilante groups of Kisunsungu,
Let us drive the invaders from Sotik-Borabu,
Until they feel kizungu-zungu,
For these Galeoz, are as foreign as wa-zungu,
Chinkororo, let us do the kuku dance
O yoo o yoooooooo – and all that I'm saying,
Is give war a chance!

Luo

Nyanza brothers to the North-
  Tik madek – the presidency was
   Stolen from you, out of Nithii, out of the blue,
    So fuck the fiss – pick up the rocks
    Of Lake Victoria, and let us sssing, in unissoon
    As in the Oldan dayz-
     'Oh Luo Biiro, ya uneyo x 2!
      As we burn down cars, motorists,
       Ukwala, Nyanza General Hospital Russsia sexsion-
       And even any loossse footballs … that we come acrooosss!
       Raila:- the presidency was stolen from ODM.
       But now, 'koro wan gi motorcade, State House and
       … kod ndege madong.' Give War a Chance!

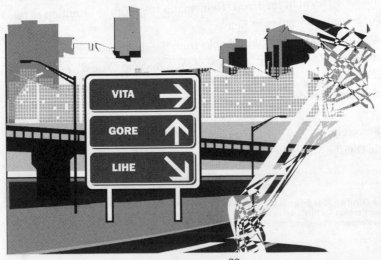

The **Luhyas**, have too many sub-tribes'
To be properly efficient, in the upcoming
Genocide – nevertheless, Mluhya,
Maybe you can start an f.m. retio station
   A Mluhya version of *De Connes Milles* of Rwanda
Exhorting the masses, to cut down the
'Brown' trees and Middle classes. 'Ata wewe Simiyu,
si yu pick up a panga? - wakati sasa umefika, kuuwa watu bure!'
and fack (fuck) the Parasa,
parasas are for peace makers
'Give War a Chance.'

Kalenjin

Ongeringe tien ua wau betusiek kap
Kuitalel arap Samoci hak
Keonde chelelenik en
Mbarenik chok.
Cut hack, choke n chop

Chemogen, the year again, is 1907,
The days of Koitalel Arap Samoei,
That was heaven.
'Beace, Luo, n Unity,' fack Moi, and
Ainamoi-

Resurrect an unelection,
   Erect a road – block,
      And castrate the head of those thieving Kikuyus
         (and the very silly Kisii) some may call it
            'decapitation,' we call it heroism, and, correcting
               Land krifance issue andi historiko in chastice …

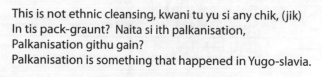

This is not ethnic cleansing, kwani tu yu si any chik, (jik)
In tis pack-graunt? Naita si ith palkanisation,
Palkanisation githu gain?
Palkanisation is something that happened in Yugo-slavia.

This is Kaitalel Arap Samoi, in déjà vu-
And what I am telling you – is 'give war a chance'

The Kikuyu.

They say we moge-koyos stole the erection
No form-frem. Ata Kibaki alisema,
'niliambiwa nilishinda tuuuu!'
Kwani Juja had a census, them versus us,
That concluded Juja doesn't have 189,000 vote -
Ati those numbers are huge, let me tell you,
Juja ni juju – so don't go juu-juu,
Brade sirry … we won the erection
Fair and square, and if you keep evicting us,
From our rightful acres, we'll make you see stars.
Pumbavu – Mau Mau Mungiki,
Tutavunja brade shit mbavu,
Kwani? Who are you? We are Cen-tro,
Some call as Choo-vinests – I'll tell you once,
I wirro terro you twice,
Kishwa gumu
Kumanina!

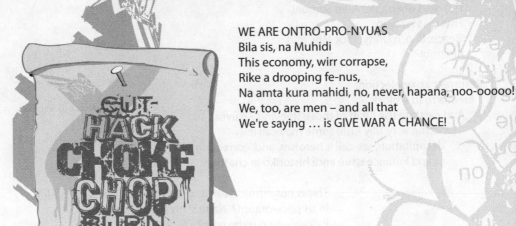

WE ARE ONTRO-PRO-NYUAS
Bila sis, na Muhidi
This economy, wirr corrapse,
Rike a drooping fe-nus,
Na amta kura mahidi, no, never, hapana, noo-ooooo!
We, too, are men – and all that
We're saying … is GIVE WAR A CHANCE!

Sadly, Mombasa road going damn South,
Is not as exciting as the road north to the Rift
So I'll exercise rhythmical thrift and give those people only three verses
Tip-tip, Amani Mukamba,
Lakini Machakos, kweli kuna hamani,
Tip-tip, Ho-ndee M-Kenya,
Hili-pata vice-presidency, Kalonsa Musyoko,
Ata kama. Lyndani Johnnyston alisema
'vice presidency hisi not worth a picha of womu shita!'
Who takes a pho-nglaf of shit?
My name is Kalonsa hand I want to tell Koffi Annan, for heaven's sake,
give war a chance hand go hand aff ha coffee n bun, horr sumthin,'
cos we haff a ouse to burn
yew peace making mouse. Give war a chance.
But where are the Maasai, the Zulus of East Africa?
The fierce noble savage warriors of mzungu love,
In all this affray? Where is William ole Ntimama,
Is he lying low, like an envelope, in Narok, or is he
ad hoc, like an antelope, running wild in Eldoret?
If Kantai can tie a tie
Why kant Ntimama ole Tip Tip, mabibi na mabwana,
GIVE WAR A CHANCE!!

Tony 'Smitta' Mochama is a poet and journalist who lives and works in Nairobi. A Law graduate, Tony is also a vodka connoisseur and gossip columnist extraordinaire. He has a collection of short stories titled The ruins down in Africa, and a book of poetry called What if I am a literary gangster?. He is a member of the Concerned Kenyan Writers group.

GATHARA'S WORLD

During the first 100 days of 2008, Kenyans lost their laughter and that loving feeling – hundreds were killed, thousands displaced. With mainstream journalism engaging in a peace jamboree and setting its own agenda, and literary narratives nothing more than an indulgent dance, photography seemed to capture the complexity of the time. The thought of humour seemed frivolous, satire surreal – at least before Gathara's World. These cartoons have what Kenya needs: a mocking knife edge-iness, bathos and pathos, a real mirror to the absurdity of those times we all want to forget but cannot afford to...

WE CALL UPON OUR SUPPORTERS TO
MAINTAIN PEACEFUL DEMONSTRATIONS AND NOT
LOOT AND DESTROY PROPERTY...
WE STAND FOR PEACE AND URGE YOU TO NOT
KILL INNOCENTS...
WE BELIEVE IN A UNITED KENYA SO PLEASE STOP
ETHNIC CLEANSING...
WE ALSO REQUEST YOU DON'T
DESTROY THE ECONOMY...

JANUARY 5

I live in a middle class housing estate, only a few hundred metres from the Kibera slums. Yet, the place is in no need of police protection. None of the rioting mobs has ventured close in spite of the lack of a police presence. While looting, chaos and death have reigned within the slum, we have been carrying on as normal, only slightly inconvenienced by the fact that the supermarkets, restaurants and bars were closed.

THE VULTURE IS A PATIENT BIRD

ODM-K

JANUARY 9

JANUARY 17

It is sadly ironic that the very clique that used mass action so effectively against Moi in the 90s is now banning that very tactic. We have truly come full circle.

JANUARY 18

Just when we thought the Big Man Syndrome was gone for good, Africa's latest reformer-turned-dictator, following in the footsteps of others like Uganda's Yoweri Museveni and Ethiopia's Meles Zenawi, is now rolling back more than a decade of hard-won freedoms in a desperate bid to hang on to power. The so-called wind of change that was supposed to be sweeping the continent is petering out in front of our eyes and with it go our hopes and dreams.

I am fast tiring of all the excuses our so-called leaders (on both sides) are employing to avoid having the necessary talks so the current crisis can be resolved. So what if Kibaki chose Kalonzo and Karua to represent him? As Yitzhak Rabin noted, one does not make peace with one's friends.

JANUARY 21

GATHARA

BEFORE WE START (SNIFF!) LET'S OBSERVE A MINUTE OF SILENCE IN HONOUR OF ALL KENYANS KILLED IN THE POST-ELECTION VIOLENCE!!

BOO-HOO-HOO-HOO!!

POLITICIANS

MEDIATION PROCESS

JANUARY 30

Military helicopters have opened fire over the heads of warring gangs in Naivasha. Question is: Is Kenya in an undeclared State of Emergency? Having seen pictures and heard media reports of the army patrolling streets in Naivasha and Nakuru, and curfews in these and other areas, I think the police have lost the ability to impose law and order. If this is the case, I wish the government would declare the emergence already. It makes no sense for the Commissioner of Police to insist that the cops are on top of things when we can plainly see evidence to the contrary.

Is this the kind of country we fought so hard to achieve in the '90's?

FEBRUARY 7

We are balkanizing the nation into exclusively tribal regions in the name of peace. Historical grievances and a stolen election are being used as an excuse to commit the most heinous crimes with impunity.

Where is the government? Where are the voices of our famously eloquent civil society? Where is the media? Why are we all silent in the face of this most extreme danger to the fabric of our society?

FEBRUARY 20

Remember the arguments over the "constitutive power" of Kenyans and Kivutha Kibwana's contention that we were not necessarily bound by the dictates of a patently unfair constitution? Remember Kibaki's own push for the IPPG agreement that had no basis in our constitution?

Kibaki did not give us democratic space; he was a beneficiary of it.

35

FINDING HALF A WORM!!!

WHAT'S WORSE THAN FINDING A
WORM
IN YOUR SAFARICOM APPLE?

APRIL 2

APRIL 3

MAY 15

MAY 22

MAY 26

JUNE 13

During his budget speech, wasn't it amazing to hear Finance Minister Amos Kimunya thanking the international community for intervening in the post-election crisis to save Kenya from self-destruction? Wasn't this is the same guy who proclaimed at the time that there was no crisis?

Patrick Gathara studied physics and math at Moi University, played too much rugby, drank too much beer, and spent too little time in the lecture hall and library. He is Secretary General of the Association of East African Cartoonists; his cartoons and writing are updated regularly in 'Gathara's World,' http://gathara.blogspot.com.

Interview with Siri-Kali

*From an interview of Alfred Mutua by Ugandan journalist
Kalundi Serumaga during a visit Mutua paid to Kampala
in January, 2008.*

*The situation today – do you see yourselves getting out of what happened
since December last year – is progress being made?*

Yes, a great deal of progress has been made. We've realized that the
image that has gone out there has been very negative, much more
negative that the reality on the ground, as is always the case.

We have to say things are not hunky dory, they have not been as good as
usual. I'd like first of all to say that, as Kenyans, we're very sad that our

crisis has affected the people of Uganda...we're very very sorry about that, that politics can be used by any person to cause disharmony.

The second thing is to assure all Ugandans that the Kenyan government has been very, very serious; we have ensured that now the roads are open and nobody's being allowed to stop any transportation of goods coming to Uganda. We are providing total security to ensure that the harmony continues between our two countries and that the lifestyles of your people are not affected by Kenya's internal issues.

What about the question of the displaced people; when can they look forward to being able to go home?

Well, the situation on the ground is improving tremendously. For people to go back there are two conditions: One, there has to be a safe environment for them to go back to, and that is what we've created. Second, psychologically they have to be assured that when they go home they will not suffer just because they have gone back home. We know that as soon as a few go back and send word to others that things are fine, the majority will be able to go back home as soon as possible.

You were speaking of image earlier, and I think it's fair to say that Kenyan people have an image in this region of being effective managers, handlers of big corporations and projects. You just look at the financial services sector, the media sector, the hotel sector. Was that all just an image, or what went wrong in the situation where you had the chairman of your electoral commission saying, in the beginning, 'yes, I'm certain' and then at the end, 'I'm not sure anymore'?

The first thing you need to realize is that the image of our country has not been tarnished because of the General Election, it has been tarnished by the violence after the election. I mean, elections have been contested in our country for very many years. The problem that we faced in Kenya is the old style of African leaders who can never accept democracy, leaders who would rather use violence as a way of getting to power, using any means necessary even though there is a democratic system.

Today the American government announced that it is going to bar 10 leaders from travelling to the United States because of ethnic cleansing charges, and the Canadians have followed suit. They believe these people are organized criminals. We have applauded this very much because we know, as the Human Rights Watch report clearly said, according to its investigations, ODM leaders actually organized the massacres that we saw.

So, you are saying that this whole problem was caused by the actions and irresponsible behavior of the ODM leadership?

Yes, clearly. Because this is not the first time that we have had a contested election; we had issues in 1992. This is not the first country either – look at the US when Al Gore won the popular vote, but George Bush won the electoral college vote in a very hotly contested election. What Al Gore did was not to unleash violence or tell his supporters to burn buildings. He went to court, and he followed the procedures.

But we have this mentality in Africa, which is very sad, of some of the older generation, that they have got to unleash violence every time things don't go their way.

So you are blaming...

I'm blaming clearly the ODM leadership.

You extended thanks earlier to President Museveni for his role in this. Would you also be prepared to extend criticism of him, because in 1980 when he lost an election he didn't go to court, he unleashed violence to become president?

I cannot comment on the internal issues of Uganda because I am not versed in them, and I don't comment on Uganda.

What I'm saying clearly is this: What we are seeing in Kenya is that people organized. There is something sinister about people waking up in the morning, going and marking doors with paint, so that that evening young people can go to those doors, rape the women, cut their heads off and torch those buildings. This is clear ethnic cleansing that was targeted at certain communities to drive them away. The blocking of roads, the blocking of highways, burning of tyres, creating this image of fire so as to gain power –

So are you saying that all the displaced people of Kenya are all from only one or two ethnicities? Are you saying that there's not been ethnic cleansing in all directions?

What we are saying is that 95 percent of the people who have been displaced are the ones who have been perceived to be supporting President Kibaki, regardless of their ethnic backgrounds.

In all this crisis, do you think it would have helped if the Electoral Commission of Kenya had been able to come out with a less ambiguous, or double-sided message? Because we saw Kivuitu make the official announcement, then we saw him on the evening of the next day say he was no longer sure.

I don't think so. No form of injustice, no form of anger, no form of question marks, no form of contradictions should justify the raping of small children, should justify the burning of women and children in a church.

Let me give you an example. Two or three days later there was a church that was burnt in Kenya where people had sought safe haven inside the house of God. Young people were taken there by a bus; they surrounded it and they torched it. A woman managed to crawl out, half burning, holding her infant. They took that infant, they threw that infant back into the fire, and, chanting ODM slogans, forced the woman to watch as her child burned and exploded in that fire. This is brutality. Somebody brought those people there. Somebody funded them, with an ethnic agenda, to kill certain people for whatever political gain. The ECK chairman could have contradicted himself 500 times, I don't care. That does not justify the burning of any children.

In your estimation, what do you think the voting pattern really was?

The voting pattern was very close. We are not talking as though Raila won 75 percent of the vote and Kibaki won 25, then declared himself president. No. It was always close to 50-50. The president won by around 200,000 votes.

Given that you're talking about whoever thinks they won, they must accept that a significant portion of the electorate voted against them. Does that mean that whatever the official results coming out of the ECK say, there is a good case now for some sort of power-sharing?

Democracy, as you know, is about winning and losing. Al Gore won the popular vote in the American election; that did not mean that all of a sudden people were calling for power-sharing between Al Gore and George Bush. You can only have one president. That is the essence of democracy. Even if President Kibaki had won by one vote that would not excuse any power sharing just because a substantial amount of people had voted for the other party.

So there's no need for talks?
The talks are not about power-sharing.

Well, that's what the ODM thinks they are about.

The talks are about the way forward. The discussion of some of the issues that arose and how to solve the impasse that is there. But how do you share power in a democracy? We are saying that everything needs to be done within the constitution. Kenya is not a banana republic.

So the clear message is that the ODM can forget about any kind of power-sharing within the current government?
We've told them very clearly that everything has to be done within the framework of the constitution. If every country in the world, every time there was a closely contested election, threw away their constitution for power-sharing, we would have anarchy all over the world.

But you don't have every country in the world where the person in charge of organizing the election starts expressing doubts as to whether this person or that person won. Why are you so insistent on maintaining a disconnection between the ambiguity from the Electoral Commission of Kenya and the subsequent crisis?
Because it's very clear the crisis was perpetuated by the violence that was unleashed. The other thing that is important to note is that the electoral commission chairman has just issued statements and paid for ads to clearly say that he never questioned the credibility of the elections. He has come out and even taken some media houses to court for running with the idea that he questioned the credibility. When he was asked who won, he said, 'as a person I am not allowed by law to say. Because the person who wins is the one that is declared by the ECK, according to the people who voted.'

So he is not the one in charge of counting the votes?
He is not allowed by the constitution to declare his personal opinion. He said, 'personally, as the ECK chairman, I am not supposed to tell you my personal opinion. But as the chairman of the ECK I can tell you I declare

the winner, that's the winner I believe in.'

Let's talk about the violence that you so emphatically denounced... Kenya has one of the biggest slums in African, namely Kibera. Don't you feel that the Kenyan economy has in its own way been inflicting violence of a different kind on ordinary Kenyan people for a very long time?

You've got to realize that for many years the Kenyan economy has been in a slump, dating from long before Kibaki's administration. We've been in recovery mode. For the first time, the Kenyan economy is growing at over seven percent. We've got medicines in hospitals, we've introduced free primary education, we've introduced the Constituency Development Fund targeting the poor across the country. According to the United Nations Development Programme, poverty has been reduced by over 10 percent in the last four years in Kenya.

Is it true that the Kenyatta family owns an entire district where a lot of saisal is grown, in the process of which they displaced an entire tribe of people called the Taveta?

Well, it is true that the Kenyatta government has been recorded in the Ndungu Report on Land Acquisition to have acquired large tracts of landing during their era. Those are issues that have been dealt with and are being dealt with, and some of these issues are the ones that we are talking about in the negotiations. But it wasn't only the Kenyatta family; the Raila family also grabbed large tracts of land.

The question is, how come some of you have ended up so fantastically rich and the rest of you are so incredibly poor, and yet you talk with pride of having the largest economy in the region?

Well, I don't know if you have been to Kenya. I think you are speaking from a point of ignorance here. Because if you go to Kenya and you talk to Kenyans about the last five years, they will tell you that we are poor, but things are getting better. Kenyans are creating wealth across the whole country. Talk to the Kenyan on the ground if you really want to know; don't listen to propaganda from ODM and others.

The real point is this: Kenyatta didn't own much of his land before he became president. When you say 'aquire,' what do you mean? Do you mean he bought it? Did he buy it with stolen money? Did he steal it? What do you mean?

There was a period of time after the colonial powers left when land was given to Kenyans who had taken part in the Mau Mau struggle. It was in that region that such people and families were given huge chunks of land all over the country. This has been reported in an inquiry very clearly so that these anomalies can be corrected.

If you look at the Taveta people that you're talking about, the land that was grabbed was basically part of the national park. We're not talking about land where people existed who were pushed out. So we've not had those issues; the first time we've seen people being pushed out of their land is with what is happening right now in the Rift Valley by honourable Ruto's supporters.

You mean there have never been clashes before in the Rift Valley?
We've not had clashes against people being pushed out. We've had them in the 1990s, when they were organized by the government of President Moi, of which Ruto was an active member at the time.

It's the same crop of people who were with Moi who organized the land clashes in the 1990s who are today organizing the ethnic cleansing with ODM.

So how do you explain the fact that one of the loudest voices in support of President Kibaki's candidature this time around was ex-president Moi?
That is something that is for Moi to decide. We were shocked when Moi started supporting us, because we've been very tough on him. We've been very tough on his sons, we've been very critical of him. I mean we told him to go and attend court –

But you never arrested him for anything.
Well, there was that immunity that applies to former heads of state. Moi stood up and said I will support President Kibaki because I have seen what my former protégé Ruto is trying to make of Kenya.

But if you are so passionately against the violence which Moi endorsed in the 1990s, why wouldn't you come out and say we are not prepared to be politically associated with this man when he came out in support of your campaign in 2007?
The point clearly is this: during the 1990s clashes, families were being displaced and moved, but we did not see the same degree of ethnic as we

are seeing now. Some people got killed, but it was not as horrendous as it is now.

What we have learned is this: History repeats itself. A mistake was done initially of not convicting all those people. If these people are not brought before the International Criminal Court for crimes against humanity, they are going to do it again and again, and who is going to suffer will be my children and your children.

Do you really think by not addressing the massive theft that took place during the Kenyatta years and the Moi years that you are somehow going to create enough wealth to remove the poor from poverty?
I think it's an anomaly to think there was wealth that was stolen and taken away so much that that's what needs to be recovered to create wealth.

When you are trying to grow an economy, it's like growing a business. You look at areas where you can support different structures to ensure that people are able to move from poverty. It's not a matter of taking away from certain people and giving to others. It is, however, very important to get money repatriated and get money that was stolen brought back. That is why this government set up the anti-corruption commission.

But I can tell you, no recovery of funds is going to make the people of Kenya rich. What is going to make the people of Kenya rich is stability, is economic policy that has already been there and reduced poverty by 10 percent.

So, what you are saying is that even if those people who stole the money stay with it, you can go ahead with your economic program?
The money that was stolen is long gone; the people who stole it are long gone. People who are rich in Kenya today are not rich because they stole their money. They are rich because Kenya created an environment of stability that enabled them to make a lot of money.

Kalundi Serumaga is a Ugandan journalist who spent much of his childhood in Kenya. He lives in Kampala, where he works as a media columnist and radio talk show host. He is a member of the Concerned Kenyan Writers group.

SOME FOR THE RECORD

If one examines the record of public comments on Kenya's electoral crisis, one of the most striking qualities to emerge is the universal absence of regret. No one, it seems, feels they did anything wrong.

This is remarkable for an episode that produced about 1500 cadavers. More than a quarter million people were chased into refugee camps and as many more forced into the homes of friends and family living elsewhere in the country, to say nothing of the economic consequences that are just starting to register. Somehow, if the reported statements of politicians and civilians alike are anything to go by, this was all a result of standing up for the truth.

Of course most people have more to say than what the media has time to report. This was the oversight, understandable or otherwise, that the *Kwani?* Testimonial Project was designed to address. It's worth stressing that we never meant it as a witch hunt; we weren't seeking to extract confessions or level accusations. What we wanted was simply to record, in a single document, statements of *what happened* from people involved on all sides of the conflict. From ODM and PNU supporters; from people who threw stones, and people who had stones thrown at them; from farmers and nurses and hustlers, Luos and Kikuyus and Kalenjin...whatever name they went by, we wanted Kenyans to speak for themselves. We wanted them to speak at length and not be reduced to a brief quote in support of someone else's story.

This had to happen quickly, before people could forgive and forget. Because judging by the last 45 years (to take the short view), few of us truly do either. The collective amnesia that so easily settles in and reduces history to a vague euphemism – "our little mistake," to use a Presidential example – has time and again been swept aside when the opportunity came to remember and avenge.

So in March, we armed a team of young writers with voice recorders and sent them across the country to hear what people had to say. When they returned in May, the government had just put Operation Rudi Nyumbani into action, thereby hoping to erase the final and most glaring testament to this country's self-betrayal.

By then we had almost 200 testimonials to sift through, each of which merited a book of its own. Yet compelling as the finalists were individually, the point of the exercise was to lay these accounts side by side; for people to see them as parts of a whole. There are no ultimate truths to be found in the stories that follow, no clear strategies to help us avoid a similar disaster when the next election strikes. But it is our hope that, taken together, these testimonials articulate an essential quality all countries have to accept before they can work as a nation: Unity.

ARNO KOPECKY
Kwani Online Editor

MATHARE

Irene Mueni

How old are you?

20 years.

Why you are living in this IDP camp?

I was living in Mathare and had a Luo boyfriend. I had my own house
but was staying with my mum, who was unwell and weak. Even after the
violence started we didn't know there was a place we could run for refuge,
so one day, as the violence was in its early stages, tear gas was thrown
near the area we were living, and Mum could not stand it. She was taken

to Kenyatta Hospital, where she died.

Before the elections, my boyfriend and I had a good life and nobody imagined anything nasty would happen after we voted. During the campaigns he would ask me who I would vote for and I would say I would support whoever won.

On election day I voted for Kalonzo since I am a Kamba.That day my boyfriend came and said our relationship had ended because I had not supported Raila like he wanted me to. He even said he was to come and force me to join the Luo crowd who were throwing stones at rivals and destroying property. I told him that was something I couldn't do.

That night my boyfriend came with the landlord. They said since I had refused everything they had told me, they had no option but to rape me. Up to that time I had been a virgin. I loved my boyfriend but had not had sex with him.

I was living with a friend of mine at the time. They wanted to rape her but I begged them not to since they didn't know her and she was innocent. It was better if they raped me again. They repeatedly raped me and then ordered me to leave, carrying nothing.

We went to the Air Force camp, where a policeman introduced me to some Red Cross officials who took me to some clinic for treatment.

I have kept it a very big secret, and I have told it to only a few people. When I go to the hospital, I just leave as if going for a walk. I still fear what will happen in the future... I even wonder whether I will be married since I hear no man wants to marry a woman who has been raped.

Charles Mwangi

How old are you?
  I am 22 years old.

How did you end up living here in an IDP camp in Mathare?
  My original home is Burnt Forest, but I used to take maize that I bought

in Narok to sell in Eldoret. During the elections I was in Narok with a cousin, a driver and the turn boy of a lorry I had just hired to transport the maize. When we got near Kericho, we found a bridge we normally used blocked and decided to turn back and pass through Mai Mahiu to get to Nakuru. On our way to Mai Mahiu we found another roadblock, this time manned by soldiers who were escorting vehicles from there because of the disturbances. Once there were enough vehicles for a convoy we were eventually escorted to Mai Mahiu, but before getting to Nakuru someone told us the situation there was just as bad.

The driver and my cousin suggested that we should head for Nairobi and sell the maize there. They said they knew of a place to store the maize till we found a buyer. I knew my cousin had once lived in Nairobi, so I agreed.

We got to Nairobi around 8 a.m and went to St Teresa's in Eastleigh. There, my cousin and the driver informed me that the place would be risky for Kikuyus, and asked me to alight so that they could go and store the maize and come back for me.

I told them I did not think I would be in any danger because of the relative calm, but they consulted a passing stranger in Kalenjin, which I don't speak, and the man approached me saying: 'Just try and see what happens when you go in there as a Kikuyu.'

I agreed to be left behind as long as I remain with the turn boy. My cousin added that since the two of us were to be left behind, they would have to hire some men to offload the bags and that needed money. I gave them Kshs 3000 and was left with Kshs 10.

We waited till late in the afternoon, and the conductor said he couldn't wait any longer. I asked him how he could leave me there as I was new in Nairobi and he retorted I was not his brother - that our relationship was a business one. He left, and I decided to follow the lorry towards Eastleigh. I followed the main street up to the end, but my cousin and the driver were nowhere to be seen.

I went back to St.Teresa's and walked up Juja road until I reached the KAF barracks where a group of people were camped. Because I had nowhere to go I joined them. When I called back home there was no answer. It dawned on me I had been conned.

How long had you known your cousin?

Long enough. We had been doing business together for some time. He was a farmer and I was the broker – I used to purchase maize from him and sell. I think he was influenced by the driver.

Tell me about your family.

We are seven children in my family. I left home on December 12.

You say you called home and found there was no one; did you eventually make contact with your family?

I have talked to my dad who told me that they had been attacked at night. The assailants had tried to burn him in the house, but luckily he was able to escape through a back door they had forgotten to lock, and he hid in a flower bush. They torched the house, and he hid in a dry borehole till he managed to escape to safety the next day.

Do you know who burnt the house?

Yes, they were our friends and neighbours. The Kalenjin had started threatening us in 2003 when my father was constructing his house, telling him he should go and build his house in Central Province. When they came to burn the house they taunted him: 'Didn't we tell you?!'

Michael Waba [Ugandan]

How old are you?

I am 52 years old.

How did you become displaced?

I am victim of the clashes between Luos and Kikuyus. Luos felt that Kikuyus had rigged the elections; at the same time, Luos said Museveni had congratulated Kibaki on his winning, and that's when we Ugandans were attacked.

How long have you been in Kenya?

For 10 years.

Were the attackers just after Ugandans?

Ours was a double tragedy. We lived in a plot owned by a Kikuyu and as the Luos were destroying his houses they discovered we were Ugandans and used the Museveni issue to also attack us.

Had you ever seen anything like this before?

This was the first time I have witnessed violence of this nature. In Uganda war is not tribal, it does not involve civilians; it takes place between soldiers and rebels. Civilians are insulated and can escape. The problem with tribal-based violence is that you have no idea who to trust. Your neighbours can turn against you anytime. It's so crazy.

Did you have friends of other tribes before the election?

We were living as different tribes, Kamba, Luo, Nandi... We were good friends who even discussed politics without any hard feelings.

Did some of the neighbours who turned against you first warn you?

The people who attacked us were individuals we knew, acting as a group. There was nothing we could do.

Stephen Kioko

How old are you?

I am 30 years old.

Where were you living before the elections?

Ngei, Huruma estate - where I still live today.

Where were you on election day?

I was here in Huruma. I cast my vote on the 27th and went to join friends for a drink. My wife was pregnant and had voted earlier and gone back to the house. In the bar we entertained ourselves by trying to predict who would win. Everything was normal.

On the 28th, tension started building in Huruma, but there was still relative calm in my immediate neighbourhood. The men, however, had armed themselves with pangas, bows and arrows and were waiting for any eventuality.

Many shops remained closed, especially kiosks where we could buy greens and vegetables, and by the 30th we had exhausted the stock of food in our house. Someone advised me that I could buy food at the Kariobangi roundabout.

My wife was too afraid to be left alone in the house, and we went with her there where we bought food. On our way back, we found the path we normally used blocked by about 300 ODM supporters. Farther ahead, we could see what we thought were PNU supporters approaching.

Having lived in Huruma for long, I know so many shortcuts and alleys and I used these to get my wife to a friend's place where it was relatively calm. I sneaked back to my house and fetched a bow and some arrows and joined the PNU gang – we managed to chase the ODM people away and they never attacked the area again.

Do you think violence is necessary at times?

Violence is not good. One can get hurt or even killed. But then again, if you are attacked you have to defend yourself in any way possible.

Did you use any of your arrows at that time you were fighting?

Yes, I shot some arrows. When I am provoked I can use them very well.

Do you have regrets perhaps your arrows hurt, or God forbid, killed someone?

I have no regrets - the other side would have done the same. It's called self defense. It's supported by the law.

Kezia Wambui

How old are you?

I am 36 years old.

Where were you living before the elctions?

Mathare, Bondeni. Even after voting I went back to the same place until we were attacked.

How did it happen?

We were attacked around 3 a.m. I was in the house with my husband and a cousin when we heard people knocking and shouting, 'Open up.' I asked who it was but they refused to identify themselves. 'If you don't identify yourself, I will not open up,' I said.

They eventually broke down the door after we exchanged more threats. They claimed they did not want to hurt me, and raped my cousin dragging out my husband who I never saw alive again. They chopped him up and threw him into the river, warning us of dire consequences if we tried to rescue him. Later, they threw a petrol bomb at the village we were living in so I ran away to the camp.

What do you think caused the violence?

Tribalism. The Luo don't like losing. The Kikuyu, on the other hand, are proud. There was also incitement, especially in the Nandi region, where some people may have felt the Kikuyu are wealthy and should be chased away.

Before the elections, did you have friends and neighbours of other tribes?
Yes, we were all mixed, Kikuyus, Kambas Luos and Gisus.

How is your relationship with that neighbors and friends today?
I came to realize that those neighbours were not good people because they are the ones who betrayed us. We were attacked by outsiders from Baba Ndogo and Ngomongo. I wonder how they knew who I was.

At the time the government was not working; there would be GSU trucks passing all over though the fighting continued unabated inside the slums. I didn't understand what was happening. I was totally confused.

Anna Njoki

How old are you?
I am 31 years old.

Where were you living before the elections?
Mathare.

How did you find yourself displaced?
It all started on elections day, the first time I cast a vote. On the 29th people started saying that Kibaki had rigged the elections, and tension started building everywhere. I moved to the Moi Air Force base for safety and stayed there for some time till we heard that calm had returned and that we could go back.

When I went back, my house was invaded by 20 people. Ten of them started ransacking my house while the other 10 took me to the banks of river Ngumba, in Mathare, where eight of them raped me. Before the other two could join in, some neighbours came and rescued me. They took me back, stark naked, to the house.

I was afraid of sleeping in my house, and I asked them to take me to the chief's camp, but they assured me of their protection. That night I didn't sleep and by 5 a.m. I was awake and headed to the chief's camp. When the Red Cross heard my story, they took me to the NCCK Huruma Clinic. From there, I was transferred to Nairobi Women's Hospital where I was cleaned and admitted for a week.

Where was your husband during the attack?
Somehow, he saw the attackers coming and ran away instead of coming to warn me. He left me in the house.

Has this changed how you feel about tribe?
No. It's the Luo who attacked me and it's the Luo who saved me. I love them very much. I was to be beheaded after being raped, and they saved me.

Samuel Munene *is a young Nairobi poet and short story writer. He holds an economics degree from the University of Nairobi.*

57

"NAKURU"

**Muthoni Geoffrey Mwangi, Form Four student at Nakuru Boys
High School**

How were you involved in the election chaos?
When the violence broke out and the Kalenjin were seen approaching
our village, the elders ordered all the men who could fight to protect the
village. I was also called upon. All the women and children were taken
to a church, then the men armed themselves with pangas and rungus.

The Kalenjins had bows and arrows. Our objective was to push them as far away as possible from the women, children and our property. We also used stones and would wait till they shot all their arrows at us then counter-attack with stones and pangas.

During the fighting I saw one of the attendants of a place we went to watch movies struck by an arrow and die. Also, a guy called Maina was killed by his best friend, a Nandi fighting on the other side. Before dying, Maina pleaded with his friend saying: 'Don't kill me, I'm your best friend.' But the friend went ahead and killed him. Because our numbers were few and the Kalenjin had reinforcements, they defeated us. They took our cows, destroyed our electronics and burnt our houses. We were being pushed towards the church, but luckily the police came to our rescue. That was about 7.30 pm on December 29. After that they put up a police camp in our area and promised not to leave.

What was the role of women and children in the chaos?
Some of the women and children came out and gathered stones, putting them in heaps; then the women would carry them in their baskets to the men who were fighting. Also, when we were pushed to the walls by the Kalenjin, the women would incite us by saying that if we couldn't fight and defend them like men, we should give them our trousers and let them fight. This kept us going.

Do you think violence is sometimes necessary?
I asked one of my brother's friends why they were fighting us; he said there is a time to be friends and a time to be enemies.

Mercy Murugi, a volunteer working at the IDP camp in Nakuru's Afraha Stadium

Were you involved in any of the violence?
I was not involved, but I witnessed a lot. I remember one Friday when young Kikuyu men attacked the Luos in Langa Langa, where I live, and in the Ponda Mali area. They would force every man to strip naked and those who were not circumcised were killed.

Do you think violence is sometimes necessary?

No, it's not necessary, especially when people lose their lives and property. Look at this tent [points to a tent in the IDP camp] with seven children who do not know where their parents are. Many other families don't know where their mothers are, wives don't know the whereabouts of their husbands, and some are still missing their children. All this because of violence.

Do you still fear that more violence could erupt?

I'm afraid because this camp is predominantly Luo; and you can't go telling everyone that you are a Kikuyu here. I only give people my first name, Mercy.

What concerns do you have about this IDP camp?

In the IDP camp, cases of HIV/AIDS have really gone up. This is because many young people here have lost hope for a better life and are having unprotected sex. Also, each tent holds two or three families leading to frequent quarrels between children and cleanliness issues between different families.

Naftali Lepo, a 14-year-old Turkana from Rongai, Nakuru

What was an average day like before the election?

I spent most the week with friends, playing all day and coming back in the evening – this is when we were not in school.

Were you involved in any of the fighting or did you see any after the election?

I only saw people fighting. It all started when some people came to our area and lied that Mungiki had been brought into the area. The Kalenjins then armed themselves and waited; they had arrows. When the Mungiki never showed up, the Kalenjins started evicting the Kikuyus. They burnt their houses, cut them into pieces and shot others with their arrows. I saw one Kalenjin man killed by the Kikuyus during the fighting. The Kikuyus who didn't die escaped to the police station. We were protected by the youth and some old men from our area.

Are you still afraid?

I used to wish that darkness would not fall as I would have horrible nightmares of us being evicted. I still have nightmares but not as frequently. I'm also afraid of being chopped up by the Mungiki.

Moses Nginya Nderitu, 18-year old student at Nakuru Boys High School

What was an average day like before the election?

Before December I would wake up at six a.m., milk the cows and take the milk to the dairy, then go to the shamba till 11. I would then do some chores in the house and do some reading later on.

How many tribes lived in your neighborhood?

Most of my neighbors were Kikuyus, Luos and Kalenjins.

Were you involved in any of the fighting or did you see any after the elections?

On January 1, raiders attacked our area at noon. They burnt schools, homes, shambas and took cattle and electronics. One of my aunts was feeding her cattle and was shot through her stomach with an arrow. The attackers also hit her in the mouth with a rungu. My friend's grandmother was also killed and her head cut off. She was 80 years old. There was no transport to carry her to the mortuary, so she was covered with blankets and kept in a house so that she could be buried her the next day.

That night, the raiders came back and burnt the house she was kept in. The next day we found the bones of her remains, which we tried bury, but as this was happening the same raiders struck again, forcing people to run for their lives. There was no time to bury the old woman properly; her remains were just thrown into a hole and covered with a little soil.

Kevin Koros, a 20-year-old actor from Lakeview, near Nakuru.

What was an average day like before the election?

When I was not working or rehearsing with a theatre group I belong to, I would visit a friend and we would have a good time together.

Were you involved in any of the fighting in January?

I was only involved when the people in our estate decided to watch over our area and protect everyone in it. The estate consists of mostly Kikuyus with a few other tribes, including Luos, Luhyas and Kalenjins like myself, but this did not prevent us from working together to protect our lives and property. We worked as one because we believed that it was not people from Nakuru who had brought the violence but other people in the IDP camp at the show ground, Kalenjins from elsewhere and the Mungiki.

I saw someone being killed. It was in town at the matatu station called Kalenjin airport because the matatus there carry people heading into the North Rift. The IDPs who had been evicted from Eldoret were very bitter and were going around looking for Kalenjins to avenge their losses. They came to Kalenjin airport because they knew that's where most of them board matatus to go home. Unfortunately, one man was caught by the group. They beat him up and stabbed him to death. I was not noticed because I look like a Kikuyu.

Lin'Gabo Samson Opanda, 19-year old student at Egerton University

Were you involved in the elections chaos?

I was not involved, but I witnessed a lot of it. When the violence started I remember being seated in town with five of my Kikuyu friends at around two p.m. when all shops and businesses owned by the Kikuyus were closed. Thirty minutes later, youth appeared singing in Kikuyu.

The Kikuyus in Ponda Mali knew what was about to happen, but other tribes were kept in the dark and caught off guard. I felt betrayed because I was seated with five Kikuyu friends and they did not even hint to me that I should take cover. When the Kikuyus came we quickly ran to our houses. I hid myself on the ceiling of our house because the youth targeted mostly men from other tribes. From where I was, I saw a man who had gone to pick his son from school, fearing the violence, captured by the Kikuyu youth who had already started burning and killing people. The man with his son, a kid in Class Seven, were stopped and mercilessly put on fire and burned to death.

One of my neighbors was also killed as he tried to save his brother. Though an ODM fanatic, he could speak Luhya, Luo and Kikuyu. Seeing his brother about to be killed he tried to plead in Kikuyu but this did not help - they were both killed.

Do you think violence is sometimes necessary?
Violence is not a joke. Once you experience firsthand what it can do, you never want to think of it as an option.

How many neighbors and friends do you have today that belong to different tribes?
Most of my neighbors, Luos, Luhyas, and Kalenjins, all fled. Many died. I lost three Luo friends who were fleeing Ponda. I will never ever trust my Kikuyu friends again.

Ogutu Joshua Muraya is a thespian and a student in International Relations at the United States International University.

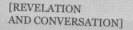

"KISUMU"

Paul Odhiambo, 31

How did you become injured?

On January 9, I was at work trying to get my daily *omena* as a *ngware* guy and a crowd of rowdy youth were demonstrating on Oginga Odinga Street. Tension at this point in Kisumu was pretty high as police had been ruthless over the election period. I can't remember everything right now, but I remember the police arriving on the scene and everybody started running towards the spot where we *ngware* guys normally park. The police followed hot on our heels. I had a customer on my bicycle and did not concentrate on the thudding footsteps coming my way. Then ... it all happened. The police fired a shot into the fleeing crowd, and I felt as if some mysterious force had gotten hold of me and thrown me right into a open nearby sewer. The person I was carrying was hurled into the sewage, but was not hit by a bullet.

How did you get to the hospital?
I don't remember anything, but I am told that after an hour the police came back, bundled me into their vehicle, and rushed me to Nyanza General hospital. I fell into a coma.

How long did you stay in a coma?
(Paul opens his mouth and stammers, but nothing comes out. His wife Eunice Anyango answers.) He could not talk, eat or recognize me for almost three weeks.

When were you informed of your husband's fate?
Three days later, I came to learn about his fate from a friend who had been to the hospital. I had spent a lot of time trying to find out where he was. Was he seeing another woman? Or had thieves beaten him to death somewhere? I didn't know what had happened to him. Then the friend came with the news concerning his whereabouts, telling me that he had been shot by police in the riots and was fighting for his life in Nyanza General Hospital. I rushed to the hospital and found a man who could not even recognize me.

[Paul regains his power of speech] What exactly happened?
The doctors said two bullets had gone through my head, and one was still lodged in the brain.

What treatment did you get while at the hospital?
Because one bullet had gone through my head, the nurses only treated the wound that was left by the bullet.

When did you realize that another bullet was still lodged in your head?
I felt relief after I was discharged from the hospital, but after a couple of weeks I started experiencing strong headaches. One day I collapsed as I was having a bath. I was taken back to the hospital and admitted for three days when they mistakenly treated me for malaria. Things got worse till they did a scan and discovered a bullet still lodged in my skull.

What did they do about it?

The doctors said that the bullet was in too delicate a place to operate. They said just touching it would kill me.

Are you angry with the police?

The police should not have shot at people who were unarmed and running away. That carelessness has turned me into nothing. How will I feed my children? I am scared that my wife will soon tire of caring for me and leave – I am no longer a man. I can not even perform my conjugal duties.

Why haven't you taken a case against the policeman who shot you?

What can a poor man like me do? I do not even know the logistics that are involved.

Judith Kemunto, a 21-year-old Kisii living with her Luo husband and their nine-month old baby at St. Stephen's cathedral, a makeshift Kisumu IDP camp.

Where were you living before you came to St. Stephen's?

We lived in an estate in Naivasha, a two-room house with electricity.

Were there tribal tensions in your old neighborhood before the campaigns started?

We were the only non-Kikuyus where we lived, but no one had any malice towards us. We had been living there for almost a decade and had never experienced *vita za ukabila* (tribal strife)

What finally happened?

I was in the market buying *sukuma wiki* for lunch when the violence broke out. It was shocking. Up to then I had assumed such violence only happened in places like Kisumu and Eldoret and never Naivasha. At the market a woman selling fish almost got killed because she came from a different tribe and was thought to be an ODM supporter.

I left the market and headed straight home with my baby tied on my back. On the way I met a *jirani* coming from the estate. She told me not to go back, that my house was already being emptied of all its contents. The culprits wanted my husband but would certainly vent their anger on me. I was very afraid. I immediately regretted marrying George in the first place. Then he called from work and told me to go to the police station.

How far away was that?

Nearby, but it felt like miles. I passed many burnt bodies along the way. Then I suddenly heard a man's voice commanding me to stop. I turned around and there he was, carrying a panga. I realised that it was one of our neighbours from the estate. He recognised me and was shocked. Knowing that I was Kisii, he did not touch me. He asked me where my husband was and I told him that he was still at work. I reached the police station around four in the afternoon.

Even there our safety was not guaranteed because the Mungiki threatened to invade the post and deal with all of us. People started making transport arrangements to their ancestral homes.

What was going on inside the station?

We held a harambee at the station and hired a lorry and the police escorted us to Kisumu. Along the way we saw burnt houses, tyres everywhere on the roads, human heads used as road blocks.

When will you go home?

We will stay in this camp for as long as it takes. My husband was born out of wedlock, so he has no *dala* to go back to. He cannot go back to his mother's people. We cannot go back to Naivasha unless our safety is guaranteed. Besides, what are we going back to? Our house was burned down with everything in it.

Do you think you can forgive your attackers?

It is hard to forgive. What if they are not in the least remorseful? I can only forgive if they acknowledge the evil of what they did and apologize. Even God forgives only those who ask for forgiveness.

Daniel Oballa is a spoken word artist and a student of Political Science and Literature at the University of Nairobi.

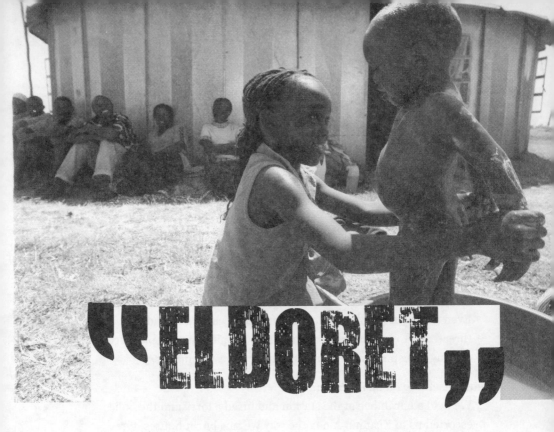

"ELDORET"

Michael Rop, 29, a farmer

How was your life before December?
I am a small-scale farmer here in Eldoret. Before December I was farming in the village of Kuinet.

Did you have friends from other communities?
I had friends from the Luo, Luhya communities but no Kikuyus. I have always disliked them since 1992 when we fought and chased them from the rural areas.

What happened in December?
We started our violence against the Kikuyu long before the eventual tally was released. When the results were announced we had already poured into the roads, torching anything that belonged to a Kikuyu. It was easy to identify such property because we are small-scale traders and milk vendors; we know exactly who owns what property along the way to town.

Schools, hospitals, churches, houses; anything owned by the rival Kikuyu community was razed. We found at least 1000 men armed with crude weapons meeting at a shopping centre to plan their attack. The meeting was chaotic because no one wanted to listen. Enraged youth kept marching towards town, leaving behind a trail of destruction.

Some youths were interested in looting before burning. They could be seen carrying home TVs, computers, generators, fridges and other gadgets even though they did not have electricity in their homes. The police recovered some of the stolen property from one of my neighbours called Maritim. They came directly to his home with a list of things they knew was stolen, as if they had a tip-off.

Will you ever be able to live with Kikuyus?
No! I would advise them to sell back their land and go away. Even if they resettled we will fight again in 2012.

Vincent Murei - 27 year old high school teacher

How was your life before December last year?
I led a normal life and taught in a local school with students from various communities.

Did you have friends and neighbours from different communities?
My girlfriend was Kikuyu and lived in a nearby village. I had several friends from other tribes. Before then we related freely. Since the clashes broke out I've been separated from my fiancée. She now lives amongst the displaced in Limuru. I can no longer interact freely with her, and my interaction with Kikuyus is regarded suspiciously within my community.

Had you seen anything like this before?
In 1997 there were clashes between the Kikuyu and Kalenjin, but they did not reach the levels I witnessed this year.

What happened after the elections?
After results were announced, young people got angry and burned nearby houses and property associated with the Kikuyu. Fadhili Academy, owned

by a wealthy Kikuyu, was set ablaze by three young men even before the results were out. The attacks were spontaneous, even in the nearby villages. Initially they involved a few young people. I was surprised because I was not aware of any such plans.

Some unknown people came to our local shopping centre and tried to calm irate members of the public. One said: 'Lets stay calm until we get a full result from them' – referring to the ODM headquarters.

The following day in the morning a lot of people assembled again in Kuinet shopping centre. People started deliberating on attacks on the Kikuyu community in the neighbourhood and in the outskirts of Eldoret town.

I remember seeing two lorries arrive with covered number plates carrying angry youth singing that they were going to war. Soon after, a group of about 1000 youth wielding all kinds of crude weapons urged everyone to go 'finish the enemy.' They blew horns and all kinds of whistles.

I joined the group and we marched to Kimumu, a place inhabited by Kikuyu. Luckily the police had been dispatched to the junction. A big argument ensued, as a large section of youth did not accept the request by police officers to turn back. Instead, they vowed to march on because they had already walked 20 kilometres. Some were ready to confront the police.

Other members of our group were, in the meantime, destroying everything in sight. Roadside houses and shops were vandalized, as some specialized in looting property. The police were forced to shoot in the air to disperse the crowd.

I began feeling uneasy and slowly retreated behind the mob when one of the protestors throwing stones at the police was shot down.

Why do you think people reacted so violently?
It seems the violence was not only a result of the elections. It appeared more of a fight for resources, with the Kalenjin community looking at the Kikuyu as more favoured in terms of government appointments. This included funding from the Ministry of Youth and loans from microfinance institutions like Equity Bank.

Land was another big subject. The Kalenjin are bitter because they have never been able to move and settle in Central Province, yet the Kikuyu were settled by previous oppressive regimes in the Rift Valley after the 'locals' had been displaced by the colonial government.

How has your life changed since then?

I have had to break up with my girlfriend because we could no longer trust each other – I feared rejection from both sets of parents. A colleague I taught with had her property destroyed and has since been transferred. There has been no replacement, so our workload has increased.

There was a three-week delay in opening the school and we fell behind in our curriculum. My school had students from various communities. Since then, there have been far fewer Kikuyu students.

Do you still talk about politics these days?

Yes I do, though with people I know. It is a way of life and concerns the issues affecting us daily. My greatest fear is that if the issues that caused our woes in December are not addressed the same might recur in the future.

Franklin Kipkirui is an industrial engineer at Unilever East and Southern Africa.

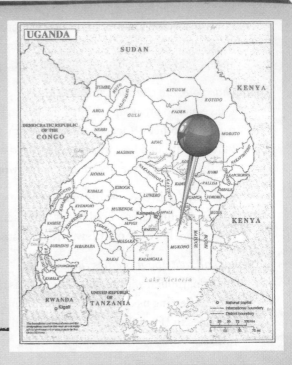

David Kaiza

'Alley-C-Ray,' I catch the cadence despite the sharpness
with which the word was spoken and the roar of the bus engine.

'*Aleesire*,' I write it down. '*Brought.*'

'*Aleese*,' I translate it into Luganda.

Later, when he has wolfed down his bananas, I show the
notebook to my neighbour.

He gives one look, points and says: 'It is written with an E'.

'A-L-E-E-S-E-R-E,' I spell it out. Have to see things from
the perspective of the natives. It's a good mood inside the bus.
Under the early rains, the high hills are a deep, lively green and
the sky's depth of blue well-clouded. For this bunch of Banyoro,
it must feel good leaving Kampala, for the Banyoro people
of western Uganda have little liking for the more numerous,
talkative Baganda of central Uganda.

Living daily with sounds of Baganda speaking their
language, Luganda, spoken Lunyoro feels like going into a
familiar yet enchanted land.

FROM THE LAND OF ANAKA

'*Amazi*,' Baganda sputter out the word for 'water'. As if to show how to make music, Banyoro temporise - '*amaizi*.'

Lunyoro's '*omuka*,' – singular for home – is pronounced so abruptly it ends up sounding like 'smoke' to Luganda ears.

Lunyoro is Luganda set to music, a verbally polyphonic, pleasant sound.

A rotten comparison: Luganda is not even my language, and I am judging Lunyoro through its ears. How very easily it creeps up on you, this century-old disease of colonial scholarship. I am supposed to be different. I am African, level-headed; take people on their own terms. Yet like so many before me who came to Bunyoro through Buganda, I am doing this.

Bunyoro still suffers the problem of not being Buganda enough; its temperament and pride made the British bleed heavily before taking the place in 1899. Unlike Buganda, Bunyoro refused to sign away its kingdom for either gun or mirror.

Her NYANGIRE (NO), asserted in bloody wars lasting many years fending off British colonialism, has come to be as idiosyncratic as NON, or NYET - an N word not for turning – a word that central governments have been weary of.

And Bunyoro paid for its refusal. They say they are the poorest people in Uganda. They say no one travels to Bunyoro because it has no roads. Its poverty is said to be its definitive adjective. I am told the most quintessential word here is *enugu* – social envy.

Nothing is as telling as me travelling there for the first time. I have distant roots there. And I was not even travelling to Bunyoro proper. I was travelling into the Bunyoro of its legend and myths, the Bunyoro of folk lore – which presumably is the version of their country peoples everywhere prefer.

'What is the difference between Luganda and Lunyoro?' I ask my neighbour. One of the Kampala hardware traders who also keeps a farm in Masindi, the second district of the Banyoro, he is most typical of frequent travelers here. Already he has shown me how to bargain down my bus fare; look as if you have your own car; look impatiently at the other buses;

start to walk away.

'The language is a bit slippery,' he tells me, pushing his hands out in a sliding motion. 'You have to maintain your stability. You take time talking. It is not like Luganda where you can jump jump.'

'*Omusaija aleesire amaizi*,' I string my first sentence in Lunyoro. '*The man has brought water.*' There's rhythmic variation in that, a lifted cadence above the atonal Luganda '*Omusajja aleese amazi*'.

Countless Banyoro friends have tried teaching me the language; couldn't go beyond *Oreirota (good morning)*. They retain the hardness of K and G: *KirunGi; not* Luganda's *chirunji*.

I try these words on my tongue. I don't have that stability. I only feel like I'm putting on verbal airs. I must have a Muganda's ears. It is easy picturing a *musajja* (man). '*Omusajja enyini*,' Baganda say. '*A real man.*' Sounds masculine spoken in Luganda. Say *musaija* and the man, now tagged with that ankle bell 'I', becomes a clowning dancer.

Even the landscape agrees. An hour out of Kampala, traveling through Kiboga, a district an hour northwest of Kampala, Buganda's hills go crazy, becoming massive blockers off of horizons. Yet the moment we get into Bunyoro, the land starts to undulate – O-shaped hills pulverised into topographic 'I's.

'Kiboga used to belong to Bunyoro,' my neighbour tells me. I blink. I know little about Bunyoro.

Even at the best of times, Bunyoro and Buganda never saw eye to eye. These hills, continuously fought over, must have changed hands many times – O flattened to I, then re-split; how many *Kasajjas* became *Kasaija* and back again?

The 'I' in my own name now feels like a tribal mark.

The land does not just flatten out. It gets dreamy as the bus pounds along. That faint blue horizon, so distant, is the escarpment of the Western Rift valley, and is called the Blue Mountains; it is the Democratic Republic of Congo. Those palm trees of River Kafu; such ethereal build up. We plunge. It goes.

We heel up. It returns - the Kafu basin, a mock Rift Valley. This must be how the music builds into the language, for is it not the land that gives food that also provokes the muse in us? Such a mystifying esplanade the thousand palm trees raise up. How their fronds stroke those hills, this army of paint brushes. This creator of folklore.

And Bunyoro is a land of myth. An engaging one is that long ago, the birth of the twins who founded Bunyoro-Kitara and Buganda caused an empire to disintegrate into several kingdoms.

But the most riveting myth narrates the appearance of a fair-skinned, long-haired people of magic and spells. They came here for a season, the story goes. One morning, when the people woke up, they had disappeared – a final, self-deleting spell. Only in this landscape can you come up with a story like that. How lovely the land is. A whole people to disappear! That's biblical; *and the land opened and swallowed them up.*

Another myth is that Bunyoro has a royal drum, handed down by the gods which contending princes had to fight for to become king.

Yet there is also a very real twist to Bunyoro, which is the reason I am travelling. It is said that a lot of people in Bunyoro are not Bantu, but that centuries ago the northern Luo crossed the River Nile and settled here. There are so many Luo words in Bunyoro – Luo the language of short, bi-syllabic staccato words (*amooti, adyeri, olimi, araali, atooti, ochaki, oyo, okwir)* – that no one places the Luo connection in league with disappearances. It is all the more fascinating for in the history of Uganda, the Luo and the Bantu hold each other in such contempt it is amazing how a Bantu people could bear even give themselves Luo titles.

Being partly Luo myself, I know that to be Luo in Uganda is to be a walking question mark. So much of Uganda is defined by the numerically superior Bantu-language speakers that they are themselves UGANDA: Ugandans are a noisy, talkative lot when the Bantu are a noisy talkative lot; nice, welcoming and civilised when the Bantu are wearing that hat and a cheating, dishonest lot when a Bantu-speaker behaves like that on Kampala Road. It is an arrangement that leaves the Luo quite out. After a century, to be Luo in Uganda is to not be in, when not out, then to be critically present. It is as if the difficulties the colonialists had in subduing the Luo, and the subsequent failure in turning them into proper colonials translated into a permanent status as outsiders for the Luo. Even now, an attempt at defining Ugandaness brings a weary northward glance.

For 20 years now, one of the most violent wars in the world has embroiled the Luo people.

And in a country where southerners sit in government, to be Luo in northern Uganda, the heartland of Luo-ness; to be Acholi or Lango is to be suspect, encamped or dead.

Except in Bunyoro. Bunyoro is one place where to be Luo is to be inside. I have always found this curious. In any contemplation, it is a matter of some seriousness. The infamous 'unstable' in the politically unstable Uganda arose from the Bantu-Luo failure get along. You had to have been a 12 year-old school boy in 1987 to fully grasp what it felt like when your skin colour and posture attracted and held glances on the streets of Kampala for meters at a time. You had to have had a tire draped round your neck and set on fire in 1986 to grasp why this journey is so consequential for me.

At its height, Bunyoro-Kitara was one of the most powerful and sophisticated empires of pre-colonial Africa, a fact now only associated with the West African empires. Of pride it lacked little. Of confidence, it possessed, in the end, too much. Its fall made the news in Victorian England and cost the British a lot to dismantle. Hence, in Bunyoro-Kitara, you feel something rare for an African – the guilt-free, triumphant dignity which only the bravely-defeated can feel. It approaches irony.

Often, one group will reject another at the local/ethnic level but take pride in their story at the continental/racial level where its people become transformed into Africans/Blacks. Bunyoro was a fierce enemy of Buganda and people in Buganda instinctively react to that. But the story of Bunyoro was of

African determination. At this level, Buganda then embraces Bunyoro as heroic.

No one says precisely when the kingdom started, but there are those willing to say it was there long before Islam became a religion. Much of the East Africa that came to be the British and Belgian colonies was once Bunyoro-Kitara.

Today this past is seen through the drama and savagery that convulsed the kingdom in its struggle to remain independent of British colonialism in the 1890s. Yet it does not quite start there for the drama itself is seen through the career of Bunyoro's last real king.

Omukama (King) Kabalega began his reign violently around the time Oscar Wilde started to be noticed in London and ended it even more violently a year before Wilde died. (He was born 10 years before Wilde). Yet again, his entire career is seen through the last six years of a 20-year reign when he led his people against colonialism. The war that would mark his passage into posterity was well underway by the time *The Importance of Being Earnest* premiered in London.

In taking Bunyoro from Kabalega, Britain was to lose 10 percent of its fighting men. Interestingly, some 2000 kilometers north of Bunyoro, around about the same time, the British were laying to ruins Omdurman in revenge for a humiliating defeat years earlier by the Mahdi. Kabalega was to be captured in 1899, exiled to Seychelles till 1923 and Bunyoro to never be forgiven by Britain. As recently as 2007, the government of Uganda had to persuade Bunyoro not to spoil the visit of Queen Elizabeth to the country with a planned demonstration. It's tense. One hundred years since British forces waged a war Bunyoro now says was genocidal, the British crown has been taken to court. Bunyoro is demanding trillions of dollars from London in compensation for lives, land and property destroyed then.

The war that Lord Kitchener waged against the Sudanese of Omdurman has been retold several times as a measure of how savagely vengeful the colonialist could get when beaten by a 'primitive' army. It is told because it was a war against a

Muslim people. The war in Bunyoro surpassed that of Sudan both in duration and extent of destruction. But it was a war against a people who do not belong to a politically significant group, just one of the numerous incidences not told because of the remoteness of the places where they took place.

For Ugandans, Kabalega is forever frozen in memory as a black and white figure on a throne: the regal aspect of his confident, aloof, imperious gaze captured in a photograph, becomes also the imagining of Bunyoro-Kitara. A curious detail in that photo, which is the way details have of throwing photographic interpretation wide, is how much polished to a shine is the leather shoe – maybe a size 10 - showing underneath his robes. Bunyoro was perhaps not manufacturing patent leather shoes but it had for centuries traded a great deal with the coast.

Hence, an entry into the six centuries of Bunyoro-Kitara is a tight squeeze through this peephole. It reveals little, for it is said that the height of Bunyoro's achievement came not in the 1890s, but perhaps 500 years before that when through a yet un-detailed ingenuity, its princes spread out to become rulers of other lands and peoples.

Distant now, unrecorded but passed on across the 20-odd generations, the very foundations of these kingdoms are in dispute. Legend describes the appearance of a strange people some 600-700 years ago. European anthropology and archeology say those strangers were of Caucasian extract and hence capable of setting up the government systems that were by any measure, rather elaborate and enduring. The claim is dubiously pre-war Darwinianism, an attractive speculation powerful enough to have drawn even the attention of the Nazis.

Bunyoro, too, combines the complex and often impossible relationship between Bantu and Luo language speakers. As similar to the south as oil to water, the north, settled mainly by the Luo-speaking peoples of dark skin, reserved character, and a diet that sets it culturally apart, they are citizens of a Uganda too driving for southern acceptance.

A country the size of Tanzania might have handled this

history better, for having less geography than history has not helped Uganda much.

The texture of this history is woven into the rhythm and beat of words that come with it: *Kabalega* the name of power, *Babiito,* the central dynasty of that power, *Oyo, Cwa, Nyimba, Duhaga,* the names of Bunyoro-Kitara kings; *Disappear,* the curious description of what happened to the Cwezi; *Cwezi,* the legendary dynasty thrown out of the empire (and existence it is sometimes said) by the Luo in about 1400. *Luo:* the trail I am on. *Emin Pasha, Sir Samuel Baker:* colonial agents whose appearance marked the beginning of the kingdom's absorption into Uganda. *Abarusuura:* name of the famous army that Kabalega led against the British. *Empaako:* word means endearment name, perhaps the only place in the world in which people are called by a praise name. *Nyabongo, Nyatworo, Rukidi-Mpuga;* perhaps the most evocative Ugandan names for seven centuries.

By far the most potent word, *Babiito,* is a word like none in Uganda. But first an aside: like so many words in southern Uganda, it is a misconstruction. The *Ba* that prefixes *ganda, ntu, nyoro,* is a false prefix. Rather the definite article 'the' pressed into the proper noun, it introduces a booming, perhaps forbidding sonority to southern and western Ugandan ethnic names.

Outsiders made the mistake. But in these parts of the world, often shaped by more powerful outsiders, we adopt their mistakes as the right way of calling ourselves. To write 'The Baganda' is in effect to write 'The theganda'.

Neither do outsiders have to be of European stock. When Baganda travelers went to Teso, that ethnic group with some similarity to the Luo who are also found in western Kenya, they could not hold the Teso 'L' on their heavy tongues. 'Soroti', they trammeled over Solot (a rock under which Soroti town sits). 'I come from Soroti,' the Teso have said for decades. I will stick to the mistakes now in common usage.

Babiito, in any form - *'Babiito', 'Ababiito' Jabiito* or the *Biito* - correct or otherwise, vibrates with power, its potency rammed down for centuries into the minds of Ugandans. A legendary yet living dynasty, unmatched arbiters of power, the Babiito were for five centuries the formulators and wielders of authority and are said to still occupy all the thrones of Uganda's kingdoms.

Babiito are found in Hoima, so I headed there, Hoima, also the heartland of the Banyoro.

The journey is over in three hours.

Hoima disappoints.

Derelict beyond belief, its streets dusty, corners suspiciously smelly, it is a typical Ugandan town. Rather than legendary warrior-kings, I am invaded by an army of secondhand-shirted, bicycle-taxi riders who have not heard of deodorant.

'Are you Luo?'

'We are not Luo. We don't even think about them. In fact we don't like them. Obote and Amin* brought suffering.' Amooti is categorical. He has a taxi. He also agrees to translate for me. We make friends. 'People here think they just kill their own people,' he explains, referring to the two-decade war in northern Uganda.

In nearly all of Uganda since 1986, most people are proud not to be Luo. But being Luo is as much about the language as a certain kind of appearance. Idi Amin Dada, president of Uganda from 1971 to 1979 who brought a notoriety Ugandans hate, was a Kakwa from the West Nile. But he was tall and dark. To be Luo is to be northern, so the eastern Luo are thought not precisely of as Luo.

'I am not Luo,' Amooti tells me.

'*Amooti*,' I say.

'Yes?'

But I was only greeting him. His name comes from the Luo word, *Amoot* (greeting), the Os slow, drawn out.

'Madi? We don't have a Madi language department,' the secretary in the Institute of Languages at Makerere University tells me. 'You go to the Department of Luo. *Aanti*, it is from up there, we lump them together.'

'Where can I find Luo people in Bunyoro then?' I ask Amooti.

'Those ends of Kiryandongo, Bweyale side. Abachope,' he says. 'But there is trouble there. The Balalo have taken over the land there.'

He corrects me. 'It's not Lunyoro. It's Runyoro.' His U is equally drawn out, the Os quick stabs. Later I am told the language is Runya-Kitara.

Two groups not thought too highly of then – Luo and the nomadic, cattle-herding Ba*lalo*. The Luo people who occupy northern Bunyoro are also referred to as Ba*cope*. The story is told that during the Arab slave trade, the men ran away, and when the slavers asked where they were, the women replied 'There are no men' – *'Coo pe'*. A story of desperation has over the ages become a comical reference, a reductive quip that subtracts the dignity of this Luo group now referred to as *'Chope'*. A fascinating aspect of strife-ridden places in much of Africa is how tragedy can be transmuted to comedy, perhaps the therapy which leaves Africa unburdened by unbearable memory.

I am in western Uganda now, and I am reminded that it is only here that ethnic background hardens into a stifling atmosphere of castes; skin colour and shape of nose vetted like moral crimes. *'We are not Luo.'*

It's only my first afternoon. I consider my notebook: obviously there is complexity in the relationship between Banyoro and that Luo connection. But before the 1400s, there had been another heritage, the shadowy Cwezi, preceded by an even more shadowy group, the Batembuzi whose dynasty is said to have lasted 22 kings. No one knows who the Batembuzi were, less even who the Cwezi were. It is the Babiito who are well-known because they are still on the thrones.

You can't trust what's given as fact. Accounts say the Cwezi ruled for less than 50 years, from around 1350 AD to 1390 AD before the Babiito took over. Others say it was

1500 AD. The Buganda kingdom started simultaneously with Bunyoro. Buganda has had more kings because it is said that contenders for the throne rarely waited for the king's natural death. It is said that between the two Cwezi kings, there was an interregnum when the kingdom was headed by a regent. I am not too keen on facts anyway. As a story teller, it is the common man's narrative that excites me. A history belongs to a people. How they use it to shape their self-image and how that in itself comes to shape power is fact of another kind – not measurable but it draws lines and fences between peoples, forces them to transmute events into myths.

The Luo trail is an attractive one for the immense impact their passage through these regions as they migrated from the Bar el Ghazel in Sudan, had on the peoples they came into contact with. Centuries later, they are still viewed with a mixture of reluctance and hostility. But it is also the story of meaning, identity and projection at a time when local identity is imposing itself against global uniformity.

The same factors that led the Luo to leave the Sudan are still active; the wars between the Arabs of Sudan and the Africans in Southern Sudan and Darfur as well as the Sahara desert, are the same that led to the Luo migration.

It is the impact of man on man. But it is also the impact of environment on human affairs.

The Bar el Ghazel is the prehistory. Still continuing is the character of Bunyoro. Narratives about ethnicity in Africa tend to present identity as absolute. But co-option, compromise, adoption, splits and crossovers are more the norm, a consideration intensified by the difficult relationship that Bunyoro has with its Luo past.

I doubt this will be easy. There have been 100 years of Christianity in Bunyoro. A large sugar cane plantation here has defined Bunyoro and put it on the business pages of newspapers – which was about all it managed to do since 'Kabarega' was hot in Victorian English pages. That is, until oil was discovered here. I can picture headlines in *The New Vision* and *The Monitor*, 10, 20 years from now: *'Bunyoro radicals sabotage pipeline', 'Babiito barons caught siphoning oil.'*

Then there are the telephone companies: MTN, Warid, Uganda Telecom and Celtel's colours are a uniform of houses, not just here, but all over Uganda.

Christianity, the big plantation with its colonial baggage, the multinational telecoms companies with their crass globalism, the oil company and its explosive, rancid capitalism – these obscure the memories of what I am looking for. In this respect, I have also come to a New York or Paris or London marketing executive's outpost. How many of the replies I will receive will have been shaped by a Nokia ring tone or that line *'Celtel, Everywhere you go'*?

How much of the past will be read through 100 years of Christian parochialism? How much will be a reaction to the loss of hope in Uganda as a country, rather than Bunyoro as a society?

So far, I have a word – *Enugu*. But Banyoro's complaints about underdevelopment I read to mean 'not as affluent as Buganda'. If they want to see actual poverty, let them travel to eastern Uganda, or even take a second look at Buganda. After a century of neglect, even the Banyoro refract their self- image through the Buganda prism.

Whatever authentic sound I hear of Bunyoro's Luo past, it will be through these thick walls, a bland echo saying as much about the walls as the quality of the sound itself.

SATURDAY

Rukuraato Hall is an arresting building. Massive pillars, exo-skeletal, the architecture post-war Brutalism but like so much of Bunyoro, derelict, impressive in structure only. Erected during the reign of Omukama Tito Winyi – 26th on the Babiito throne – in the 1950s and 60s, it housed the Bunyoro-Kitara parliament, the *Rukuraato*.

It gives a glimpse into the last of the confidence Bunyoro once projected. It sat its clan representatives. Now it seats local government councilors.

Araali sits there too. His seat is a broken 1960s design steel chair, now listing and half leant against the wall. This affords him a cozy, sofa-like tilt. He spends much time here, looking down as visitors approach the raw concrete hall. At 11 o'clock, it is shining pleasantly. A handful of cows crop the lawn. Palm trees once meant to rarify the air now look afflicted by the dereliction. Even the cattle look derelict. But Araali is the most derelict of all. He is in his late 60s, already wasted bodily, shirt unbuttoned, septuagenarian geriatrics unimpressive, collapsed plexus muscles like a bunch of chapatti fold over an ungainly tummy.

He speaks little English.

'He says you are going to use the information to make money,' Amooti translates.

Araali blinks insulted at the 2000 Uganda shillings. Even 12,000 shillings is too little for him to persuade someone to give us a book.

'At that price we can only read half the book,' Amooti translates.

Araali sulks. He has the casing of an audio cassette in hand, the paper slip on which he was calligraphing the letter A as we came up.

The history book is a pamphlet in Runya-Kitara which contains Primary Three social studies history. It is many years since those days, and I listen to the interrupted, quizzical read-the-Runya-Kitara, translate-with-difficulty-into-English which Amooti is doing.

Araali is absorbed on the letter C. Amooti draws his forehead.

Neither likes being interrupted. This is something I am starting to learn here. The Banyoro I have met so far are an assertive lot. When they start a sentence, they must finish it. I feel a bit of *nyangire* in this ram-rod straight walk, this hard stare into your eyes I have not met in Buganda.

'H.'

I am told the story of palace intrigue in 1870:

'Before Omukama Kyebambe Kamurasi died, he wanted Kabalega to succeed him as Omukama,' Amooti translates.

85

'A meeting was held on succession attended by Omudaya, Dwetakya, Kasami, Nyukahia, and Rwigwirwa. But Nyaika did not attend.'

'Who is Nyaika?'

'He was Kabalega's brother who wanted to become omukama.'

Kabalega became king at about the age of 24 and died at about 77 in 1923. By all accounts, he was a very grasping man, said to have lost his throne to a rival at 27 and grabbed it back before long. A king had to be constantly on the watch. Bunyoro never had a crown prince. Being born to the king gave you a running chance for the crown but weak-wristed princes never made it. The story is told that in Buganda, kings resorted to killing their own sons in order to remain on the throne a bit longer.

'After the burial of Kamurasi, Kamihanda, who also wanted the drum, sent his men, to trick Kabalega. Kabalega arrested and hanged all of them. He sent others. Kabalega hanged all of them. By this time, all the clan chiefs were on Kabalega's side. One man who was not, called Omudaya, said 'this Kabalega is a problem'. He escaped from here with all his cattle before Kabalega came and took the royal drum.'

Araali has printed an O. He stops and places a hand on the book.

'He says we have to add more money.'

'We have no more money. Look, I know how Kabalega became king. Can you tell me about clans and groups in Bunyoro...?' I stop. Araali has added L and I ask, in Luganda: 'Lwaaki owaandika Acholi?' 'Why are you writing Acholi?'

'Acholi visitors came here and left us with their music.'

This is the conversation I want. Araali notices his influence going, and he looks distracted. So many researchers come here keen on finding out about Bunyoro-Kitara; is it true these kingdoms were founded by Africans or by a branch of the Caucasian race? Were Cwezi black people or white people? Were they Egyptian or Ethiopian? Surely Africans are incapable of building such elaborate government systems? So many

THIS IS SOMETHING I AM STARTING TO LEARN HERE. THE BANYORO I HAVE MET SO FAR ARE AN ASSERTIVE LOT. WHEN THEY START A SENTENCE,

THEY MUST FINISH IT.

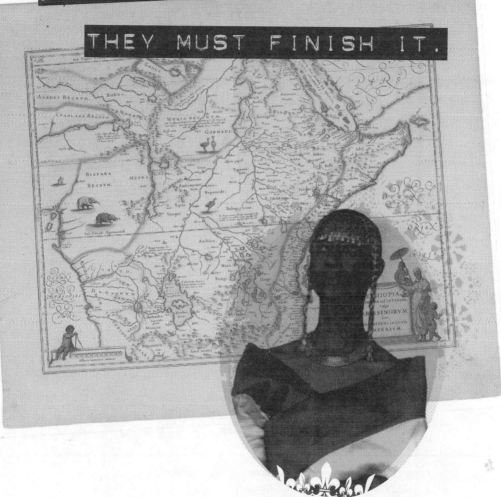

questions. All Araali has to do is charge a fee for them to listen to a translation of his books. This book is history as hardware catalogue, but it is in Runya-Kitara and translation gives a sense of depth and authenticity. They pay too much money.

'Acholi are our ancestors.'

He prints the last letter, an 'I'.

I notice the flowers he has drawn round the cover.

'How did they come here?'

'The Bacwezi had lost power and the Babiito took over.'

'Babiito?'

'They came from Acholi.'

We are midway through the building, some four meters off the ground. A quiet town, it is even quieter this Saturday.

'They are *nkorogi*, royal cattle,' Araali points at the animals. 'They roam and eat from anywhere they want.'

But my thoughts were suspended in mid-air, not at the cattle. You couldn't tell the lineage by looking at the scrawny ribs.

'I thought most Banyoro were Luo?'

'Only the Babiito are Luo. Only the rulers. The founder of Bunyoro-Kitara kingdom was Rukidi Mpuga.' Amooti scans the book. 'His twin brother Kato Kimera founded the Buganda kingdom.

'The Bacwezi lost power and disappeared.'

'Where did they go?'

'They just disappeared. No one knows. We say '*okwegoromora* – to disappear.'

'The Babiito did not defeat them in war. I heard there was war?'

'There was no war. When the Cwezi disappeared –*goromora* – the Babiito came and took power from the Baciita.'

'Baciita. But Baciita are Banyankole?'

'They are a clan from here.'

'How did Babiito take power from the Bacwezi? I heard there was a war at the time?'

'Oh, the Babiito, they were very intelligent people. Oh,

those people, they are very very clever.'

'And the Baciita?'

He laughs. 'Ah, the Baciita, they are a laughing stock. People say they sold the royal drum for food. They had no command.' He balls up a hand and flexes the muscles on it. 'They did not have power.'

'So you are saying there was no war?'

He creases his forehead. 'They sold the royal drum to the Babiito for millet. I think they were hungry.'

'What happened to the Baciita?'

'Nothing. They are still here. They are the keepers of the royal regalia. They are the ones who crown the kings. They sit next to Babiito in power.'

'I want to meet a Mubiito and I want to meet a Muciita.' Babiito describes both clan and lineage. A single member is a *Mubiito*, which also means prince or princess. I start to sense some tension between the two clans, Babiito and Baciita which is an exciting lead, or be it to a sideline story.

Amooti smiles and looks directly at me.

'They are very compricated people.'

This is a very complicated myth.

'There are those who pretend to know more about the history of Bunyoro,' Mr. Muhuruzi, keeper of the royal regalia of Bunyoro-Kitara kingdom, tells me. We are sitting in his compound. There are visitors around. Despite introducing myself only to him, a guest or two drops in to make points about Bunyoro. Again it is that forcefulness I am now recognizing. In Buganda, whatever is not liked is called '*Akanyoro*,' diminutive for Bunyoro. There are Banyoro who still refer to Buganda as *Muwawa*, which is the name it had as an outpost of Bunyoro-Kitara before it broke off.

Muhuruzi does not answer my questions. He tells me why it is not possible at this time. He prefers I speak to the prime minister. It is Saturday and his son is getting married.

We leave when his lunch arrives. I take one last look and I

see a plateful of questions.

'It's *emukaaro omugoro binyobwa*,' Amooti tells me much later when I enquire. *Millet meal with smoked meat in groundnut butter sauce.*

I consider. For 22 years now, with the people of Ankole (Banyankole) dominating the political, economic and military power in Uganda, the enmity that built up with the northern peoples from whom they took power has extended to hatred of all things northern.

I puzzle. A man of the Baciita clan, also the president's clan, eating smoked meat cooked in groundnut butter soup with millet. From my experience, Baciita don't touch northern food. But those are Ankole Baciita I am thinking of. How was I supposed to know Bunyoro had its own Baciita? How do you recognise it when, physiologically, a people no longer resemble their nominal brothers? Muhuruzi does not even look Ankole. I would have mistaken him to be from Apac district in the north by his looks. And the way he took to the food, the way he handled the millet in his hands, is something I am very familiar with.

Later in the evening, I was to get an answer why this was the case, and to understand something of the polished politics that kept Bunyoro powerful for so long and which drew in diverse peoples.

We try for a Mubiito. We try two. They are not at their business premises. We try a third and a fourth. Nothing. We try telephones. I am told as princes, they don't like to be accosted just like that. None pick their phones. Babiito, I am beginning to think, have also disappeared.

'Babiito are also very compricated.'

Perhaps they have disappeared till Monday.

The day lengthens to a hot afternoon. Too many things are not adding up.

All that remains of the power it must have once had is the openness of the grounds, and the tall trees. I picture a ghost parade of bristling *Abarusuura* the on these grounds, regarding us as we approach the palace grounds. I feel the ancient presence of nobles, in royal ranks forming a ring around Kabalega. They all have his face, skyward gazes that don't notice our presence. Bunyoro is mostly gently flat, which makes the massive hills, not too many of them, stick out even higher. Royalty here was not defined by sitting on the highest hills like in Buganda. It is too open, the trees not clamorously tropical like in Buganda. This is tropical savannah. In northern Bunyoro, as you approach the Kabalega National Park, is a great tropical hardwood forest called Budongo. The name itself echoes Luo phonetics. After just a day, I feel I have never understood Bunyoro because I am starting to recognise too much of the Apac I grew up in. The Bantu I know tend to be more self-effacing, more ready to take back their personality to give you room. Here, the slightest attempt at taking that room is reacted to instantly. It varies from totally ignoring you, to that sharply taken breath which I am starting to understand is a warning that you are getting uppity. This difference with the Buganda I live in, seen in so short a time, is elemental. It is an almost hostile sensitivity, this sharpness.

I imagine what the 19th century explorers Dr. Emin Pasha and Sir Samuel Baker, trying unsuccessfully to colonise these lands for Egypt, must have felt approaching these grounds back in the 1870s. Stomachs churned, gazes furtively ferreting out the defenses? Making reports for the Emir? Did they look forward to that millet with smoked meat and groundnut butter? Perhaps the first man they accosted also had the pet name Amooti.

Those hills must have served as observation posts. A suspicious-looking, thin-faced white doctor wearing a red fez and pince-nez, or a heavily bearded, beefy white knight spotted and up goes smoke from hilltop to hilltop. But maybe they drummed. I am thinking of American westerns because it is where I have seen smoke used as military signals.

Now all hilltops sport radio and telephone FM masts. Still transmitting information after so many centuries.

Rather than *Abarusuura* there is only wiry grass waving in the wind. We approach the royal tombs and I cannot avoid feeling we have gone back to the 19th century. There are the ranked royals still – Omukama Tito Winyi there, daughters of Kabalega, important relatives. All their graves encircle the royal tomb. Inside there, alone, lie the remains of Kabalega.

There are *Abarusuura* of sorts here still – but of a modern army, the Uganda People's Defense Forces - who are building a perimeter wall around the tomb. Before we go through the fence, we stop at the cenotaph erected to mark the spot where Dr. Emin Pasha met Kabalega on September 22, 1877. It is a white-washed set of rings about six feet high, the rings in smaller diameter as they pile to the top. A ring pyramid.

This place, this whole area, this historical bend in time, has the rousing name – *Mpaaro* (palace). But there is no palace now, only wilderness, and the wall and the tomb.

'People used to steal the reeds around the tombs, so they are building a wall to protect them.'

Lesser royals have crosses over their graves. The Kings' graves, much larger and elaborate, are topped by spearheads. Kabalega alone lies in the tomb. The humped grass structure with entrances at both ends is barred. His very stature and reputation raise him higher now than all the 22 kings before him. No other king – there have been four since his downfall – is likely to challenge that.

The tomb is under repair. Thatching grass lying in heaps defines a reconstruction site. I am told the kingdom cannot afford to maintain this place, so the Uganda government – the army – has taken over the duty.

We introduce ourselves to a young man who calls the keeper, a man of some age called Andrea. Both men are in dirty work clothes. They are covered with grass from the cutting and the re-thatching. They spend their time here. We sit under the jutting eaves. Kabalega lies just four feet behind the wall. His name is perhaps the biggest Uganda will ever produce. Waves of vagueness from not feeling too real wash over me.

I now know that it is the commoners who are reluctant to

directly say they have Luo ancestors. For the royal clan people, this is a matter of distinction. So I ask Andrea if indeed the Babiito came from Acholi.

'Every year at *Empaango*, Acholi come here to perform traditional rituals and dances,' Andrea says. 'They come in many numbers and almost take over the whole ceremony.'

Empaango is the kingdom's annual cultural gala held in June.

'*Nyoro*, that is a word from the north, I do not know what it means, but when the Babiito came here, that name was given to this area. Nyoro-Kitara.'

I have studied with a number of Acholi called Kitara, but that could have traveled from here to Acholi, rather than the other way.

As a keeper of the royal tomb, Andrea has the most polished way of speaking. He keeps a certain dignity, an economy of movement and an evenness of tone which makes the words 'high priest' come to mind.

'The Big Man who is resting here, his very own mother was an Acholi. The names of our royals are Acholi; Oyo, Ocaki, Olimi, Rabwoni. Tooro broke away from Bunyoro, but they are part of the lineage. The current king of Tooro is also Oyo Nyimba, like the one in Bunyoro. It is only in Buganda that they decided to change their names, but they are of the same lineage.

'Bunyoro was a very powerful kingdom that extended to Karagwe and the southern shores of Lake Victoria. When we hear Saida Karooli sing, we recognise many of the words she is using.

'In Bunyoro, it is mostly the Babiito who are Luo. The chiefs were also Babiito.

'Bunyoro was very advanced technologically. People were making hoes, spears, pangas, knives, all of iron and steel. This made it very difficult for the British to subdue the kingdom. When they took over, they shut the iron and steel works down. They took Bunyoro backwards.

'Kabalega was a very clever man who never wanted to be fooled around with. He saw that if he agreed to sign agreements with the British, that it would be *baligotaisansa* – an ambush.

'It was difficult. You could not just say no to them. But when they agreed, they would attack some of the British soldiers and destroy them.'

'But people also say that his war against the British did not help Bunyoro?'

'He was not a man who wanted to be commanded. He would never surrender. That was his blood. You see even Kony does not surrender. He wants you to agree with him, not defeat him. I think it is in the blood.'

I wince at the crassness of the comparison with the notorious rebel Joseph Kony. But when it is Andrea saying it, there is a clerical evening out.

'When did the Babiito actually come to Bunyoro?'

All three, Andrea, Amooti and the young man look puzzled.

'Maybe the Babiito were always around,' Amooti says.

'Why were they able to take over and rule for so long?'

'These were men of substance,' Andrea says. They were very very intelligent. They were generous. The people liked them.'

It is what I keep hearing, this intelligence of the Babiito. But is it not the case that royalty wherever and whenever has been exalted for even giving life?

I am showed samples of the ferrous rocks once smelted into pig iron. To have had an African kingdom here mine and work iron so much without the presence of European tutelage puzzled colonial anthropologists, for colonialism was justified on the grounds that the black peoples were technologically inferior. The young man brings the rocks from the tomb caught on the magnetic end of a cannibalised radio speaker phone.

Another titular name drops in, *Abacwa*, said to be constructed from another Luo word – *Cwa*. I like this because it was my nickname as a boy. There have been kings called Cwa in Bunyoro and Tooro. The grandfather of Ronald Mutebi, the current Kabaka of Buganda, was called Daudi Cwa, appointed as an infant king when his father, Muwanga, was forced from the throne at the same time as Kabalega. The Buganda throne made a rapprochement towards Bunyoro to gang up against Britain. Too late. The Christian missionaries had by 1890 totally eaten up the fabric of Buganda.

At one point Andrea says, 'people say he was Jomo Kenyatta's father.' I have heard this from many Kenyans, but I find that hard to believe. It must be from the resemblance.

'People come here with their problems,' Andrea says. 'They come here on their knees to pray at the shrine of the Big Man here. They go away, and their problems are solved. We pray for Obama to win the elections. If he wins, we will be very happy.'

They laugh out loud. The mention of Obama lightens the mood, and we prepare to leave.

I am allowed a last glimpse into the shrine. How very silent it is inside there. All this dereliction which touches even this tomb – the inscrutable heap of regalia said to have been used by Kabalega as instruments of power now lying over the grave itself covered in bark cloth, all the dust - I now see as antiquity, a kind of earthy eulogy to a man who refused to bow his head to the loss of centre his land was to suffer with his fall. Andrea holds out a hand to prevent me getting in.

'Shoes are not allowed in.'

Those who enter, go on their knees. He was sent to Seychelles a fallen monarch. In death he became a god.

There's not a single item of modern industry in there. Kabalega was a man from a wholesome Africa and in interment remains untouched by the trinkets of his adversaries. Even in death, his aura of nobility touches profoundly. For the moments I stare in there, it is as if there was never any colonialism, that the Union Jack never went up on this land, that despite everything, we never got touched because he refused to sign and those 100 years never erased the shabbiness with which the English forced themselves on this nobility that was unimpressed and remains untouched by their imperial presumptuousness.

This feeling persists even when we go back to town. I start to wonder if you can really colonise people when they say NYANGIRE. The claim that you are doing them a favour crumbles. Everything you do beyond that is banditry. Proper colonialism must touch the soul, brow beat the mind. When after Christianity and Shakespeare, people approach that shrine on their knees, and an Andrea prays there for the fortunes of an American presidential candidate, then colonialism never really happened. There was only murder. There was only robbery. An armed occupation. This dereliction I have seen now looks different. It is the dereliction of buildings and roads. It is the dereliction of what colonialism forced on a people who chose to die free men.

Colonialism is a cooptation of the willing.

I am trying to come to terms with the subtleties of Bunyoro – this duality – of the people praying at the grave of a man whose bloodline was strenuously maintained away from their own, from an area they now say they do not want to be associated with. Bunyoro is confusing me.

Later, back in town, at a restaurant-sports-bar with a match between Newcastle United and Reading on TV, I ask Amooti: 'Banyoro are very proud of Kabalega?' But I know the answer to this question already, and I am unsurprised to hear it again.

'Very proud,' Amooti says, and I know he means it. Going to Mpaaro has affected him as much as me.

'But he also left the place very poor?'

'He was very proud. He could not accept the white man. He refused to give away Bunyoro.

'We have become small people. Bunyoro has nothing. It's as if we are here, and we are not here; as if we are there and we are not there.'

Alone, my thoughts turn to questions of identity. It is hard, ultimately, to reach a bottom. Only in logical constructions can things add up. I have lived in southern Uganda since 1988 but it is as if I never knew where I was. Now explanations stir and move towards clarity. The itchiness towards northerners, specifically to people with names starting with O, starts to have a convincing foundation that goes beyond the crass politics of post-independence decline. Here in Bunyoro I feel the fortunes of ethnic groups covering not just present-day Uganda but going into present-day Congo, were decided by the power struggles that took place that long ago. Time has buried so much.

In six centuries, ages come and go and so much loses meaning. It is only now with the intensified ethnic politics that buried pasts get exhumed. Andrea speaks of 'Acholi', yet scholars say that word entered usage only about a century ago. It is reading the past through the present. Luo becomes Acholi because Acholi has been in the news now as an identity on the other side of politics.

Even outside of Uganda, the northern war has focused more attention on the Acholi than any other group in the country. Buganda used to be the most-talked about group in the heyday of colonialism. The war and the extent of hatred with which it has been waged snapped the world's attention several times in the direction of Acholi. There is a war-weariness there which I first came into contact with in the late '90s. Back then there was a feeling of being a condemned people: *'Wan Acholi,'* – *'We Acholi,'* carried a depth of despair and isolation which will take time to dissipate.

Until this afternoon, this was the only reality I knew about Luo. In six centuries, a Luo past becomes meaningless, and is only resurrected because pressures redefining ethnic and political boundaries are fast dissolving and redefining relationships.

Reaction to colonialism inspired nationalistic favor particularly in Buganda, in which the king was central. Kings were 'loved.' In prior centuries, they would simply have been government, no matter what ordinary people felt. You were born with his authority hanging over your head like the sky, and you could no more desert it than opt out of walking under a sky. In any case, the fact that the monarch 'came' from somewhere else, not 'here,' was part of his elevation. To have descended from that land beyond the raging river and great lake, would have required a falsely sublime association with the land beyond. In the 15th century ordinary people would never have dreamt of traveling that far to find out the facts.

Outside of myth and legend, real economic and social circumstance should explain what precipitated the 'disappearance' of the Cwezi. Historians refer to inequality and tyranny as definers of life in the period prior to Babiito ascendancy.

There are modern day parallels to draw from. It is only within these regions of present day Uganda that social inequalities can be deep and permanent. The terms used to describe people on the lower rungs sound horrible; Mu*iru*, singular for Ba*iru* from the root *Iru*; under-people, untouchables of Ankole and Bunyoro; Ba*kopi* of Buganda and Ba*hutu* in Rwanda and Burundi. In monarchies, you need barons and dukes. Inevitably this means there must be corresponding underlings. Stepped on, forced to swallow spittle, they will raise arms against the hierarchy and if a force comes from outside offering a new order, they will ally with it.

A big mystery is why hardly anyone in Bunyoro seems to know the meanings of place names. These are simultaneously of Bantu and Luo construction. There is a county in north Bunyoro called Kibanda with a sub-county named Panyadoli. Kibanda a Bantu word, Panyadoli, Luo.

The first king was Rukidi Mpuga, Rukidi a bastardization of the Luo name, Okidi, more common in Lango than in Acholi. Ocaki loosely translates from Luo to English as pioneer, but in daily usage is also the imperative 'let's commence.'

Oyo is a masculine name common in the north (Ayo for feminine).

Okwir is a man's name; *Akwir* feminine.

Empaako – pet name – makes sense in Luo when stripped down to *'Paak'*; *'Wa paak rwot'*, the religious say in the north; *'Let's praise the lord'*. There are Bantu words not even Banyoro understand. For instance, that hottest of them all, Babiito, no one knows.

'It is the name of a clan from Lango,' Bunyoro-Kitara

spokesman, Henry-Ford Mirima told me.

'It means royal clan,' Amooti told me, lamely. Can living history really give you anything convincing? I start to suspect that I am going to find not self-image, but self-projection. Amooti said: 'The word Hoima comes from the name of a place called Oyima, in a sub-country called Kigorobya. The white man could not pronounce 'Oyima'. He said 'Hoima'.'

Self images are often a casting into the future, a projection of intent in which the backward glance is attempt at legitimating a claim. It is a glance that cannot be made too far for the suturing it can reveal. But the paucity of a claim is less a sign of mal-intent; a claim is also a plea for survival. A projection of strength then must spring from a fear of fragility. There's less truth in the firmly set; the claim made with conviction is more a result of uncertainty. The truth seems to lie in the *ad hoc*, the provisional, in the in-between spaces of various claims. There's less certainty in this incompleteness, but in it is also the willingness to discard even the basic facts when doubt comes.

Society cannot cope too much with the circuitous route back to the first man, the last primate to evolve. The story has to be edited down to a mythical river, a mountain, a kind of false bottom to cushion memory and forgive the crimes of ancestors.

Perhaps societies that succeed are those that construct singular narratives of origin.

Saturday ends vertiginously. Of course I have always known the story of Bunyoro, but I have never known it as a continuum. It was pre-independence antiquity. And here is a point: the introduction of flags and national anthems were a new mythical beginning for African societies, a healing to cure the deconstructing impact of colonialism. In these new myths, ancient quarrels between African societies sprung from backward systems that left us vulnerable to European power.

New first men – new Kintus – in the shape of a Nyerere, a Kenyatta, an Obote, rose from the ether of pre-beginning to found new peoples defined by coats of arms and passports.

Coming to Bunyoro has burst this founding myth for me. Here, with the social realities going half a century, Uganda's, and perhaps the failures of Rwanda, Burundi and Congo are starting to add up. How? The wars and massacres that have taken place in these countries all revolve around the ethnic strata leveling the communities. They are strata of being 'original' and being 'foreign'. It is here in Bunyoro, the Bunyoro of Bunyoro-Kitara, that immense past, that I hear peoples being described as 'disappeared.' There is something prohibitive in that expression. A whole people to have disappeared! It sounds suspiciously euphemistic. A people cannot vapourise. Even vapour coalesces and returns as rain. I start to feel that the differences everyone in Hoima talks about, of the mighty Babiito and regressive Cwezi, is more than passing parlance.

Not much else is explained beyond these mythical narratives. But the academic mess surrounding that story is enough to make one suspect at least a cover-up. It does not help that those who promote Cwezi pre-eminence are also European scholars. Whatever they have said, their linking of the mythical Cwezi with Egypt and the larger Europeanisation of the pyramids has been heavily attacked by scholars who also say they are trying to deny black peoples their achievements.

Hence the actual facts about why these lands changed dynasty from the Cwezi to the Babiito remain in contention. Whatever calamity approaches, people don't just walk away from power. Secondly, the distance between the Luo and the Bantu is such that it is also hard to comprehend why the Bantu embraced them as their rulers. Power is something you fight to occupy.

Something horrible might have been done to them as they escaped, and this 'something' is more acceptably described as a 'disappearance.' The depths of ethnic hatreds in the greater regions of western Uganda, Rwanda, Burundi and eastern Congo – which were once Bunyoro-Kitara – are such that only a tragic eruption could have precipitated it. But this is only conjecture. Even here in Bunyoro, I doubt I will ever really get to the bottom of it. After all, I am interested in finding out the manner in which history is used to build self-image and define social bonds.

Yet I feel my vertigo comes from wanting too much definition from the indefinite. It is also a reaction against the politics of ethnicity. Travelling to a place where you don't speak the language can grate on your nerves. It mixes excitement with anxiety. If you traveled to a war zone like northern Uganda, the sheer tragedy of the people you are meeting can have a devastating impact on your mind. Bunyoro's war was a century ago. But to come here to a proud people, to ask them 'are you Luo,' is trying. For many people in southern Uganda, it is an affront to be described as Luo-like. It takes two to three days at the least to settle down into this kind of work, time during which you have properly managed to recognise body language, to learn where the limits are set.

When Bunyoro realised it could not beat the Maxim gun, it fought to the last soldier to protect its honour. When it ran out of ammunition, the army retreated to a rock from whose height they rolled boulders down at the British. This in itself is such an attractive story that it stands outside politics and begins to describe a certain kind of aesthetic. It is not the kind of story we hear of Africa that honour was so highly valued. The Africa we know is the Africa seen by western scholars and media – their yards of film scripted on continuing the Tarzan-legend, a cinematic fraud narrated over and over that it has become TRUTH. If then you meet a Kabalega, he becomes untruth because he is outside the narrative.

Now that I have met a few people and observed gestures along the streets of Hoima, I am looking beyond the initial shock of dust. Try as I might, I have a fear of dirt that still surprises me. After just a day, I have lost my anxiety. I begin to think: Oh, that man's head is shaped like mine, that kind of posture is mine. The man in the shop who spoke to me in Lunyoro looked askance when I couldn't reply in his language. So I begin to read this place from this personal perspective as well. This produces a stupid smile and I start to feel silly, as though I have become a fake. It is ironic to feel that I fit in for much of my life; I have gotten used to being an outsider.

Later, when I got to understand it even better, I was to walk away really angry and thanking God I was not born here.

After only a day, I also start to see that Bunyoro's myth is not so much an attempt to dress up the past. I also see myth-making as an art form; a formulaic presentation that handles its material in much the same way as versification transforms a landscape into rhyming lines. It offers a chance to withdraw from history and climb into art.

In any case, you can't walk into history. At 11 o'clock, under the African sun, the present is so present; you are constantly getting thirsty, hungry, negotiating for lower fare that history seems a remote kind of fraud. Even ethnic tensions, thought of at 11 o'clock, can seem superfluous. All becomes tenuous. The asking of questions at such moments seems too much. Why not? After all, peoples seem to know they have common ancestry, but the imperatives of survival force them to coagulate into a tribe to fight for what does not come easily – land, grazing, water. Myth is that important coagulant. The trauma of killing another for food must be healed by first casting them into the role of the Other; otherising as expiation against the monstrosity of what has to be done. How easily a tribe splinters into clans, clans into families; even within families there is no guarantee that the bond will hold. Did not a cataclysmic family split occasion the splintering of the Luo family?

How even easier does the reverse happen, that a family becomes a clan, a tribe, a nation.

I can't sleep too easily because the wedding in the back gardens of the hotel starts to get noisy. Ugandan weddings go on till morning.

They turn on the music. I get up to listen. They are playing one of the more famous songs of Uganda, an Acholi track popularly called *Ajolina*. Ah, these Acholi, I say of the Banyoro. The track is a forlorn regret of lost love. But its delivery is forceful, very rhythmic, inventive and hard to forget. I smile weakly, seeing that these troubled questions are just mine. Me, an outsider. Look at it. It makes sense. It is their heritage. The disturbance is mine, my ignorance, for travelling the highways that cross Bunyoro for a quarter of a century without stopping to consider that the place had a personality. If I have had problems with being Luo, it is because I know what it felt like being a northerner in the south. I have only come to a place that is more subtle than Kampala.

Then I spring to my feet. Another one of my favourite tracks is on. It's *Ekitagururo*, just as fast, just as famous as *Ajolina*. But it's Ankole – nomadic herdsman's music. I was wrong again. What appears to be duality of heritage is only an outsider's perspective, born of the chauvinism of a present that thinks its hatreds are so elemental as to extend into the past. But I go out because in this unassuming town, this sounds like a party. When a party gets this noisy, you can gate-crash it. They ask for invitation cards only when the sun is up. Even the gatekeepers must be drunk, I figure and head out.

The man at the gate is a hotel hand I have made friends with. 'Big wedding eh,' I say to him. I remember Mr. Muhuruzi. 'Is it Muhuruzi's son?'

'Yes. Patrick Muhuruzi.'

'Who is he marrying?'

'Margaret Mpuga.'

'Mpuga? That's a Mubiito name?'

'She is a Mubiito.'

I am stunned; an Ankole man marrying a Luo lady? But immediately I start to feel foolish again. Coming here and pressing these Hoima people to tell me about their ethnic identities feels like tribal incitement. I feel subdued. Is tribalism not merely a colonial construct of divide and rule, while for centuries Ugandans crossed and re-crossed tribal lines? Are not historians right in saying that using the word tribe is meaningless in Uganda and that there are only language groups?

Even the cultures are exchanged, I think, for look at that loop of rope between two poles, the ones Banyankole use to bear gifts for the bride's family. All this asking about identity starts to smell like a Kampala political unease which I carry with me. These people live their lives oblivious of tribe.

The music stops. The couple approach to cut the cake. A strange thing happens. The Kinyankole gift loop starts to explode, bright white light that dazzles everyone. I miss a beat. They are the firecracker rockets which the Indian *Diwali festival* has made ubiquitous in Kampala. My mind does a loop. If you look too much for patterns, even clouds will resemble maps and human faces.

Sunday brings even more quiet. I am leaving Hoima today. I understand less now than I did at the beginning. I don't trust anything anybody has told me. They are as ignorant as myself. Worse, I am beginning to distrust my own conclusions. But I have been told that if I meet Burhandi, I will not need to ask further questions about Bunyoro-Kitara.

I ring up Burhandi. The sound of the voice assures me that he will know what he is going to say. A former headmaster, he tells me, and repeats again and again that he can only see me at 10 o'clock tomorrow.

Suddenly I have a whole day free. We go out of town.

GULU

The break happens quite high up, some three quarters of a kilometre from the bridge. Beyond that point, where you see the water as part of the horizon, the Nile is still a gentle, if driving mass of water. Then the break, which is the where the drop begins lowering the ground into the Rift Valley, transforms the Nile. It changes temperament. The unrelenting stomach churning plunge begins. The Karuma bridge is built at a point which, from bank to bank, is less than 50 meters wide. It is this funneling which seems to make the river rage with anger.

Densely wooded savannah, aged granite rocks, baboons and roaring rapids mark this point in a hard-edged realism that in the dry season can seem hostile. It is the second climatic zone the Nile crosses in its 3000-plus journey that will see it power through a desert, cross the 23 degrees longitude, and advance to the very edge of the winter zone.

As if the Karuma funnel were an affront to its forceful reputation, the Nile turns ugly. Here at its most ferocious, the whitened, driving rapids are as far from a drinkable liquid as water can look. Horror stories of buses, cars and trucks plunging into it are still told years later. Just getting across the bridge feels like a narrow escape from certain annihilation. How it crashes, rises, bashes, and breaks into rock-sized sprays inspires not so much wonder as fear.

If you have just heard the story of northern Uganda of the last 20 years, the passage over Karuma Bridge feels like a passage into human passion and fury. The silence that crossing the bridge imposes will stay lodged firmly as you begin the journey to Gulu.

Once you have crossed this bridge, you instinctively know you have entered another country. The school signposts carry the black, yellow and red of the Ugandan flag, just so you remember you have not.

Temperamentally, the country you enter just crossing this bridge sets you on edge. It has its great stretch of sunshine seasons that lash down towards the end of the year and stretch well into the next.

It is not the climate that is most telling. Instantly, you notice the absence of people. With the climb out of the Karuma depression begins this silence which was once also a prayer that the bus does not break down, that no one crosses the road ahead, that it is only the sound of the engine you hear and that if there is a loud popping, let it be a tire going off. It is some 70 kilometers to Gulu town itself, covered within the hour, but it seemed the longest section of a journey stretching nearly 300 kilometers from Kampala.

Even without an active war still going on, habits formed over two decades define this as a war zone. For war has marked this place as no other place in Uganda. Two armies – the hand, lip and ear-cutting Lords Resistance Army and the constantly at-war Ugandan Army – pulled and pushed aimlessly across these lands that go on till the Sudan.

Fire-gutted bus frames blackened and reduced to sitting on the chassis, bodies stretched across the road; that was the journey to northern Uganda starting in 1986.

Karuma has always been a kind of border, for unlike its East African neighbours, the boundaries between the Luo-speaking groups and the Bantu-speakers is so firmly marked by the River Nile perhaps the role it plays in creating the mentality of separateness has not been fully discussed. Uganda is a northern and southern bank country.

Now across this river, I see the hand of nature in the Bunyoro-Kitara story. At the height of its cruelty, the climate here does not make these lands look like the kind of place to which you might want to migrate. Not here the depth of soil and broadness of leaf you find in Buganda. There is only one rainy season here – stretched out in the middle of the year, unlike the south where there are two lengthy ones. Dotting the homesteads of the north, a sight you rarely find in the south, stand the ubiquitous granaries (*dero*) that a young man builds in his freshly cut home before he has children and which he and wife must keep filled through the year with grain and pulses.

Together with Bunyoro, these Luo-speaking areas of Uganda never got on with the British. It was nearly a decade after Britain had colonised the south that they managed to take the north in fierce battles that drained and left little love for either side till colonialism came to an end. If Bunyoro was left under-developed, northern Uganda was maintained as an outer territory. It was the place to which colonial officials were sent when the Governor wished to punish them.

It is still the sort of place government and NGO workers avoid coming to.

In the two and half decades after independence, Uganda was run by northerners, two of them Luo speakers. The breakdown in military discipline, the random murders and robberies that started in the 1970s and intensified with the 1980s civil war, widened the divide between the two sides. The sound of Luo brought associations for southerners that meant only fear.

Beyond Karuma, the story of Bunyoro-Kitara makes sense. The breadth and force of the River Nile has for ages been a natural barrier that kept first Sudanic Arab slavers out of the southern Uganda and for two decades stopped northern rebel groups from crossing into the south. With Lakes Victoria, Kyoga and Albert, it is a natural barrier that will let a people form their relationships into organised political systems. It seems that the most difficult barrier to taking control of the south for the Babiito, so many centuries ago, was not overcoming its armies but crossing the river at all in large enough numbers.

Northern Ugandans have little in common with southerners; in appearance they are taller, leaner, athletic and darker-skinned; in manners very reserved. Gulu town comes at a stage in which the landscape is already preparing itself to become the Sahara desert; the big-leafed thickets of the south become here tall, single-standing heat-weathering trees, shrub taking over from bush, grasses stiffening into hardy spear and elephant bushes.

The people, too, appear to have been stiffened by nature itself, for here is none of the raucous, celebratory bonhomie of southern towns. An alert watchfulness in reserved postures is the people. To drive north from south within a morning is to learn that you have to speak differently, that here too much camaraderie breaks pace with a space defined by stoicism.

'The fare is 6000,' a motorbike taxi man wheels his machine for me to sit. I try to bargain and realise that it is not too polite to bargain here. *'Ladit, wel eno,'* he tells me *'That is the fare sir'.* 'The distance is great,' he adds. When we arrive, I can't believe how modest his demand was. An instinctual attentiveness that misses little. I approach people. They hear my Lango-accented Luo and reply in English. Acholi-chauvinism, it was once called; only their late coming Luo, younger than Alur for instance, is Luo proper; *'Acholi are Luo class A; Lango, Luo class B'.* Several times, their relationship to the Lango people was edgy and the fall of northern rule was less from loss of military capability than the breakdown in Luo unity.

The bus ride from Masindi has me stiff. I came here because there was no ATM in Masindi. I intend to go to Nebbi where I will find the Alur people.

I go to the ATM. I am glad there is only man standing in line. I am weighed down by my bags. I stand behind him. He enters. I am approached.

'Line caake ki kan kuu,' the lady tells me. *'The line does not start here.'* She points into the tent in the court yard. There are perhaps 50 people who looked like they were waiting to open accounts with the bank or something. Gulu is a hot town, so the bank erected a tent for its customers. The ATM line gets so long (salary time) customers are provided a bench.

They watch me in silence. No one says anything. I am expected to see my error. I do not. One person comes up to tell me. Back in the south, a furor would have broken out, abuse flung at me. Not here. In northern Uganda, still waters can run deep, will take long to stir and be unpleasant when finally disturbed. I apologise, and they nod in acceptance.

I decide to look for a room first. I walk away. On the road, the Sir Samuel Baker Secondary School football team drives past. A student is blowing a triumphant horn, modest really. But faces turn in its direction and there are comments. *'Mono gin ma gi mito, raa'.* 'They just like to show off.'

I should have known. But years of living in the south have made me forget how to behave here. Southerners cause offence with their often talkative presumptuousness and will not know it.

I go to a hotel in town, a lodge. Despite the return of peace, I prefer to sleep right in the middle of town, cheap, not always too clean, but safe.

'I still have no money but can you give me a room so I can leave my bag? I will check in later.'

The lady shows me a room. The rooms don't have numbers. They have names; Brazil, Nairobi, China, Beijing...I go to Beijing. It is my third time coming here. It feels less foreign when you return to a room.

Leaving, I stop at her desk and ask: 'Can you give me a chit to show I left my bag behind?'

I am taken aback by her reaction: 'Do you think I can steal your bag. I have a good heart that is why I gave you a room. If you think I have that kind of heart, then it is also the kind of heart you have.'

In the hotels, they are more professional. This is a lodge. But I can't sleep in the outskirts.

I may be reading too much, but I quickly recollect that the greatest insult here is to let on, however discretely, that you don't trust a person's integrity. For the two nights I am here, the lady and I don't talk too much.

I just asked for a chit.

If anything defines differences between northerners and southerners, it is the stress the two place on social etiquette. A business-like curtness is all that a greeting is here. At the height of its civilisation, politeness in Buganda was unequalled anywhere. It started the moment you laid eyes on someone you knew – no matter how far away, the women dropped to their knees, the men cupped hands, bowing. '*Mbulamusizza,*' it started with a shout (good wishes to your health) given the distance. It was not the greeting proper. It was the entrée. The greeting was never made. It was performed, a marvel that never failed to melt a foreigner's heart down. Buganda charmed generations of visitors; Arab traders who could not contain themselves, European scholars who clapped and hurrah-ed for a century and built them schools and a university in return.

'*Mbulamusizza*'. Thence commenced a mastery of niceness which was pure torture *a la politesse*. When they walk to within speaking distance, it must not give the appearance that the woman has actually gotten off the ground, nor the man stopped bowing. When the business of the visit has to be broken, '*I came to get*', was rudeness unimagined. '*I thought I might come to*,' the circumspection begins and without letting it out, without any impression that a thing has been said, it gets transmitted. In Buganda culture, people did not say things. They transmitted their thoughts. But if the meeting was lengthy, and if nothing was said, then the finale, the departure, topped it all. The social etiquette evolved to give the impression that you were so terribly afflicted with shame at the thought of approaching another; even more ashamed at having to make a demand. When the time to go came, you then had to demonstrate that the attention you received was so immense you hate to leave. So begun perhaps the most arduous avoidance of actually saying 'Good bye'. A winding circuitousness, a lengthening, '*eraade*,' *eh*, '*kakaati*' '*eeh*', '*bwekityo*,'; '*eeeeh*', the walking away performed crabwise. It is abominable to turn your back on the king; not even to a friend. '*Eeeeeeh*' '*Munnange*' '*eeeeeeeeeh*' '*Kaale*,' '*eeeeeeeeeeeeeh*'...

...as recently as 20 years ago, the Baganda considered it rude to end a conversation. As the joke went, two Baganda went on greeting, genuflecting, bowing until the other's head disappeared behind a hill. To get anything done at all, they needed a hill to be close by.

In Busoga, it got worse: when two Basoga run out of niceties, a litany of relative's names came up, how are they, how is the second cousin, how is the dear mother? Relatives also run out. How are the goats then; are the chickens doing well; the goat produced; eeeh? And how are the kids doing? Cultured Basoga, when they meet foreigners ignorant about this, irritate by wanting to know why and when you cut your hair. With

Basoga friends, we wisecracked; 'how is the first horn of the first goat doing; how is the second horn of the first goat looking ...and is the first pod of groundnut in the heap faring well? Is the third pod...how are the bed sheets...'

In towns now, the mile-long avoidance of the words 'good-bye' in Buganda has been edited down to a tossed off '*Ki*' (Chi). Baganda grandparents coming to the city go into shock when grandchildren throw off school bags and without kneeling, rap '*Ki, Jajja*'.

Northern Ugandans with their curt, head-shaken '*oreme*', a culture in which even a little smile, let alone show of endearment is unbearably personal, came across to southerners as indescribably barbaric, a wild people who must not have grown up in proper homes.

The exiling of the King of Buganda, Edward Muteesa II in 1952 by the British colonial government and later the abolition of the kingdom in 1966 occasioned a period of darkness – this lost glory of Buganda less a loss of kingship as a loss of good manners. As a sign of how things have changed, even northerners now find Baganda rude.

Muto'no pa Lajur is an old journalist hand. He has been *The Monitor* Bureau Chief for years, a veteran of war reporting, a man who maneuvered government and rebel threats in equal measure. I drop by to greet him and maybe get an Irumba-style dialogue. Then I should move on to Nebbi tomorrow.

'Do you know anyone who might tell me about the link between Bunyoro-Kitara and Acholi culture?'

'Yes, there are many people, many elders.' He ponders a while. 'There is an old man, Mzee Napthali Ocuc. He is the chairman of Ker Kal pa Ayira.'

I am interested.

'But it is not a link with the whole of Acholi. It is only the Ayira clan that has that link.'

I am more interested.

He points out where I can find Ladit (Mzee) Ocuc. As I

walk, I think I have made a connection. *'It is only the Ayira clan.'* Again that contraction, pushing the hot potato into someone else's hands. *'Oyima clan brought trouble to Lango,'* they said of Milton Obote's clan. I spoke to Oyima: *It is the Akena family.'* Now increasingly in Kampala you hear; *'It is not Banyankole in power. It is Bahima.'* Among the Bahima; *'It is the Baciita who are in power.'* Among Baciita, *'It is Museveni and his family.'*

There has been a war in Gulu for 20 years now. But more than Hoima or Masindi, this is a flourishing town. More vehicles, more people, better and bigger motorbike taxis. At the height of anti-Acholi feelings in the country, it was said that the Acholi benefited from the LRA war. How come they are developing like that? But Acholi also have the biggest number of Ugandan exiles who send hundreds of millions of dollars home each year. Rejected at home, their money from abroad has become the single biggest source of foreign currency Uganda receives. There are so many NGOs here. NGO money is de facto economy. More to it, Acholi is also now the gate way to Southern Sudan, hotel rooms constantly filled up.

'Oh, you were in Juba,' you meet a lost friend in Kampala. 'Money, eh?'

Perhaps it is the first time in millennia that out of that direction is now coming opportunity, not refugees. Had it been like that centuries ago, there would have been no Luo migration into East Africa.

How much of my conclusions are a reaction to the war; how much of the public character here is born of a chastening, soul-destroying war?

The town's population is inflated from rural populations that poured in from the fighting. 'You would find children lined up there, at night till morning,' the girl at *The Monitor* Bureau pointed at the verandah. The world press gave them a captivating name, which shamed the government. 'Night commuters,' the epithet went.

But I am not new in Gulu like I was in Hoima. First coming here in 1982, I remember what it was like before the war.

Beginning in 2000, I started to report on the war. Slashed ears, chopped off hands, abductions into Sudan and broken families were at times more than I could bear. Yet I came. And when large camps spread all over northern Uganda, and the entire countryside from Acholi to Lango to Teso emptied of people, I sensed a danger brewing up for the whole of Uganda. If the peace talks had not started and the war kept pushing people, how would they react to the Southern-dominated government? Would a 500-year history once more have been re-enacted?

But there was a peace talk. Today Gulu is exhaling. It was scalding hot when I arrived. But after lunch, it rained heavily. It is a cool air now. The papers are loudly announcing that in two days, Joseph Kony will sign a peace agreement. It is as if I have come at the right moment.

Napthali Ocuc is patriarch of a large homestead, just outside the town, the huts spread out. And amidst these, amidst the wet, slippery ground, the smell of beans and cassava boiling in pots, the smell of groundnut and simsim roasted and pounded in pestles – the right way - the intoxicating smell of he-goats and their droppings and children angling down mangoes from the giant mango trees, I could not have met Ladit Ocuc in a better setting.

Suddenly, I sense that after nearly a week, this story is no longer a word game, not anymore an uncertain poking about for faint trails. It's as if this side of the Nile will fit ball and socket into Hoima. It is with a gathering sense of finality that I walk through the thicket of huts. My heart pounds. For the first time I am weary that I may fail. Suppose I don't find him? Suppose I find him and he says there is no Luo connection with Bunyoro-Kitara?

I find him, a man in his early 80s, still strong, clearly observing my approach with the bearing of a man 20 years younger.

'There are many, many connections,' he tells me. After nearly a week, this is like a triumph.

Like men of his generation do, he scans me for genealogy and background. The one pleasure of having nearly all my grandparents having different ethnic backgrounds is the look of confusion I see on people's faces when they want to determine where I come from. Experienced readers of ethnic stereotype from all parts of Uganda have looked and then given up. It is about the only nice thing about being ethnically ambiguous. His eyes tearing off my face, Ocuc asks where I come from. I tell him.

'People from Apac travel yearly for rituals in Bunyoro,' he looks elated, saying this. In other parts of the country, saying I came from the north used to end with a glum-faced genealogist or the sharply-withdrawn handshake, the face of amity packed back inside its mask.

'*Acholi, Lango, Nyoro, pe ti lapoka poka,*' Ocuc says. '*Acholi, Lango and Banyoro are one people.*' He tells me he knows many people around where my grandfather settled.

'We meet with them in Hoima during *Empaango,*' he says.

But it is getting dark and we have to meet tomorrow.

To explain the war in the north, anthropologists talk of 'Acholi culture'. Some explain that because the north was not a kingdom area, its people never learnt to be obedient to authority; this said with the jargon-wrought authority of sociologists and anthropologists as if there have been no wars in other parts of the world and by scholars who will not hesitate to throw a barricade in the streets of Paris or New York at the slightest hint of government arrogance. For some years, I nearly accepted this. It is until Saturday last week that I was exploded out of a lifetime of assumptions.

Crossing the Nile on this trip now has the texture of the proverbial, for I begin to have a sense of history I never had before. Much of what I have been told I find disturbing. A lot of what is disturbing was to strike me later, and to give me a sense into what goes on underneath the surface of African countries. There is so much history tightly packed in that would make more than just Africans respect this continent if only those who know the continent started to find out. Certainly for me now,

CROSSING THE NILE

ON THIS TRIP NOW HAS THE TEXTURE
OF THE PROVERBIAL, FOR I BEGIN
TO HAVE A SENSE OF HISTORY I
NEVER HAD BEFORE.

Uganda has taken on a tantalizing narrative quality. Things are not what they seem to be.

For peoples here, kingdoms are southern oddities. But how much do they actually know about those kingdoms; how much do they know about the manner in which their kin, crossing the Nile centuries ago, rearranged the lives of southerners with a permanence which took colonialism to unpack? There is no indication that they know and even less that they care.

My explanation hits me hard. How many times in the south have I personally been let know I was being overbearing, demanding too much? I choose these words carefully because I am presenting my own perspectives. But this trip has forced me to see things from southern perspectives; I have thought of the lineages of southern kingdoms, the princes and princesses and the way in which the Amootis respond in the face of nobility. So now I also see that it is perhaps this apparent lack of interest in Southern affairs, this unawareness of the extent to which the Luo shaped the south over such a long period of time, which is perhaps the immense, naturally arrogant and un-mitigating superiority which might lead one people to sit on others' thrones. But I also see some other difference. The friendly and ever-commodious amity of the south contrasts sharply against the utilitarian and almost-humorless serious focus of the north.

How many times have I heard it said here of southerners that they are 'weak-willed banana eaters', people too short and inactive to 'manage'? *'Bad gi pe'; 'They have no strength in their arms.'*

Back then, this slighting meant little beyond simple parlance. Today it vibrates in a sinister beat.

Obviously, northern Ugandans today are not their ancestors. It is a place in utter social collapse. Twenty years during which war broke families and the world turned its back on Acholi has had an impact. The war is a kind of wall here, an echo that warps discussion of Acholi. The entire north has felt it, but the enduring damage is heaviest in Acholi:

My friend Okello, whom I have seen only three times since 1987, once told me 'I am going to call myself Calvin. Because of my name, I cannot make it in life anymore.'

It is the kind of self-revelation to which you cannot reply. At school, it was reputed, there had never been a mathematician of his brains before. So many people like him now live in North America and Europe.

It is the story of the group of boys I interviewed in 2000 who had scars on their bodies, and in the psyche, who had carried guns and marched into the Sudan, who had been forced to kill fellow children. It is the story of the girls in 1996 abducted from a school and forcefully turned into wives by the rebel ranks. It is the story of Bar Lonyo in which 300 people were hacked, shot and burnt to death.

'We are not Luo. People hear about the war in northern Uganda but they don't care. They are killing their own people.'

At the height of his war, Joseph Kony demonstrated the worst stereotype southerners have of northerners. *They are killing their own people,* always reminds me of the malnutrition which at its height in 2003/04, was said to have killed more people and children than the war did in all its two decades; babies in Medicins sans frontieres tents with bone joints and ligaments showing under flesh wrinkled like fabric.

'Why is that war allowed to continue?' expatriates asked.

A certain kind of war culture has crept on the north. Pushed and blamed for a war whose motive few people seem to understand let alone show interest in, dialogue about the war is not broached in conversation. But you have to know the place well enough to tell that people are skirting a great hole in their lives, that gestures and glances or lowered heads and certain types of smiles are comments you are not going to hear in speech.

I hear about Okello and learn that finally, he has a job. But like nearly everyone, he works for an NGO. The war has created a pattern people are finding hard to pull out of. With the return of some peace, people under 20 are being asked to return to homes they have never been to. It is said that some resistance is being raised against return, away from World Food Program hand outs. *'Boo Kec,'* a comical expression describes this.

'*Green vegetable are bitter,*' the resistors are dubbed. '*Cho pe*'. It helps to understand that such humor is necessary to put the past behind.

From the South, the land of the Luo speakers is an undivided 'up there'. In Teso, they rail against the Acholi for Kony's war. 'Even when you are drinking *marua (millet brew)* an Acholi wants to rule the conversation,' I was told once. In Lango they say the Acholi deserved their war because it was a group of Acholi generals who overthrew the second Milton Obote government in 1985 – Obote a man from Lango. In Acholi, there is no passing the buck.

Or so I thought until with the peephole of Bunyoro-Kitara, I sensed the sensitivity towards the centuries of history which here, is also brought up to explain the war: '*It is only the Ayira clan*'.

But in the end, there is never a there. A search for social-fixedness becomes an unwieldy race for the horizon. However hard and fast you lunge at it, it is still in the distance.

'*Kaiza, from Apac?*' a politician I was interviewing once quizzed me. '*Are you one of those people hiding their identities in southern names?*'

For thousands of young men, a chance to jump on a bus and get to Buganda is like a Muganda's chance to jump on a plane and go to London. A job as a security guard is a passport to undreamt of income.

If Bunyoro-Kitara was the height of Luo achievement, northern Uganda is easily its lowest experience.

'...WE COME FROM THE LAND OF ANAKA...'

'The migration of the Luo was a wave of very large movements. It started in Sudan and spread out. Long ago, they settled at a place called Kilak, under Got Kilak. The Luo spread out into Tanzania, into Kenya. The Luo found in Tanzania and Kenya outnumbers those found in Uganda. There are even more in Sudan.'

I have come to talk to Ladit Ocuc in the offices of the palace of the head of Acholi clans, Rwot Acana. Northwest of Gulu town, it stands on a hillock. There are no hills here, only large thors that mark the horizon. These horizons, ruler straight that sometimes peter out into blue, then grey, become indistinguishable from the sky. As we parted yesterday in the evening, he motioned with his hand 'Let's meet when the sun is about that high.'

My interpretation of 'that high' was liberal for he says he has been waiting for me.

'Long ago, in a place called Te-Biito, now in Purongo division, Amuru district, a young woman named Owila Latworo fell pregnant. She was unmarried. When she was questioned, she said it was a man named Kyomya. The matter was investigated by the clan, who is this Kyomya, where does he come from. It was later found out he came from a place called Kibanda. The family gathered a large group and crossed the river, carrying the girl to look for Kyomya. They were fully dressed and carrying music instruments. They announced their approach blowing horns and playing much music. The people of Kibanda were frightened and run away. The family stayed to wait the birth. When the girl gave birth, she had twins. They were named Opio and Ocen. They had on their bodies, the white birthmarks which are sometimes found on the people of Bugisu. It was also found that this Kyomya was the brother of the king of Bunyoro. The king was called Wamara. When they heard about this pregnancy and presence of Ocholi, they run away from Bunyoro.

'The people of Bunyoro now had no ruler. They saw that these were the children of a prince and decided to make Opio Rwot. He was given the name of Rukidi Mpuga.

'His younger brother could not stay, so he gathered his men and marched down to Buganda. Buganda had its own ruler. Ocen had many heads of cattle and a lot of food. He was a rich and generous man and in Buganda, he fed the people. He gave the women milk for their children to drink. They were very happy and liked him. When their ruler asked about this man, who is he, where has he come from, the people replied, he is a kind man who has brought us things, (*en nwo otero jamii ma pol bot jo me Buganda. Okelli wa jamii. Kintu, kintu*, they kept saying. They called him Kintu because he brought things.

'Their leader saw that his people were turning away from him and so he left and said, if you want him to be your ruler, then crown him.

'This is the man who was given the name Kato Kimera.'

Ocuc keeps a constant face when talking. Now he draws his forehead heavily and speaks. 'People of Luo never took those thrones by force as they are now saying. It was a peaceful thing.

'It is the culture of Acholi that a ruler does not mistreat his people. A chief only rules through the will of the people. When a stranger shows up in his court, he is welcomed and fed. The chief's court, is the people's court. The chief rules with the will of the leaders. Everyone gathers in *Kacoke Madit* (parliament) to give their mind. It is how we want the war to be ended, through talking, not by force. In Acholi culture, when you kill another man, you are not sentenced to death. You must pay the dead man's family. A young man will marry with the dowry and his child given the dead man's name. *Dano dong ocer* (the dean man is resurrected). In Bunyoro, Babiito set up *Kacoke Madit*, which they called *Rukuraato*. In Buganda, they called it *Lukiiko. Loc ka me Ocweji ca nwo pe obedo loc maber;.* ' (Leadership under the Cwezi was wrong). It is for this reason the Luo were welcomed.'

'Is Biito an Acholi word?'

'Biito is a tree, a tall tree that has many roots going up. It looks like *Ituba*.'

'And are these trees still growing here?'

'They grow in many places.'

'Is the original tree still growing?'

'I saw it myself in 1952 before it fell.'

I look out. Out of the windows. The land so flat. Suppose you poured water on the ground, can it flow at all in that flatness?

Ocuc has not finished talking. He tells me: 'When the government fell in 1986, Ibingira said 'You used to say *Ocweji* had disappeared, that *Ocweji* had died, now *Ocweji* have resurrected. It makes some of us think the war on the people of Acholi is because of these stories. But the thrones were not taken by force.'

I have avoided sounding impatient for a week. 'This place they crossed the river, can it be found?'

'It is found in Anaka, in Amuru.'

'The trees still grow there?'

'They grow there. It is a place called Purongo. If you go there, the people will show you.'

When later I leave, when Ocuc walks me out, leaning heavily on his stick and we are in the courtyard, and he points the walking stick into the hills far away, light blue in the distance and says 'That is Patiko, where Samuel Baker stopped and built a fort,' I feel an immense pressure rising in me.

'They encircled Acholi after many years. They broke the will and culture of the Acholi and turned Acholi into soldiers. Acholi were not allowed education.'

I leave and I walk. I walk past the motorbike taxis. I keep walking. I get hot and sweaty. But I am only looking at my feet. When I reach town, I don't stop. I keep walking. It is hotter even and I am sweating heavily. When I stop, it is because I have run out of town to walk through. But I feel I must keep moving. I get a vehicle and head out. I must keep moving. There is a climax now, there is a tangible thing, the myth has yielded form and I keep moving.

Later, two hours later, I start to doubt the wisdom of this sudden impulse, to move so suddenly. You have to be in northern Uganda to know that you must not set out on a journey that will trap you away by nightfall. For a tree. This tree of giant proportion with its aerial roots has become a holy grail.

Yet had I not always known it? *Te-Biito, Biito.* How many parishes in the north are named after trees most common there; *Te-Tugu, Bar-Tugu, Te-Oboke* (where my maternal great-grandmother lived). Again it is how words hide inside another tongue. Up here, letters K and T when they appear before the last vowel, get softened. K becomes H in *Oleke, Aboke, Kabaka (Olehe, Abohe, Kabaha))* T becomes a kind of hard R, rrtrr, a hard grind; *Oborrtrre (Obote)*. In southern tongues, its *OboTe, BiiTTo*. I saw it because Ladit Ocuc said *Biirtru* and I saw a tree I had always known.

'Onyoro call Latworo Nyatworo. Labongo they say Nyabongo.'

Te-Biito is about 15 kilometers north of Bunyoro, on the other side of the Nile's rapids. I muse; Sir Samuel Baker would have passed through it in the 1870s when he went to see the falls to later be named Murchison Falls.

But its not that I am thinking of. After a week of doubts and uncertainty, seeing this tree starts to feel like a climax. My summit.

But I can't get round it completely. With the heavy, early rains, I come alive to the fact that this place, which is deepest Acholi, was until a year ago, a dangerous place. Caught now on the beat of finding a tree, I also connect this war to my story. I see the clouds and connect them to my story. The whole world revolves around a Banyan tree.

We drive beside the railway tracks, which is bush, trees growing between the tracks. It strikes out wide into the bush to return shooting across the road, appearing and reappearing as if it too wants to become part of my story. *A long time ago, a white skinned people came and laid down iron snakes in the grass.*

With the anti-Acholi of the 1990s, it was *'The Acholi are a secretive people.'* A politician saying loudly on a radio talk show, *'Luo chauvinism must stop. They think it is their prerogative to rule.'* Have I run into the secret, will a tree reveal this to me, this day?

This land so vast. How it undulates, how it builds up all round, how over it clouds explode into gigantic, floating mountains. Wind-cropped trees immense flat heads. Eucalyptus trees are dancing girls at *Dingi Dingi*, elegant limbs that hide, reveal, hiding, revealing the land beyond: light green, dark green vegetation. Neither man nor beast. In all strangeness as if caught bathing naked, roofless walls of abandoned homesteads race backwards outside the window.

Shrubs. Like herding elephants, the huts of refugee camps teem humanity. Alero Langol camp, so many huts bunched together; a woman holding a saucepan bending about to enter a hut; so many boys in running motion and a ball going up. They race out of the window to reveal more width of wilderness; that quad of landscape running long, tilting so evenly dipping into a valley for another quad to run. Heaven is one place. Earth is down here. How odd that green earth becomes dense blue in distance and by degrees, pales to light blue to grey to become sky. *Owila Latworo. '...Obiga telayo, we come from the land of Anaka; we had dreams, we had hope...'* I hear Geoffrey Oryema's voice and this enchanting, bewitching land, is all of his music.

In Anaka, in Purongo division, 15 kilometers from the place called Te-Biito, I am told: 'It is national park territory and many trees have been cut down. You will need a letter to explain what you want but it is past working time now.'

David Kaiza *is a Ugandan writer based in Kampala. After working as a journalist for several years with the* Daily Monitor, *he took a two year hiatus from writing and became a metal worker. This story marks his return to the pen.*

Travels through KALENJINLand

Binyavanga Wainaina

To get a matatu to Baringo, you have to get to *Ogilgei* –
which is the name of a notorious bar, and more: throughout
Kalenjinland, the plains, and rifts and mountains and towns –
inside State House and its circles, among Special Branch police
with their grey shoes and red or white socks, and shiny suits
with a KANU party badge near the pocket; nearly everywhere
the two million people, of various related languages and
cultures called Kalenjin, whether they be in Texas working for
an IT company, or in the hills of Cherengani shaking bones
and wearing cloak of skin for a ceremony, *Ogilgei* in Nakuru
means a lot. Across the road from the bar, just 10 metres
away, are 15-seater Nissan vehicles that go to various places
in Kalenjinland. So this noisy corner, not 20 metres square, is
a sort of Kalenjin national nerve centre: you can land, dusty
and tired, from Texas or Kabartonjo, and ask around in your
language for *mursik*, or porridge, or to be updated on all the
latest politics, or negotiate, if your tongue is adroit enough,

to meet the President; or a good traditional healer, or a
trustworthy doctor, or your missing cousin, or a guy who knows
a guy who speaks your language who can find you a tractor to
hire, or a friendly policeman to help your court case disappear.
When times are hot and there is conflict with the Gikuyu, this
is a place of safety – or danger – for you can hide here, and be
hidden, or be sought out here. If you stand outside the bar, a
soft mist of Kalenjin babble rises. To the outsider it has a slight
falsetto, not high, flat – sounds are sharp sticks hitting wood,
hard g's and b's are soft porridge, gurgly, and a force defined in
secondary school physics class as a bush or a bull, because that
is where p becomes b.

If there are riots against a perception of Kalenjin threat
– which means that people feel that State House is being
ethnically xenophobic – people will know to head to *Ogilgei*.
To attack this small place, even with loud banging noises, is
to speak loudly to the nation of Kalenjins, and directly to the
President.

There have been ethnic clashes here: In 1991, and 1994. We
all know Moi and his people were at the centre of it: shoring
up his support among the Kalenjin by creating paranoia about
the Gikuyu, the Luhya – all neighbouring tribes. They use the
cheapest and most flammable political tactic: the outsiders are
out to get you, if you give them an inch. There is enough tinder
here, from Kenyatta days and before, when the Gikuyus were
seen to benefit disproportionately.

But ethnic clashes never really have to do with the noble
quest of the oppressed. In Kenya, it is always the poor who
get killed and displaced by the poor, and only to serve the
territorial needs of the political elite. If Gikuyu petty traders
are kicked out of Maasailand, Maasai politicians can grab their
assets. Those who really steal from Kenyans, in all our political
regimes, have never had their wealth challenged. As people
become poorer and more desperate, the politicians escalate the
paranoia, for fear that, one day, the crowd will stop and turn on
them.

Not 10 metres away from Ogilgei, you are in little Somalia,

126

which merges with little Mombasa – because the mosque is nearby – and so spicy things to eat can be found alongside sweetmeats and incenses. Behind Mombasa Stores, a Swahili grocer, and right next to the mosque is Nakuru's most famous whorehouse, also referred to as Mombasa Stores. Any teenager knows what you mean when you say Mombasa Stores.

I walk down, past Zoom Zoom, where we used to eat ice cream, past the Rift Valley Sports Club, an ocean of green cricket fields, and brown tennis courts, marked with white chalk, waiters who have worked there for 40 years, and Mwangi, the chef, who has been making cheap English food (fish and chips, shepherd's pie and others) for 46 years and who talks about the days when you would be beaten by settlers in Nakuru town if you were black and seen wearing shoes within club grounds. Behind the wall are Tipsy and Nakuru Sweet Mart, twin restaurants, one a bakery and vegetarian thali restaurant and the other serving burgers and chips and the best marsala chips in the world.

I stop to get a cup of marsala tea, and a grimy face with brown smelly teeth presents itself in front of me: Wainaina! – he shouts. I am embarrassed, I can't remember his name. He is waving a rag – a group of young men have been seated here for thirty years fighting to wash cars. This particular young man has been a street kid since I was a child. He and his brother operate from the market which is two streets down – both of them are fond of my mother and my brother Jim. He has a new car, Jimmy does, I am informed, and he helped me very much, very much. Your brother, he! He has a good heart. Your mother is very strict, but she always helps, and your brother has a good heart, he never forgets me. You have grown fat...you were in Botwsana right? No, South Africa, and how is Mandela? An almost empty bottle of glue sticks off the side of his face. Things are rough these days, he says, there are people coming down from Molo and places, the Kalenjins are coming for Gikuyus ....there are even Maasais hiding in Nakuru...are you driving the 505?

I can remember the first day I met him and his brother. I

was 7 or 8, and it was the first time I had ridden my bike into town, with my brother. I was exhausted, and hating it: my brother loves exercise and I don't.

But I loved the idea of being allowed to be next to Jimmy. My lungs were burning as we peddled, but my heart was twin purple fluorescent tubes of happiness. My sister Ciru and I are like twins, maybe too close for me to feel love so violently. My love for Jimmy, and my desire for approval from him, disables me.

So, by the large patch of loudly trading voices and hooting vehicles opposite the market, we were peddling furiously, when we saw, spread out on the dust, two long bodies in ragged shorts and nothing else. Their ribcages stood like hills, skin patchy and blackened with dirt, bruises and scars. In the full heat of the dry high altitude day, they were motionless, and my brother turned to me and said, 'they are dead,' and my heart stopped, my feet flailed and I toppled, scratched deep by the bicycle chains. I did not want to look to see if their tongues were hanging out, because that was, in our childhood language, the utter confirmation of death. I squinted at the bodies, and one of them jerked up, red swollen eyes caught mine and I squealed in fear and he started laughing, not so different from how he is laughing with me now.

I am not afraid now.

Drama unfolded at Nyandarua County Council on Thursday afternoon when a chief officer swallowed a bankers cheque for Sh1 million only a few minutes after being suspended. Civic leaders were dumbfounded at a special full council meeting when the officer grabbed the cheque and swallowed it. Chaos erupted as councillors wrestled with the treasurer in a bid to retrieve the cheque. Mathingira ward councillor Margaret Wambugu was bitten as she tried to retrieve the cheque and was rushed to a local hospital.
- The Standard

1995

The road shoots out into the distance, knobbly grey
tarmac, straight and true, and making equal: Nakuru town; the
Agricultural Showground; the dead straight line of jacaranda
and their morning carpet of mushy purple on rich, brown
damp earth; President Moi's palace and its attached school in
Kabarak; plains of grain and cattle; stony, sky land, hot and
dry; a pile of lonely casks of fresh milk, slowly souring by the
side of the road; another pile of recycled bottles filled with dark
beer-coloured Baringo honey, waiting for a market that is not
coming; an arm reaching out to show off a wriggling catfish
to the odd city car; a huddle of schoolgirls in purple school-
skirts swollen by the wind into swaying polyester lampshades,
giggling; goats seated in the centre of the road just past Marigat
town; dried riverbeds; and the plains of grain and cattle as we
head towards Baringo; groups of shining vaselined people walk
or cycle by the side of the road, to church, sometimes 10 or
more kilometres away; 10 or 12 tribes, three lakes; the whole
unbroken line of human evolution here, in the base of the Rift
Valley, as I head out to Pokot.

This road was the promise of a president t his people. The
honey projects, the milk, the irrigation scheme not far from
here that once produced eggplants the size of small pumpkins –
all these things failed to make wealth; to find markets.

The only durable success is the school, Kabarak High
School that provides some of the best high school education
in the country and has created a meritoclass of Bright Young
Kalenjins now in banks, and government, in Wall Street and
teaching at universities all over the world. Moi has invested a
lot in education all over Kalenjinland.

I got into the early matatu to Kabartonjo at dawn, and got
the front seat, next to a plump woman in a thick prickly sweater
and a massive handbag. She is reading the Bible, and chatting
to the driver – in Kalenjin, which I do not understand, but
which I love to listen to, the soft t's and baby softness of it, and
how it is spoken always with the mouth yapping up and down
in the grip of a full smile, a smile sometimes made poignant by

a gap in the bottom teeth some men have, like the driver.

When I was a child there was a season of Sunday drives like this. My father had committed, one year, to playing golf in every Sunday tournament in the country. So come Sunday morning, we would be tearing roads up to make tee-off time. Mum hated golf, and golfers – and this whole expedition – and although we often did not attend church in our home town, she often insisted we go when we were on such trips, which we hated. Trips were for other things.

This particular Sunday, the plan was to launch ourselves into a frenzy of splashing and swinging and sliding with fellow golf children and lick tomato sauce and molten Cadbury's chocolate off hot fingers and generally squirm and bliss around. Uplands pork sausages.

But Mum must find a church first.

We end up in just some corrugated iron church, and the heat and light is blinding and people are jumping up and down and singing what seems to me to sound like voices from an accordion.

I do not know what this religion is.

But it is unseemly.

I do not like accordions.

We sit. All hot and in Sunday sweaters and collars and Vaseline under the hot iron roof, and people spit and start, and this is because we are frying, not because God is here. In the front, there is a line of young women dressed in long gowns: bright red and green, with a stiff cone rising outwards up their chins. They are bouncing up and down. Up and down. And some of them have rattles, and some have tambourines and they are singing and sweating in that gritty dusty Kenyan way – not smooth and happy like America-on-television.

And the man in the front stands in the pulpit, sweating and shouting.

The Catholic Church I know is all about kneeling and standing when everybody else kneels and stands and crossing and singing with eyebrows up to show earnestness before God, and open mouth dignity to receive the bread. Some women will not put out their tongues for the priest – this is too suggestive. They will cup their hands and receive bread, and put the bread demurely into their hands and move back and bend one knee briefly before fading back to their seats, adjusting headscarves before sitting, kneeling, standing. Kneeling. Standing. Massage rosary. Service ends in 57 minutes.

This service goes on and on. Mum is shushing us a lot. Why does she come here? What is she looking for? Jimmy is quiet and looks pained. Mum, dressed in a simple elegant dress, her hair professionally done, with her angular Tutsi face, looks out of place here. She does not seem involved; her face is set.

People are dressed in wild robes: orange Peter Pan collars, neon blues and golds and yellows. And I am curious at this clang of music and God. And heat. Why does hot sun music clang?

And somewhere, things reach a pitch after we have given money, and people are writhing in the heat and shouting in the heat. Words are flowing from their lips, like porridge, in no language I know. Some people just hiccup for 20 minutes. In the front eyes are closed, tears are flowing and hand-made bottle-top tambourines rattling at full slapslapslap, the tin roof church is so hot.

And people have stretched to be *integrated* into this heat and clang. Have found a commitment. Not us though. Our hot wet breath and moisture is now dripping back down on us from the roof. Some faint. I want to drink. What is she looking for here?

Then – some are moaning, others whisper, music softer, honeyed panting, tongues lolling, and the pastor's hands are spread out and he is swaying, and the tambourine is soft, and soon we spill out, and people are talking to each other and shaking hands solemnly and we go to swim and lick Cadburys chocolate off our fingers.

We drive past the turnoff to Kabartonjo. There the road rises a few thousand metres in a few minutes. To our left, in the hills up there, is the series of humps called the Tugen Hills that run all the way to Kabartonjo, from where you look down from a great height on the Lukeino triangle, on the lakes of this area, the deep Kerio Valley. On a clear day you can see past Pokot lands to Turkana. The Lukeino Basin has for long been thought to be a good candidate for finding early hominids. The Turkana, who live not far from here in the hostile desert in the north of Kenya, are many things. They are also the world's oldest society, all 500 000 of them. A few years ago, it was discovered that the Turkana are the most genetically diverse people in the world, more diverse, they say, than all the populations in the world pooled together.

When I got into the matatu this morning, the conductor, a young shabbily dressed man, had been slapping the vehicle, eyes narrowed and shrewd, sometimes urging people on with his hand on their back – sometimes grabbing people from the side of the road, all the time in Gikuyu – bawdy and rustic, laughing hoarsely when somebody shrugged away in annoyance. We left, and he marinated chatter in Gikuyu, and in Gikuyu-accented English.

We had just past the police post at the industrial area when the driver turned to the young man sitting next to the door in the back seat of the 15-seater Nissan and addressed him in Kalenjin, and he replied in the same language. I was so startled I turned back and his eyes caught mine and he laughed, then broke into Kalenjin for the benefit of the passengers, swinging his chin to point at me, laughing softly, his smile now open and friendly, teasing, rather than mocking.

I notice this less and less, and often only after travelling. The man's body language, his expressions, his character even, change from language to language – he is a brash town guy, a Gikuyu matatu guy in Gikuyu, and even in Kiswahili. In Kalenjin his face is gentler, more humorous, ironic rather than sarcastic, conservative, eyes more naked to vulnerability. Easier to shock, easier to anger. By the time we pass Kabarak, the newer passengers are helped in with more courtliness and less rush, things piled on the roof, one older woman is helped in, his eyes respectful.

Some frail old threads gather as the woman sitting next to me sighs, long, in the middle of saying something to the driver, her shoulder slumps, and she says, "Msllp, ai, aliniuthii" – the Msllp, a sort of pulling in of saliva – a completely familiar movement, and one I haven't seen in years. The thing about it is how complete it is; it is not just the sound that she has, it is the way her neck swings, her shoulders move up the droop quickly, as she says, oh, that man! He really offended me, her slack shoulders say, even now she can only soften and succumb to this offence, for like me, or you, she suggests, we are vulnerable to being offended and being defeated by the offence: and this moves us all, for she has told us all too, that she trusts our common reaction enough to know that we too, would not put up a wall of pride at offence, or begin an escalation of conflicts. We sigh with her. For a moment we become a common personality, and she is chatting back and forth with people all over the matatu.

In the soft quiet following her shrug, if she turns back to me and asks me some small intimacy, that my individual would not appreciate, my common person will find himself being gracious and open.

..and it occurs to me, just now, that all the movements she presented, are, like *Ogilgei,* a national capital; a small tool that can be used to elicit an act of grace, in any part of this country, where neither our anthem nor our tax base, nor our language, nor view of the world is in any way universal.

I look out, and there is a horizontal placenta of cloud, dirty pink and brown, and somewhere in this distance, shafts of cloud-coloured rain is falling; on both my sides there is a wall of blue mountains, the escarpments of the Rift Valley. Some ragged-looking cows stand staring at us stupidly, and there is a trail of goat shit on the road.

It comes from every direction – shrapnel climbing up my arms, warm pools at the base of my stomach, a pulse of rising heat in my temples: the feeling of home.

They say, those scientists who know these things, that our smartest nerves are mirror neurons. They fire when we watch sports, or watch somebody dancing.

Our brains have been this big for 200 000 years – most of this time, we have lived within a few miles of where we are right now, the Rift Valley. But it is only 40 000 years ago that the "Big Bang" happened, some sort of critical mass in which tools, tailored clothes, religion appeared. Some speculate that some sort of genetic change also happened to the brain.

We have become used to thinking that until we learnt to write, human beings struggled to build a scaffolding of knowledge and ideas to carry them, and spread them.

What a defense of good!

That the patterns we spread around, we pass on, as efficiently as title deeds carry realty; we can pass on ourselves through our grace, down generation after generation. We spread even simple motions, movements, defences, loyalties.

But grace is a funny thing, and I don't mean just the grace that refers to swans. Because if we are sitting together, in this vehicle, and somebody's motor neurons fail to fire (maybe there is a Bavarian sitting with us) when this woman shrugs and her soft phrase pierces the silence, and group chatter rises, and she begins to speak to the whole vehicle, and this Bavarian person says something poisonous, like, 'please shut up Madam, can't you see I am reading?' – and the moment this happens, this man senses the small shift and stiffness inside the vehicle, the sudden silence of 15 chattering mindingownbusiness people, and his body is now numb, fingers do not know what to do as they fidget, and throat clears, gurgling defenses, he knows exactly what mood he has spoilt, but not at all what she said or did, or what that meant.

So, he may choose to stretch out a hand which we are all so suddenly acutely aware of – it stands outside this common experience – a naked thing wriggling in empty space.

It is scary, and we are tense, as this foreign object reaches forward. Perfectly physically familiar, this hand becomes an immediate animal threat, an inhuman object. It knows this and is tentative, and those long pale wrinkled things that spread like a fan from a palm, flutter for a moment, and then pat the shoulder of the woman, too hard or too soft, somehow not right, and she jerks sharply with an inhale of breath to catch his eyes, which are jumping now, clueless, and he looks down.

And this immediately releases our tension. He mumbles, sorry, sorry mama, and there is silence for a moment as we let him marvel with us, his own bravery, standing naked of mirror neuron empathy in thorny space and time, and finding his way to us blindfolded.

And somebody, the conductor maybe, and this becomes a truly appropriate word – *conductor* – will send us all into a new series of patterns by saying hallo *mzungu,* and jerking about in a deliberately unpatterned way, but close to our idea of a foreign Bavarian clumsiness, and we all burst out laughing at this joke with no punchline, constructed only out of movements that are incongruous, a word I am already associating with my brief religious ideology, based entirely on patterns and mirror neurons, and capital places like Ogilgei, and capital people, and conductors.

During these minutes, we climbed up the whole wall of an escarpment, drove past lakes and parks and towns, and these remained invisible as we registered with no conscious attention little sighs and slumping shoulders and a pat on a shoulder.

And so, I register the irony of a swaying conductor, moving to be righteously German, doing it ever so slightly wrong; he is confident enough in the smallest of signals to suggest that he is not proposing violence by this parody but is defusing awkward patterns, killing their threat. Ad we all get it, even the imaginary cliché Bavarian leans back and laughs.

Timing is everything, said Miles Davis.

Binyavanga Wainaina is the founding editor of Kwani?. He holds a Caine Prize for African Writing (2002) for his story 'How To Write About Africa,' and is a contributor to such international publications as National Geographic, Vanity Fair, Granta and many more. This story is an excerpt from his forthcoming book, Discovering Home.

Arrows
Marjorie Oludhe-MacGoye

Arrows
  are meant for silence, subtlety, precision,
  surprising with supple venom,
  quivering with pent-up anger
  or the propitiatory violence of the hunter.

Arrows
  may strike desire, quash rivalry, mark bounds,
  display a skill, direct a scout,
  exploit an ancient craft,
  convey wind-conscious cunning of concealment.

But these arrows
  foreign, purchased with malice aforethought,
  followed by fire and pillage,
  pointed with arrogance,
  feathered with pride, ignoring blood-guilt,

These arrows
  lacking the temper of tradition,
  do not embody common cause,
  can obey other bowstrings
  and turn against the shadowy assailant.

Why not
  employ the weapons of the disputed plain,
  pangas to clear the thickets,
  taught strings to contain edges,
  interpreters, proverbs, respect or truce?

Arrows
  impounded at the airport, choppers hover
  above the thickets scanning faces,
  jet planes whistle past bodies
  stripped for negotiation. Can we wake
  into our century, and shoot our mouths
  straight where murder is, an act of mercy?

Marjorie Oludhe Macgoye is a Kenyan poet and novelist.

137

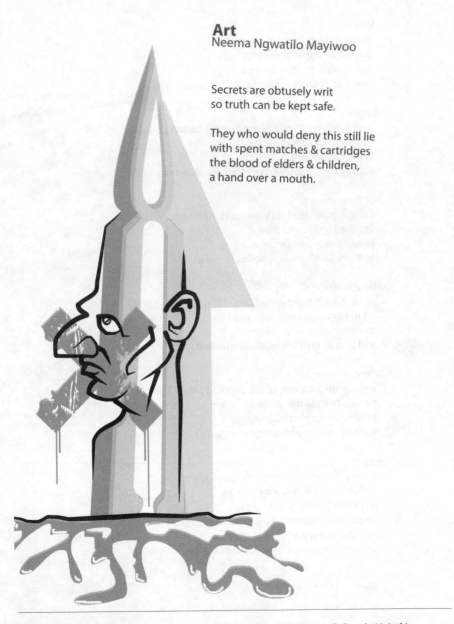

Art
Neema Ngwatilo Mayiwoo

Secrets are obtusely writ
so truth can be kept safe.

They who would deny this still lie
with spent matches & cartridges
the blood of elders & children,
a hand over a mouth.

Neema Ngwatilo Mawiyoo is a Kenyan poet and musician. She currently lives in Nairobi.

Heat, Smoke and Dust
Wilson Wahome Kiriungi

Now I miss the dust; not the clouds trailing the heels of fleeing crowds –
I miss the friendly brown sheets of earth - dancing with the wind during merrier times.
Though the dirt reddened my eyes with tears, all that cried were my eyes.
Now my heart is crying out, for my old, peaceful dusty street.

Now I miss the heat; not the smoldering sanctuary that cremated them -
I miss twelve o'clock on the equator - on us the lazying lenses beaming down.
Though the ultra-violet rays darkened my skin, all that darkened was my skin.
Now my heart is full of gloom, longing for those hot, slow afternoons.

Now I miss the smoke; not the billowing marker of mayhem -
I miss the ghostly smog of the city - man and machine getting along.
Though the fumes oft choked my lungs, all that choked were my lungs.
Now I am choking up, at the memory of the normal chaos.

Wilson Wahome Kiriungi is a graduate of Language and Literary Studies from Moi University. He is currently living in Massachusetts, USA, and studying law.

Divide and Misrule
Stephen Derwent Partington

What does dug earth care at all about ethnicity?
A Mwangi fits a six foot hole
as snugly as Owuor.
And tell me, where's the corpse that anyone
can teargas with success?
Or did you do it to augment the tears of mourners,
                              out of kindness?
Can you tell a foe from how he skins a cow
                    or peels a spud
                           or guts a fish?
        Are these enough to skin his hide?
        Perhaps it's speech, the way she shrubs?
    And who's the carrier, his mother or his dad?
        Can we locate the gene for Enemy?
            Today, can we condone the fact
        Kikamba's only got one word for 'enemy',
                        'Maasai'?
            Reflect: that family you killed,
                it had as little land as you.
Or did you see the old machete used to cut you?
        Dented, rusty, cheap, like yours.
            Reflect on this.
This warped deflection of your anger
                        isn't justice:

        it's a coffinful of shit.

140

Media Framing, Eldoret IDP Camp
Stephen Derwent Partington

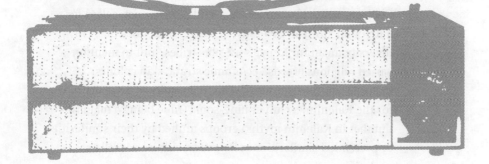

The camera was fixed on something else:
a young girl crying,
much as babies always cry, with food, without.
There was a sombre drone of muzak
and a lilting-voiced narration.
Some producer was determined we should weep.

It seems one toothless homeless woman
wasn't briefed: top-left, off focus
she was doubled-up with laughter
like a woman half her age,
her bright tears streaming.
Did you notice? Did you frown, or did you grin?

Stephen Derwent Partington hides behind an isolated hill in Ukambani, where he teaches and writes poems, academic articles and other such stuff. A firm believer in the need for literature to demonstrate a social conscience, but also in the need to avoid preaching, he is a member of the Concerned Kenyan Writers group.

KALENJIN NARRATIVES

EDITOR'S NOTE

One of our main challenges in addressing the troubles of January was not only to focus on the epicenters of violence, but to also illuminate the cultures of different ethnic communities to provide some context. Just as we published a googlepedia section in *Kwani? 4* that took an irreverent thrust at the ways of the Gikuyu, and a Luo travelogue through Nyanza province in Part 1 of *Kwani? 5*, for Part 2 we have put together the following 'Kalenjin Narratives.'

In the December, 2007 issue of *Kass* magazine, Chelulei Cheison, political commentator and bio-chemist, called for a Kalenjin 'unity in diversity,' asking: ' what does unity in diversity mean for Kenya's 42-plus tribes, not to mention varied religious creeds, economic strata, skin colours, histories and geographies? What does unity in diversity mean for the Kalenjin, a club of nine-some (nine being a magical number in Kalenjin myths) groups unified by their similarities or pretended similarities in language, culture as well as evolutionary or migratory attributes?'

To help answer these questions on Kalenjin origins, identity and culture, this section includes an excerpt from Benjamin Kipkorir's book, *The Marakwet of Kenya: A Preliminary Study,* an article previously published in *Kass* magazine, and a short excerpt on the 'Kalenjin calendar' by Dr Kipkoeech araap Sambu.

THE HISTORY OF THE MARAKWET: A PRELIMINARY STUDY

By Benjamin Kipkorir

THE KALENJIN PEOPLES EGYPT ORIGIN LEGEND REVISITED; WAS ASIIS ISIS?

Following Ancestral Footsteps

There is a Kalenjin girls' initiation song that goes:

'*Ndomo rireetaab Musaiga koto mokimi emoni.*'

'Were it not for the sea of Musaiga (Moses) we would be dead.'

Why would modern day girls undergoing initiation sing about the biblical legend of Moses fleeing Egypt and leading his people across the Red Sea? Could this song have been passed down intact through a hundred generations or was it a recent addition brought in by the advent of Christianity in the Kalenjin community?

In his book, *The Kalenjin Peoples Egypt Origin Legend Revisited; Was Asiis Isis?*, Dr. Kipkoeech Araap Sambu analyses similarities in Egyptian and Kalenjin religion, culture and language to show the two communities may share a common ancestry. Religion governs man's relationship with God. Culture, through its principles and structures, manifests God amongst men, while language is the medium through which religion and culture are handed down through generations. The *Egyptians*, we learn, believed in the existence of a supreme being with many attributes that they called '*Ptah.*' *Ptah*, like the Kalenjin godhead *Kiptaiyaat,* was perceived through his attributes which were based on the communities' different experiences of God's nature. Through such experiences as redemption from external attacks, good climate, bounty harvest, light from sun, and child bearing, the godhead was given different names. The Egyptian *Ptah* was also called *Isis, Ka, Ra, and Amon,* while *Kiptaiyaat* was referred to as *Asiis, Cheebet, Kooriis* and *Ileet/Ilat.* This litany of the divinity's manifestations in Egyptian and in Kalenjin has confused many historians, making them declare African religions polytheistic, while in fact they were monotheistic.

Most of the attributes of the divinity in Kalenjin and Egyptian have similar linguistic correlations. The Egyptian term *Ptah* means 'of the beginning' just as *Pataa* does in Kalenjin. This perhaps shows a common belief that the divinity transcends all creation. Both communities believe that God created man and that he rules over all creation. *Isis,* the Egyptian attribute to *Ptah* as the creator can also be directly compared to *Asiis,* Kalenjin's similar attribute to '*Kiptaiyaat.*' Both *Isis* and *Asiis* have female attributes, as if creation were better handled by a woman. Like the Egyptians, Kalenjin believed that God, whomever they perceived him to be, established a system to govern his relationship with the community and between individual members of the community to ensure harmony and prosperity. This code of conduct was referred to as '*Maat*' in Kalenjin. The Egyptians call it *M'haut.*

African communities preserve their history through song, folklore, myth and legend. These forms of literature also serve to remind the community members of their responsibilities to each other.

One song sung during Kalenjin boys' initiation goes:
'*Kebare Kimugon ami tai....* '
'I will be at the frontline fighting *Kimugon* (The Pokot.*)*'

Once a man has been initiated into adulthood, he takes on responsibilities including defending the community. The *Maat* code governing the social grouping which this man was admitted to when the song was being sung clearly stipulates that he has an unquestionable duty to defend his land and people. *Asiis* in her wisdom set this code to harmonize the lives of community members. *Maat* is the most important element of Kalenjin religion and culture. A man who adheres to this code is rewarded and his spirit lives forever through generations to come. *Maat* means family continuity both in the Kalenjin and Egyptian communities. This form of continuity, like in many other African communities, is a totemic based social structure. *Maat* and *M'haut* as philosophical concepts are a code of conduct governing man's relationship with his community, his creator and his ancestors, or the living dead.

Dr. Sambu makes linguistic comparisons of the terms as follows:

The ancient Egyptians, and the Kalenjin, associate the word *Maat* and its derivates with 'fire', 'way', or 'path' as well as with the 'family and social inter linkage networks.' The author goes on to write that the ancient Egyptian word is preserved in the hieroglyphic as *Her-t,* meaning (as translated by Wallis Budge, British Egyptologist) path, road, tribesmen, generations, family, and kith. The Kalenjin equivalent of *Her-t, Oreet,* can be translated into the same familial and generational structures.

M'haut is the code of ethics in the Egyptian tradition. It was the concept of order in nature and society as set by the act of creation, meaning *M'haut* oversaw administration of justice, law and order. *M'haut* promised a reward to those who kept faithful to it, ensuring every member of the community carried out their duties and responsibilities with the society's best interests at heart. *M'haut* was conceptualized as a female deity, same as the Kalenjin did with Asiis. The ancient Egyptians believed she kept human beings on the straight course of justice, equity and harmony (Egyptologist Wallis Budge also interprets the word M'haut as 'straight'.) However M'haut was not autonomous to the godhead {Ka, Ra, and Amon} but some sort of interface between man and the divinity.

For the Kalenjin, *Maat* had a deeper function in addition to the ethical aspect governing the man-God-ancestor relationship. *Maat* is the manifestation of the continuity within the community. *Maat* can be pictured as a thread running down through generations, connecting the community to its ancestry. *Maat* is perpetuated through a patriarchal lineage system, a relay torch passed from one generation to the other. It is also the bond between individuals, fixed rules, and rights and duties that automatically come with a person being a member of a military regiment, which was hereditary along agnatic lines. Members of this regiment would call each other 'Maat.'

Maat is the embodiment of the cordial relationship, norms and responsibilities that are a result of one being a member of an *ibindo* (age set). There were defined roles for each *ibindo* based on age and life experience. Community governance was the old men's duty, the youth were warriors, while adolescent boys and girls herded livestock. There are eight categories of the Kalenjin age sets: *Chuumo, Maaina, Nyoongi, Kimnyigee, Kapleelach Kipkoimet, Korongoro and Saawe*. One formally joins an *ibindo* during initiation. The age groups change every ten to fifteen years. The current *ibindo* being initiated is Kimnyigee (1994- 2010). *Kimnyigee* will be followed by *Nyoongi* and so forth. Father and son cannot fall under the same *ibindo*: for instance *Chuumo* will bear *Nyoongi*. Members of the same *ibindo* regard each other as brothers and it was common to find an adult disciplining a child not necessarily his own or even related to him.

Maat through *ibindo* brings about a sense of communal responsibility to property and other members of the community. Like in the Egyptian community, we learn from Dr. Sambu's book that *Maat* in Kalenjin rewarded those who kept to it through re-incarnation, marked by naming a newborn after a dead relative. The Egyptian concept of reincarnation is found in the myth of *Osiris* – the Eygptian God of incarnation. He is believed to have been begotten after his mother, *Isis*, resurrected her husband, *Horus,* who had been killed by his evil brother in-law *Seth*. Based on the cultural, linguistic and religious similarities listed above, Dr. Sambu gives evidence to show the Kalenjin must have been in ancient Egypt at one time, if they are not kin to the Egyptians.

Among the Keiyo and Marakwet, there is a famous song praising Mount Elgon, where their ancestors are said to have come from. The story behind this song is well known and repeated often by grandmothers from the aforementioned communities. The Kalenjin at Mt. Elgon were known as the Sabinny (Sebei/Sabaot?). It is at this point that they are said to have dispersed into the various groups that they are in now. The history beyond Mount Elgon seems to have been lost beyond reach of myth or legend. According to Heroditus, so called ' Father of History,' the Egyptian King Sesostris II of the 12th dynasty divided Egyptian society into hereditary professions. The warrior class had a clan named Sebenitus, who in Heroditus's *Histories* wander into Southern Africa and are cut off from Egypt when the Sahara desert forms. Could the Sabenitus be the Sabinny, ancestral community of the present day Kalenjin? Could it be that the warrior class did not concern itself with writing, embalming the dead and building pyramids – things considered to be at the heart of Egyptian civilization?

The Kalenjin community, like their Egyptian counterparts, held warriors in high regard. Most Kalenjin legends were believed to have been warriors. Bows, arrows and spears were the most commonly used weapons in both communities. The Kalenjin have an elaborate army structure, and along with the Maasai were reputed to be the fiercest communities in pre-colonial times.

Gaston Maspero, the 19th Century Egyptologist and historian, gave the following description of the ancient Egyptian army:

'Both spearmen and archers for the most part were purebred Egyptians .....The army of King Ramases II at the battle of Quodshu comprised four divisions which bore the names of *Amon, Ra, Ptah* and *Sukhtu {Set}*... the effective force of the army was made up of auxiliaries taken from the Negros of the upper Nile...'

Dr. Sambu brings this up to make a comparison with yet another historian, Peristiany, who lived among the Kipsigis. Peristiany wrote the following about the Kipsigis military arrangement:

'The *Puriet* (*Poryeet*) is another of the social groupings into which the Kipsigis are drawn from the moment of birth. There are four Kipsigis puriosiek; *Kipkayge, Ngetunyo, Kasanet*, and *Kebeni*. The *Kipkayge* with *Ngetunyo*, the *Kasanet* with *Kebeni* are united together without the possibility of telling which one is a subdivision of the other.'

While King Ramases II army's divisions are named after the deity, the Kipsigis named theirs after four heroes. Dr. Sambu points out that the naming system of the two armies seem to peg importance to the figure four, which the Kalenjin still consider sacred. Both Peristiany and Maspero further say that the two armies employed similar offensive formation, this was also based on the sacred figure four. During the day, Kipsigis warriors would walk in a single file but broke into four *Kwanaik* (columns) commanded by the four *kiptaynek ab puriosiek* (singular *kiptaiyaat ab poryeet*- leader of the battle.)

The Egyptian army, according to Maspero: 'Once they entered the enemy country advanced in close, the infantry in columns of four.' One of Ramases II divisions was known as *Set*. This term in Kalenjin means 'an act of going to war with the aim of plundering.'

A strong corroboration to Dr. Sambu's argument can be found in the research of Weldon Araap Kirui. In his paper titled *Kalenjin, the Military Clan of Ancient Egyptians*, Kirui writes The Sebenitus are Kalenjin ancestors, and further argues the word Sebenitus is a corruption of the term Sebei, Sabinny or Sabaot, the word the Kalenjin were known by until a group of scholars from the different sub-nations (Tugen, Nandi, Keiyo, Kipsigis etc) coined the term Kalenjin, meaning 'I tell you,' to capture all the sub-nations under one group. Kirui also quotes instances where the Sabeans are found in the Christian Bible, in Job 1:15: 'And the Sabeans fell upon them, and took them away;' and Ezekiel 23:42: 'And a voice of multitude being at ease with her, and with their message of the common sort was brought Sabeans from the wilderness which put bracelets upon their hands and beautiful crowns upon their heads.' In Kirui's paper, the Sebei believe they originated from a place called *Ntrr* (Egyptian) meaning 'the holy land of God in the south.' The Kalenjin equivalent, *'Ne toror,'* means 'the exalted one,' or 'a place high up,' or better still, 'summit.' Kirui also conducted interviews with old men who told him that the Kalenjin originated in Mount Elgon, migrated north to Misri (Egypt) and came back after a thousand years.

Mount Elgon emerges as a significant place, the area where the Kalenjin stopped en route to their present day settlements. Dr. Sambu compares the migratory path taken by the Kalenjin to that taken by the post-mosaic Israelites. The Kalenjin came from Mount Elgon through present day Kakamega, Kitale, Moiben, Tugen, to Nakuru, Elementaita and back, crossing river Kipchoryaan to the famous Tulwaap Psisgiis (also known as Tulwaap Moonyis), from which flow springs where they are said to have performed a mass circumcision. Standing on the summit of the Tulwaap Psigiis (located north of Nakuru) one gets the full view of the present day Kalenjin settlements from Tugen to the northeast, Keiyo to the north, Nandi in the south and Kipsigis to the south. The post-mosaic Israelites wandered northwards in the wilderness for 40 years till they crossed River Jordan, when their leader Joshua performed a mass circumcision of all grown up males at a sanctuary they called Gilgal. The last major initiation was said to have been performed by Moses on Mount Pisgah. Standing atop this mountain, one make outs Israel's Promised Land. Mount Pisgah is also famous for the springs that flow from it.

For ages Kalenjin history has had a blank difficult for even the best of orators to fill. Dr. Sambu's book provides an elaborate map tracing the community's history, piecing together myth, legend and grounding them in historical fact. It also puts down in writing knowledge that would have been forgotten with the passing of the few remaining pre-colonial grandparents. In the larger context, the book follows the tradition of Cheik Anta Diop's *African Origin of Civilization*, whose premise is that African history cannot be told convincingly until historians dare to link it to Egypt.

THE KALENJIIN CALENDAR

By Dr Kipkoeech araap Sambu

1: THE 120-YEAR KALENJIIN CALENDAR

Perhaps nothing demonstrates ancient Kalenjiin mathematical and philosophical genius better than the high precision and complex traditional division of society into age sets and age grades. We are going to discuss the system in its original pristine format, what we are going to refer to as the 'ideal' here, the reason being that the situation, as it is now, has since varied markedly in one or two regions from the original ideal format. There are 8 age-sets, *ibinweek* in Kalenjiin, which are divided into two Houses. These are **Kaapkoroongoro** and **Kaapkipkooimet**. Each of the two Houses has four age-sets within it. Kaapkoroongoro House has: Koroongoro, Kaapleelach, Nyoongi and Chuumo. And the Kaapkipkooimet House has: Kipkooimet, Kimnyiigee, Maaina and Saawe. But the two Houses are meshed together so that both operate as one. So the order of occurrence, ideally shifting every 15 years, is as follows: **Koroongoro–Kipkooimet–Kaapleelach–Kimnyiigee–Nyoongi–Maaina–Chuumo–Saawe** then back to Koroongoro 120 years later and the cycle begins all over again.

Each of the 8 age sets is subdivided into what anthropologists call age grades, *sirit* or *maat* in Kalenjiin. These are, in order of seniority: Choongin, Kiptaru, Tetagaat and Kiptaitooin/Kiptooin.

So we need to familiarize ourselves with the two terms, 'age set' and 'age grade' and make sure not to confuse between them. As pointed out, an age set contains four age grades. These are ushered in one by one at an interval of four years. The first to be initiated when a new age set is begun will always be called Choongin grade. After approximately 4 years the initiation of the same age set's Kiptaru grade begins. This will run for about 4 years whereupon the Tetagaat will take their turn. After the 4 or so years of Tetagaat initiation, it will be the time for the last

lot of that age set, the Kiptaitooin, also called Kiptooin. After a
lapse of approximately 4 years a brand new age set begins and
the same age grade names are also freshly begun, the eldest
being, of course, the Choongin.

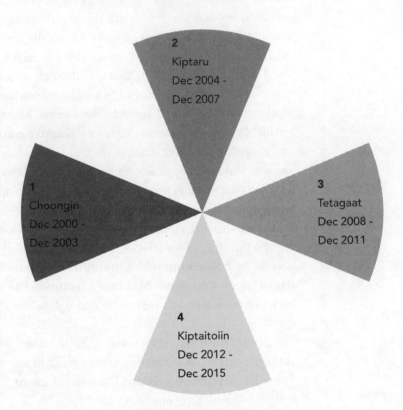

FIGURE 1

Age-grade diagram as it is today for the Kimnyiigee
age set over much of southern Kalenjiinland: Each of the 8
Kalenjiin age sets is divided into 4 cyclical age grades which
are ushered in every fourth year as in the following order:
Choongin, Kiptaru, Tetagaat, and Kiptaitoiin/Kiptoiin. The age
set being initiated now over much of southern Kalenjiinland
is Kimnyiigee and the Kimnyigee age grade being initiated

now is the second one, Kiptaru. December 2008 will usher in
the Tetagaat age grade of Kimnyiigee and December 2012 will
usher in the last age grade of Kimnyiigee called Kiptaitoiin
or Kiptoiin. The last lot of Kiptaitoiin of Kimnyiigee will be
initiated in December 2015 and Kimnyiigee age-set will be
closed to make way for the Choongin age grade of Nyoongi age
set.

FIGURE 2

The House of Kaapkoroongoro: it comprises the following
age sets: Koroongoro who are ideally the fathers of Kaapleelach
who are in turn ideally the fathers of Nyoongi, who, ideally, are
in turn the fathers of Chuumo who in turn are the fathers of
Koroongoro. The corresponding female sets' names are given
in brackets. However, upon marriage a woman adopted her
husband's age set. The children of the occasional very young
wife of an old man may end up being circumcised into an age
set outside the old man's traditional House. Thus the system

was often disrupted from family to family. Otherwise as a whole, the system worked with precision. Where the system still obtains in its original format, families are known to belong to either Kaapkipkooimet or Kaapkorongoro. The word 'ideally' is used advisedly here because in practice there will be exceptions. These are explained in the caption of Figure 4 below.

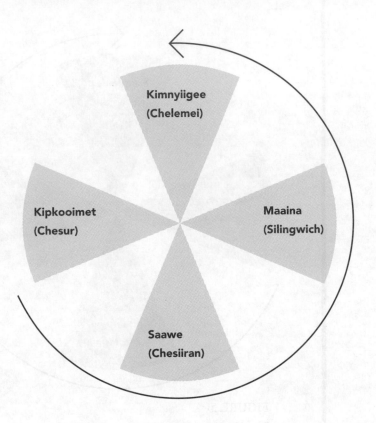

FIGURE 3

The House of Kaapkipkooimet, comprising the following age sets: Kipkooimet who are ideally the fathers of Kimnyiigee who are in turn ideally the fathers of Maaina, who, ideally, are in turn the fathers of Saawe, who are the fathers of Kipkooimet. The corresponding female sets' names are given in brackets. However upon marriage a woman adopted her husband's age set. The children of the occasional very young wife of an old man may end up being circumcised into an age set outside the old man's traditional House. Thus the system was often disrupted from family to family. Otherwise in general, the system worked with precision. Where the system still obtains in its original format families are known to belong to either Kaapkipkooimet or Kaapkorongoro for ever. The word 'ideally' is used advisedly here because in practice there will be exceptions. These are explained in the caption of Figure 4 below.

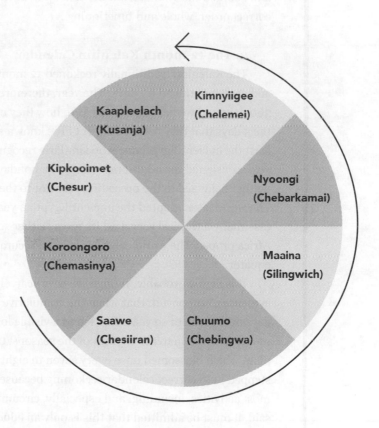

FIGURE 4

The work of ancient genius: the two Houses, Kaapkorongoro and Kaapkipkooimet are enmeshed and do rotate in such a synchronized fashion that it is not possible to tell that they are identified as two distinct houses. The entire system of 8 age sets rotates anticlockwise at the rate of one revolution in 120 years. Each age set is circumcised over a period of 15 years, then the following set is ushered in. But that scenario is the ideal and presently obtains only in North Baringo, Keiyo, Marakwet and perhaps elsewhere but not among the Kipsigiis (who lost Kipkooimet), the Nandi (who lost Koroongoro) and the Tugen south of Arror (who lost Maaina). Ironically, the Luhya, the Kuria and the Abagusii, who learnt and adopted the system from the Kalenjiin, have the system in correct order, whole and functioning.

2: The 12-month Kalenjiin Calendar

The Kalenjiin traditionally reckoned 12 months in a year and each month had 30 days. The year, therefore, consisted of 360 days and we have no record as to how they made up for the 5 days that they counted short of the known solar year. At least the ancient Egyptians, who similarly recognized a 360-day year, consigned the additional 5 days to a holiday period that neither belonged to the preceding year nor to the following one. The world later adopted the ancient Egyptian year, which, being essentially a tropical year, had its roots farther south in tropical Africa proper. The world calendar is most accurate along the equator.

It is highly probable, though we have scarcely any tangible evidence to support it, that when the cumulative loss of five days over seven or so years had led to a visible loss of a whole month in relation to the rhythm of the seasons, the setyoot plant which blossomed once every seven to eight years stepped in to correct calendar reckoning because it stopped most activities, including, and especially, circumcision. That said, it must be admitted that this is only an educated guess. Earlier writers who commented on it never tried to address the discrepancy and how it was made up for. The principal of them were: C. Hollis (1909) and Peristiany (1939). I have also discussed the calendar in my doctoral thesis (2000), in various unpublished works and in my published book (2007).

Kalenjiinland was vast and seasons varied and because the month-names were really season names, they occurred at varying times during the year. The first month of the Kalenjiin year was the month of planting, which most called Kiptaamo. It, however, coincides with February in old Nandi but with March in Belgut. The year started at different times from region to region, depending on the month of planting. There cannot be, therefore, a uniform Kalenjiin calendar, and any adoption of one would be a matter of convention for the sake of uniformity.

The Gotabgaa website: www.gotabgaa.org, has the following calendar, which seems to be closely modeled on the Belgut calendar. This was documented by J.G. Peristiany in 1939. It differs with the one documented in Nandi by Hollis in 1909. The month names are, however, uniform to a large extent, and we publish it here with that caution in mind. What we need to reiterate and remember is: these were largely season names and since seasons differed from place to place over the vast land the month names also followed that pattern even though the nomenclature was reasonably uniform.

The Emperor's New Clothes

As we were selecting the artwork for *Kwani? 05,* one particular series came our way that arrested us completely. A dozen vivid street scenes, each clearly drawn by a child's hand yet with a scope and attention to detail that brought to mind the kaleidoscopic murals of Diego Rivera, we couldn't take our eyes off. Here was the neighborly violence that tore through the slums in January of 2008, seen through the eyes of an innocent, stripped of all ideology or politics. These paintings left us naked; they exposed the absurd brutality of the post-election chaos in a way no photograph or story had managed to do.

Then we found out they'd been drawn before the election.

'Kids in Mathare don't speak their mind, they're very shy,' said Jacob Wachira, the Mathare-based artist and director of Watoto Wa Kwetu Trust under whose guidance the paintings were made. 'But they see everything.'

Wachira has been offering the children of Mathare free art workshops since 2004. In February of 2007, he started a project with over 100 of them, themed – ironically enough – 'Peace in the World.'

'I never said this is what you should do, this is how it's done. I just gave them the tools and asked them to paint their world as they saw it.'

In Mathare, that meant people marking Kikuyu houses with paint long before the election campaign began; it meant violence from Mungiki and police; pangas and bullets, helicopters and ambulances. 'These kids were observing it all – everything that shocked the rest of us when the election finally arrived came as no surprise to them. They were the best intelligence gatherers in the country.'

Ranging from five to 15 years in age and representing as many tribes as live in Mathare, the children collaborated on 48 paintings in all. The last one was completed at the end of November, 2007, a month before Kenyans went to the polls on December 27.

We thank Jacob Wachira and the children of Watoto Wa Kwetu Trust for donating the following paintings to *Kwani? 5.*

NEVER LET THE FACTS
GET IN THE WAY OF TRUTH.

... AN OLD CREATIVE NON-FICTION DICTUM

RICE
WARS

Samuel Munene

To get there, you board an Embu-bound Nissan matatu from Nairobi. Once out on the Nairobi-Nyeri road and the driver steps on the accelerator (speedometer indicating vehicle speed 100 kilometres per hour), you will be crossing Tana River or Thagana, as it is known by the locals, in an hour and a half.

You will know you have reached the Thagana when you see shirtless men with pronounced ribs, bare feet and trousers folded to the knee selling tilapia fish, still wet and dripping, to motorists on the roadside. While crossing the Thagana bridge, you will hear, exactly 10 times, noises coming from the largest broken heavy metal LP record in the world, produced as the Nissan's wheels hit the shallow drainage trenches. If you look down, you will see Kenya's longest river, a molten-lava-coloured slug crawling to the Indian Ocean, engorged with red volcanic soil from the hills of central Kenya.

After 300 metres with the heavy metal experience still ringing in your ears, you will come to Makutano, which for many years has been wavering between a small town and a large trading centre built on both sides of the road. If your driver slows down (as he should because of the numerous bumps on the road), women in headscarves with dirty *lesos* tied around their waists and *ngoma* rubber shoes on their feet will crowd around the matatu, offering the largest passion fruit, bananas, tomatoes and mangoes for only five shillings apiece.

After clearing the bumps the driver probably will accelerate devilishly as the road becomes smoother and wider, and after 15 minutes you will be on the outskirts of Wanguru, popularly known as Ngurubani.

This is the headquarters of Mwea Division.

On both sides of the road you will see green rice shoots growing in fields of black soil that extends for miles and miles, and the trenches and canals full of brown water will seem to extend to the end of the world. Occasionally you will notice some black spots, and you will be surprised to make out a group of children playing in the water or men in their underwear, bathing. In the large waterworld before your eyes, the air will dance with cicadas above the brackish water spread over several fields. There will be a lone cow, a halo of insects buzzing around her head, squelching through the swamp, drinking and grazing, a speck in this mosaic landscape of vegetation and water. Now and then, grey storks and herons will wheel and plop softly into the marshlands.

You will whiz past all this, and as you approach Ngurubani, your driver will be forced to slow down again, this time because of the tens of bicycles everywhere. Shoulder to shoulder with the bicycles, donkeys stroll; some pulling carts, some walking leisurely on the road with no inhibitions, none of them caring about the vehicles.

Look up and you will see a billboard that reads, MTUNZE PANDA AKUTUNZE (TAKE CARE OF YOUR DONKEY, AND HE WILL SERVE YOU BETTER). In November 2007, the region was identified by the Kenya Society for the Protection and Care of Animals as one of the worst abusers of animals in the country, second only to Lamu. Look closer at the donkeys' backs and sides: they carry maps of scars and fresh wounds healing on top of older ones. The men leading the donkeys hold rubber whips: steering mechanisms that lead the donkeys in a certain direction, or accelerators to make them move faster.

Ngurubani is more rice granary than town; one of three shops has sacks of rice neatly arranged outside the entrance. Plopped beside the doorways sit the shopkeepers, mostly women, idling on Kenpoly plastic chairs of the kind found in Nairobi's downtown hotels, basking and chatting in the sun. An Embu or Nairobi-bound matatu pulls them out of their seats, ready for passengers looking to purchase rice 'from the source.' Out of sight, the real sources—rice mills—hum in the distance.

Nothing much happens in this rice outpost; an elections year brings much needed relief to the unending flatness. If you were in Ngurubani in December of 2007, what you would have noticed were the posters plastered to every feasible vertical surface. Of the many faces that peered out from Ngurubani's telephone poles and tin walls, two stood out. The first was of a middle-aged man with small eyes, charcoal black hair and a wealthy, cunning smile against a white glossy background. Below the photo was the name Peter Gitau, the words KUGA NA GWIKA (WORDS AND ACTIONS). (In the left upper corner of the poster was a smaller photo of a man with receding hair, showing his teeth in a slight grimace: EMILIO MWAI KIBAKI.)

The other poster was blue. It featured a bespectacled man in a white shirt and striped tie, ALFRED NDERITU: MAN OF THE PEOPLE, and also the incumbent MP. (Again, only this time in the upper right corner, was a photo of that same man with the receding hair and a toothy grimace: EMILIO MWAI KIBAKI.)

The man charged with making sure Alfred Nderitu, the self-styled Man of the People, recaptured his parliamentary seat was David Waweru, a dark, almost six-foot-tall man with a puffy face and short-cropped hair. His habit of chewing the left end of his lower lip faster than he spoke made him seem to be lip-synching as words came from his mouth.

Born in the neighbouring Gichugu constituency, Waweru migrated to Mwea in his mid-twenties as a schoolteacher at Thiba Primary School, located in the heart of the rice farms. He fell in love with Mwea—its heat and its people—and with time began to supplement his teaching salary by purchasing small quantities of rice from his neighbours and selling it in bulk to the neighbouring markets of Embu, Muranga and Kerugoya.

Waweru was popular, in part because of his generosity; he could always be counted on to buy a few rounds for his buddies at the local. In 1995, Waweru started organizing quarterly volleyball tournaments in Ngurubani, where he donated small cash and volleyball-kit prizes. He was also invited to preside over jumble sales in churches, either as a guest or as master of ceremonies, a job usually given to those who fire up a crowd. Although he was not a politician, he was vocal on most issues affecting the area. Mwea, to him, was home, and anything that affected its people affected him. These skills eventually led him to become the Man of the People's right-hand man.

During the 2007 campaign, Waweru avoided riding in the same vehicle with the Man of the People as much as possible. There was always the possibility of something going wrong, especially as the election neared. Also, wherever the candidate was there were always hangers-on currying favour, a never-ending blame game between sycophants, accusatory outbursts and childlike sulking by campaign and staff—all of the grand drama of the political circus hovering over the candidate that deterred Waweru from doing his job. Given an option, he would have preferred to drive alone in his dark grey Toyota Camry, playing some soft music and setting his mind free.

But in the campaign convoy, no car belonged to any individual; anyone could hitch a ride in your car by pressing a little blackmail button and threatening to join the rival camp. It was The Campaign, and you had to dance to everyone's little guitar to make them happy.

Leading up to the elections in December, 21 vehicles in the convoy were doing one of their last tours of the campaign. Vehicle-hiring was one thing the Man of the People was willing to spend money on, others being his campaign posters and T-shirts. Waweru was in the back seat of the lead vehicle, a grey Nissan Hard-Body caked with a mixture of black and red soil.

Four speakers were mounted on the Nissan. The man in the front passenger seat, a dark, short man with a wide mouth and full lips, was in charge of public address. With one hand holding the microphone and the other on the control knobs, he would play some loud Kikuyu song, and just when the song was getting to the climax, he would interrupt, 'Ndio, ndio, Alfred Nderitu, Mundu wa Andu' ('Yes, yes, Alfred Nderitu, Man of the People'), before letting the song play for another few seconds, and then interrupting again, just like a radio presenter. His voice could be heard for miles across the flatlands.

The convoy suddenly came upon a crowd of 200 people. Most were barefooted or in slippers. Most of the men had their trousers folded to the knees (standard Mwea style to avoid getting wet). A group of noisy young people at the back moved from one end to another. Nderitu emerged from the vehicle behind the Nissan, bespectacled and wearing grey sneakers, black jeans and a checked short-sleeved shirt. Standing next to him was another six-foot-tall man with a sagging potbelly and receding hairline. He wore black leather shoes, black cotton trousers and a blue shirt. Behind Nderitu was another man whose biceps and broad shoulders were obvious even through his brown leather jacket. Looking through the crowd, his eyes sometimes rested on a particular character, squinting before continuing the scan, the kind of dramatic technique found in Chinese karate movies.

Waweru stood behind everyone, biting his lower lip and wearing that expressionless face you see on football coaches when they are two goals down in the 80th minute. Slowly he moved and joined the crowd. The man with the sagging potbelly held the microphone, cleared his throat and started in a voice which, despite his protruding tummy, sounded as though it came from a starving man. Waweru disliked him.

'Thank you, Nguka people, for turning up. This is not really a meeting but an opportunity to remind you that a good leader is known by the sacrifices he has made for his people. A good leader has a stake in the people he is leading.' He removed a crumpled white handkerchief from his shirt pocket and wiped the greasy sweat accumulating on his brow. He then continued in the strange thin voice, 'You all know Nderitu; you know how much he has sacrificed for you. Just to repeat the obvious, who doesn't know what he has done for you rice farmers. Who hasn't benefited from rice?'

Someone in the crowd shouted, 'Until when will you talk about rice?'

Waweru moved towards the source of the voice. Potbelly ignored the fellow and continued, 'Let us not become people to be deceived. Let us elect

Kibaki. Let us elect Alfred Nderitu. And with those few remarks let me invite Mheshimiwa himself to say a word or two. Clap, clap for the Mheshimiwa!'

With the sun's rays hitting him, Nderitu's dark glasses looked like a poor imitation of Victoria Beckham's fashion shades. Once the microphone was in his hand, Nderitu stretched his mouth at the edges with a hybrid of smile and scowl. 'Thengiu. Thengiu. People of Nguka,' he started in a deep voice with the tone of a headmaster. *Thank you, thank you so much*. Waweru moved to the back and looked at the Man of the People as he spoke.

'I think Bwana Njoroge has said it all. You people know what I have done for you. Who doesn't know how we fought the rice wars? Who doesn't know that we have been trying to tackle the land issue? Look at CDF: Haven't we built schools, hospitals and even roads? Who is better, someone who has shown you what he can do or someone just making promises, promises, promises and just promises?'

The crowd was growing bigger by the minute. Waweru was curious about what had drawn them, whether it was the sound of loudspeakers or whether they wanted to answer the numerous questions Nderitu was asking. He was not sure whether the crowd was friendly. 'I am asking you, my people, to kindly give me your votes,' Nderitu continued.

At this point the group of young hecklers at the back started shouting: 'Stadium! Stadium! What about the stadium?'

They were referring to Wanguru Stadium, which is the size of a football pitch and mainly used for sports and political rallies. Residents of Ngurubani had been complaining that the stadium was neglected and misused and had become a grazing ground for donkeys and cattle. The CDF Committee, under the patronage of Mr. Alfred Nderitu, had decided to fence and renovate it a few years ago. Eventually it had been fenced with chicken wire and the pitch had been levelled using a Caterpillar tractor. The CDF Committee then presented a bill of more than a million shillings. Critics, and many a Mwea resident, believed the cost could not have exceeded 400,000.

Everyone turned to the group that was shouting—everyone except Nderitu, who ignored them and continued with his address.

'Don't be deceived with useless things like [sic] alkohoo,' he cried, as the chants grew louder, drowning out his voice. Realizing that his efforts were futile and trying to maintain some dignity, he quickly wrapped up. 'Thank you so much for giving me your time. Remember on 27th, 'Mtu wa watu Nderitu',' he finished, before hurriedly getting into his Prado in the company of Potbelly

Njoroge and the man in the brown leather coat.

Waweru got into the double-cabin pickup, and the man called DJ started playing a song by Joseph Kamaru. Every so often came the interruption, 'Alfred Nderitu Mundu wa Andu.' Other than the DJ, no one else spoke. Waweru kept on biting the left side of his lower lip, working on his Motorola V3. He looked like a coach who had lost a game. The clock on the dashboard showed it was some minutes to six. The sun was receding into the open rice fields. The horizon looked so near and yet was so far, just like those paintings by amateur artists perennially titled 'African Sunset.'

The Man of the People's convoy reached the main road and branched off toward Embu, leaving Ngurubani behind. They drove for about 10 minutes before turning onto a dirt road and then past a smaller town, Kimbimbi, down another dirt road with a large tomato farm to one side that many thought belonged to Nderitu. That was another thing: there were murmurings that he preached water but drank wine—Nderitu himself did not believe in rice. The string of vehicles stopped in front of a blue gate that a farm worker opened, ushering them in to a half-acre compound.

The Man of the People jumped out of the Prado and headed toward the house, with Brown Leather Jacket, Potbelly Njoroge and Waweru in tow. At one end of the compound were a tent and some empty plastic chairs; those left behind in the convoy drifted toward the tent. There were about 30 people. There were only two women. Everyone was subdued.

Thirty minutes later, Waweru drove back toward Ngurubani in his grey Toyota Camry, biting his lower lip and holding the steering wheel with both hands close together. He drove silently, looking at the road ahead. He was thinking about Alfred Nderitu, the Man of the People, and Mwea, the constituency whose destiny he was trying to shape.

In 1997, Alfred Nderitu was still 40 years old and the director of Anet Enterprises, a 'general trading and construction company.' He had previously worked as a design and measurements engineer with several international engineering companies and had a degree in civil engineering from the University of Massachusetts, in addition to a diploma in philosophy, psychology and journalism. He enjoyed tennis and golf.

In those years, Mwea Irrigation Scheme was managed by the National Irrigation Board (NIB). Residents rented the land rather than owned it. Many conditions were attached to tenancy on the scheme. The most contentious was that all the rice grown on the allocated piece of land belonged to the board and could not be delivered or sold anywhere else without its authority. The board then determined how many bags to give to the farmer for consumption and how many he could sell to meet other subsistence needs. On average, this allocation was between nine and 12 bags.

Another rule, widely ignored, decreed that women could not be tenants, and once children reached the age of 18 they were expected to leave the scheme. Rice farmers were not happy but put up with the rules with little fuss since getting into the wrong books with the NIB officials could lead to harassment and possible expulsion. All this had been inherited when the scheme was set up at independence. At the time, the government had to find a solution for the many poor, landless people. It thus established cheaper schemes for settling the landless. Mwea was just one such area.

Mwea constituency was formed almost 90 percent from the Mwea Irrigation Scheme, a gazetted area of 30,350 acres. More than half of the area, about 16,000 acres, eventually was developed for rice production. The rest was mainly used for settlement, horticultural crops and other subsistence farming. Farmers on the scheme became tenants of the government through the NIB. The area under the Mwea Settlement Scheme never increased, since no extra land had been allocated to factor in a growing population. After the first generation of beneficiaries, land had to be split up to accomodate the next generation and the next, so when Mwea boys reached the age of 18, they demanded a part of the initial four acres allocated to each family, especially after providing labour on the family farm for many years throughout their school-going days.

People lived communally in villages, usually on the dry, raised areas. This was in order to spare as much area as possible for rice farming and to protect residents from floods. The crowding naturally produced an increase in population. And the work was gruelling: Planting to harvesting of rice takes about five months—six if you count the month it takes to prepare the fields before planting. Two of these months are spent chasing the birds away; families rise as early as six and work as late as seven in the evening, spending the whole day in hot fields partially submerged in water. With increased subdivision of the family allocations, the return per individual has gone down steadily, making many—especially young men—lose interest in rice farming and seek alternatives in other areas such as horticultural farming, small businesses, boda bodas, etc. Others have illegally leased their land to farmers from a neighbouring constituency who grow rice not as their only source of livelihood, but as a supplement.

When Nderitu decided to run for Parliament, despite being virtually unknown in Mwea, this was the general state of affairs. So he packaged himself as the young rebel candidate, a hothead with a message of hope and liberation. He promised to lead the farmers 'from the bondage of the board.' In the history of Mwea, no leader had ever dared take on the NIB like Nderitu did, promising to continue to do so if elected. Soon everyone was listening to this new leader who was promising to help them change their lives.

As the elections neared, many expected Waweru to declare his candidacy for the Wanguru civic seat. Some officials of the Democratic Party even approached him, promising their support if he vied. He declined but made it clear that he was supporting Nderitu for MP. Nderitu wound up beating his closest rival by a very large margin. The newly elected MP set out to fulfil the freedom-from-the-board promise he had made to his constituents. The first part of his plan involved mobilizing farmers to demonstrate against the board for as long as it took to have it change its policies.

Theoretically, this sounded like an easy thing to do, but it took some convincing, even amongst the people who had voted for Nderitu on that premise. After decades of subjugation, the rice farmers were thoroughly cowed by the NIB and found it much easier to simply criticize it than to take any action. Nderitu needed charismatic people on the ground to instil faith in the farmers, lift their spirits and mobilize them into action. With an ever-present car to the ground, Waweru heard that volunteers were needed, and he offered himself, risking his teaching career.

The two first met one evening in early January of 1998, right after the previously held elections, at a hotel in Kerugoya, Kirinyaga District headquarters. Some Mwea councillors and other volunteers attended the meeting. Nderitu spoke of his vision for the rice farmers and how it could be achieved. Later that night, he engaged in a one-on-one discussion with Waweru on the plight of rice farmers. Waweru was more than pleased by the wit, charisma and plans of the new leader. For all the years he had lived in Mwea, he had never seen a leader who had a true understanding of what was happening on the ground. The following day he started talking to farmers on Nderitu's behalf.

The first demonstration at Ngurubani town, where the offices of the NIB were located, was attended by some 5000 farmers. The farmers stormed the board's offices and unilaterally declared that they would run the scheme themselves. Police were called and dispersed the mobs. The volunteers regularly met with Nderitu to plan their next course of action and discuss how best to keep the farmers from giving up. They successfully convinced the farmers to keep on demonstrating, and the gatherings grew more and more intense. Board tractors were burned, employees were beaten, NIB buildings torched. The busy Nairobi-Embu highway was blocked again and again by angry farmers who lit fires. Again and again, the police came to engage the farmers in street battles. This eventually resulted in the fatal shooting of two demonstrators.

The deaths were the turning point in the protests. Other MPs started raising their voices in support of the farmers, backed by local and international human rights organizations. Reluctantly, the government relented and gave the farmers their land. Freedom from the National Irrigation Board was achieved at last. Nderitu became the Man of the People, and for a while he could no wrong.

Mugumo Hotel and Lodge is located about 200 metres from the main Ngurubani town. From the main road, the part of the hotel painted with black-and-white zebra stripes is visible. Inside, the hotel is divided into cubicles with names like Wanguru, Kagio and Karira. The bigger cubicles can hold up to 18 people, the smaller ones only four. Waweru chose one of the smaller cubicles, where he ordered some fried meat and a cold White Cap from one of the uniformed staff, a rarity in Ngurubani.

The reason he was there was to meet a media man who had sought to interview The Man of the People the previous day. Nderitu had turned down the request, citing 'time constraints,' probably thinking the interview futile as the elections were only a few days away. Waweru thought this a mistake and managed to convince Nderitu to write down the answers, which he was now reviewing as he waited for the man. At this stage of the campaign he was trying everything he could do to get the Man of the People re-elected.

On the next day, the last official day of the campaign, Nderitu wore a plain green short-sleeved shirt, blue jeans and black leather boots. The campaign convoy headed out to Kianjiru, Mururi, Murinduko and South Ngariama. Waweru wore a brown polo shirt, dark jeans and white sneakers. That day, he rode in the same vehicle with the Man of the People, a navy-blue Isuzu Pajero with new number plates. The driver was a man with a long face and a big head skewed to one side. Waweru sat in the front seat, next to the driver, his teeth, as ever, fighting with his lower lip. Brown Leather Coat sat behind him, wearing a white polo shirt beneath the jacket. Potbelly Njoroge sat directly behind the driver with his belly spilled halfway over his thighs. His hairline seemed to have receded a few millimetres since the campaign had started. The campaign convoy hit the road some minutes to 11, in the general direction of Embu. There was silence in the Pajero. Waweru counted the homes, trying to translate them to votes. Twenty minutes later, the convoy arrived at South Ngariama. Waweru emerged first from the Pajero. He looked at the crowd of about 200 people before moving to join them, his mind racing back and tracing the history of the scheme.

South Ngariama is a 28,000-acre piece of land bordered by three rivers: the Rupingaci to the south, the Nyamindi to the west and the Kiiri to the north. It was originally the common grazing land of the nine clans of Ngariama; during the Mau Mau years, when Kikuyus were evicted from the region, the land was abandoned and reverted to bush. After independence, the government gave South Ngariama to the Kirinyaga County Council, which in turn granted a lease to what became the South Ngariama Farmers Co-operative Society. That society has been dairy farming on the 28,000 acres ever since.

For the last 20 years, however, an increasingly bloody dispute has arisen over proper ownership of the land. The South Ngariama Farmer's Co-operative has been battling the Kenya Co-operative Creameries, which is trying to take the land back, and has also been battling representatives of the nine clans of Ngariama, who have begun a court case to establish original ownership of the land. In 1998, yet another group of clans, this time representing Kirinyaga District, sought to establish legal ownership of the disputed land. The Farmer's Co-operative also has suffered increasingly from corrupt mismanagement of its own ranks.

Beset from inside and out, the farmers of the South Ngariama Co-operative have watched as random squatters encroached upon their

11

farmland, operating farms as big as their own. They themselves increasingly are seen as squatters, with no choice but to await the verdicts of several court cases against them. Thus the South Ngariama people have long lived on a diet of wicked hope and fear. Every day when the sun sets behind the Murinduko Hills, they thank God that their grip on the land has lasted another day. For some, it's a whole 24 hours of their crops maturing, while for others, it's a place they can call home. And just as each day brings hope, so does it give birth to fear of attack, of eviction.

This was the group Nderitu was about to address. Waweru hoped the meeting would be peaceful and that the Man of the People would not get excited by the crowd and say anything untoward. When Potbelly Njoroge gave Nderitu the microphone, the crowd surged closer, clapping and screaming. The Man of the People just smiled and said, 'Thengiu. Thengiu. The battle for South Ngariama is not over. We have fought, and we will continue fighting, and unlike others I am not going to abandon you. . . . Just remember on the 27th, vote for your man, a brave man, a man of action, Alfred Nderitu. Kazi iendelee!' The crowd screamed at the end of the speech.

The convoy snaked to Murinduko, a small town about six kilometres from South Ngariama. And the message was the same: 'Remember, on the 27th, it's Alfred Nderitu, the Man of the

People.' The small trading centres of Gathoge, Difathas, Mururi, Kianjiru, Kutus and Kagio were reminded, 'Alfred Nderitu, Mundu wa Andu.'

At six in the evening, the convoy headed back to Alfred Nderitu's house in Kimbimbi. Immediately, Waweru excused himself and took his Toyota Camry back to Ngurubani. 'It's over,' he said to himself with a sense of guilt. He had felt it. He drove holding the steering wheel tightly as he looked blankly into the twilight.

Between 1997 and 2000, during the first years of Nderitu's first parliamentary term, the National Irrigation Board provided farmers with some essential services. It milled and marketed their produce, and advised them about rice farming methods; it provided fertilizers and tractors to plough the rice fields. So when farmers rejected the board, someone filled the void.

Nderitu came up with the Mwea Rice Growers Multi-Purpose Co-operative. And for about two years, the co-operative did a reasonably good job of supporting the farmers, providing them with all the infrastructural needs the NIB had formerly seen to and paying them better for their work. By 2000, however, the system had started to crack. Harvest payments were delayed, tractors disappeared, and seedlings and fertilizers became more scarce each planting season.

The Man of the People was blamed for all of this, not least for his alleged part ownership of a private rice mill that was built and created to compete directly with the one operated by the co-operative. With all these woes, Nderitu barely managed to win the 2002 elections. Since then, Waweru had been filled with conflicting emotions. He somehow felt that he had betrayed the people who had agreed to join the 'struggle' because they trusted him. Some blamed him. He also believed in Nderitu to some extent but still felt that the MP had let the farmers down by not showing proper leadership in the management of their co-operative.

He'd always made it clear to Nderitu that the farmers were not happy but gave the same excuses Nderitu gave him when he was asked what had gone wrong. Slowly he realized that fewer and fewer believed him, and Waweru started wondering whether he believed the things he said himself. Meanwhile, the NIB—which had been sidelined but never disbanded—had been restructured and rebranded, recasting itself, finally, as an equal partner, rather than as a landlord. By 2003, some farmers had rejoined the board, which now treated them with dignity and offered better prices than their own co-operative, once Nderitu's initiative.

In 2006, Waweru held a meeting with Nderitu at his home. 'What's the story on the ground?' the Man of the People asked. By then, Waweru was no longer the Man of the People's man. With time, he had withdrawn as much as he could from political activities and other projects involving the community. He had also quit his teaching job and now concentrated on several businesses he'd started, especially the fleet of Nissan matatus he owned that ran along the Embu–Nairobi route.

Waweru did not mince words during the meeting with Nderitu. The constituents wanted nothing to do with the Man of the People. They felt he had hijacked and exploited them to his advantage. Word on the ground was that he was to be voted out.

'What should we do?' Nderitu asked.

'Focus on rice, but not as the main issue and especially not among the young people,' Waweru told him.

'Can you help me?'

'I will think about it.'

Waweru left caught up between the people who had trusted him and the man he had come to consider a friend and associate. He believed Nderitu had a good vision for the farmers, but something somewhere had gone wrong. The money he was offered was good, but that was hardly a motivation. What would his friends say? What would Nderitu say if he turned the offer down? In the end, it didn't make much difference. Waweru learned that you can please many people some of the time, but you can never please them all of the time. Politics is, after all, a game of too many people and few resources.

Nderitu lost to the other candidate when the results came in.

There is a bar in Ngurubani known as Skyview Bar and Restaurant. It has exactly six wooden tables and 36 chairs. The Skyview has one television—a 21-inch Akai—and a Sony VCD player. When not showing a video of John Ndemathiu, George Wanjaro or Mike Murimi, the TV is tuned to Citizen. The Skyview is the kind of bar where you can spend the whole day watching television without a drink. If Wangechi, the hefty waitress, asks you to buy a drink, just remind her of that evening three months ago when you bought drinks for the whole night.

On December 28, 2008, if Wangechi asked why you were not buying a drink, you just needed to retort, 'Are you one of those supporting ODM?'

'Who? I would even have a headache thinking of it,' she would say, and leave you alone, for Skyview was overflowing with people watching the elections results.

Every few minutes, the female presenter on the tube would say, 'On the line we have our correspondent from Bondo; so, Oscar, what are the results?' And the reporter, if in Nyanza, replied, 'Here Raila came first, followed by Kibaki, Kukubo, then Muiru.' It would be the opposite in Central: 'This is Mwangi reporting from Gichugu. Martha Karua recaptured her seat, and Kibaki led, followed by Kalonzo, then Raila.'

By 4 p.m. on the 28th, the tally showed Raila to be leading, followed by Kibaki, with a vote difference of more than half a million.

'Even if he wins, it's okay,' someone said.

'Kwani, where is Moi, to show Kibaki how it is done?' another man asked.

'A million votes, those are many! I don't think he will recover.'

'Even Raila is a human being, maybe he will not be as bad as we expect.'

By 7 p.m., the tally showed Raila's lead widening. By 8 p.m., the patrons demanded a video of John Ndemathiu. The outcome was now obvious.

Samuel Munene is a young Nairobi poet, short story writer, and contributor to Kwani? as well as various literary online magazines. He holds an economics degree from the University of Nairobi, and currently earns a living as a freelance writer.

ITUIKA

Millicent Muthoni

For my father, Bethuel Gitu

In order to keep up the spirit of Ituika [revolution that signified the breaking away from autocracy to democracy], and to prevent any tendency to return to the system of despotic government, the change of, and the election for, the government offices should be based on a rotation system of generations. The community was divided into two communities; a) Mwangi, b) Maina or Irungu

Membership was to be determined by birth, that is, if one generation is Mwangi, their sons shall be called Maina[Irungu], and their grandsons Mwangi, and so on. It was further decided that one generation should hold the office for a period of 30 to 40 years, at the end of which the ceremony of Ituika should take place to declare that the old generation had completed its term of governing, and that the young generation was ready to take over administration of the country.
Facing Mount Kenya, Jomo Kenyatta p 101

ONE HEAD DOES NOT DIVIDE THE LAND
(Mutwe umwe ndugayaga ng'undu)

December 2ⁿᵈ, 2007, 6 pm.

Members of the Kigumo Development Initiative (KDI) comprised of
the Kigumo diaspora within and without the larger Kenya: Constituents
of Kigumo, Friends of Kigumo, Degree-holders of Kigumo, Kigumo
professionals (all legally registered associations) sit together to discuss the
dire state of their homeland. An auburn Nairobi sun drops below the ceramic-
tiled terrace of the Boulevard Hotel where they sit, the pall of calm frequently
disturbed by the after-work traffic coming from the adjacent Museum Hill
roundabout. All aspirants for the Kigumo parliamentary seat have been
invited and are present, bar one.

They have all done good – many of their life-narratives are sermons in
fortitude: they went to school barefoot, eked a life out of the three-stone
hearth, grew up on arrowroots and sweet potatoes, worked hard and got
somewhere. All are examples and proponents of the Kenyan dream. There
is a former Muthithi Primary school student who now sits on the board of
the Kenya Tea Development Authority; a former teacher who took a degree
program at Kenyatta University and now lectures at a Zetech college; the
Director of City Planning in Nairobi himself, Mr. Peter Kibinda.

Violence in the Kigumo election campaign tops the agenda. Resolution
No 1: They will not allow insecurity in this campaign. They, as erstwhile
Kigumo citizens, have decided. Childish, very childish, one of the attendees
mutters below his breath. Aspirants have been kidnapped, others beaten
up, and others have had their car windscreens smashed by groups of armed
thugs. All but one have had their posters torn down. The seven aspirants
present wear grim faces, including the incumbent, Hon. Kihara Mwangi. The
culprit allegedly responsible for all this misery is the one candidate who was
not invited – the Enemy.

'*Ngai*! Give me a high five. You are so *rost*. Ni campaigns zimefanya
upotee hivyo?' It is a light-skinned lady who works for the Coffee Board of
Kenya and is also one of the founders of KDI. She addresses the youngest
aspirant, Chefman, whose wife is said to be Raila's cousin (this has not
helped his campaign). She clutches him to her bosom. Chefman's slogan,
Like Father, Like Son, brands him as an action-oriented progeny of President
Mwai Kibaki; he has travelled all over Kigumo, distributing wheat flour
to voters and constructing roadside sheds. Everywhere he takes the flour,

women ululate five times, as they do for a returning son in Kikuyu custom. Days afterwards, however, there are complaints that *mandazis* and *chapatis* made from the flour were sour. Another candidate is said to have connections to donors and has recently been distributing free medicine in Kigumo; the old and frail constituents lean towards him. The young ones, however, dismiss him, asking where he was when they were 'falling sick for the last five years.'

The meeting starts; business cards are tossed on the table and collected like poker hands. Everyone picks up his bunch, scrutinizes and pockets or tosses into a handbag. A kettle of mixed *chai* is ordered. Tea. Everyone fraternizes for two hours, then the meeting is called to order when looks of impatience start appearing on those who have exhausted their fount of small talk. The chairman, a grizzled middle-aged man with a static buzz in his voice, gets the group's attention.

'KDI will not support any single candidate. All we are looking for over here is that professionals are consulted and involved in the rallies.'

'When the leader of the pack limps ...' he starts ... 'the animals never get to the pastures,' the rest finish in unison.

'We want a strong leader who will work with ...eeh ... us, stakeholders. You will forgive me Mheshimiwa, (to Hon. Kihara Mwangi, the incumbent)... but eeh ... we as professionals have long been ignored.'

'There are ... eeh ... auditors, planners, lawyers, businessmen, engineers, and even ... eeh...' he looks around to see who he has left out and sees a raised hand.

'Yes ... teachers. All pillars of Kigumo society.'

Hon. Kihara, fondly referred to as 'Bishop,' opens his address with a prayer. The men take off their hats, mostly cowboy Stetsons.

'We ask you, Lord, to give us one mind because a divided army falls by the first blow. Let not the devil bring hatred and bloodshed in our constituency...' After a few more pleas for peace, he finishes with a resounding Amen! The Bishop starts off with praise for the KDI's noble venture. His gaze is piercing, his back straight, his palms firmly set on the table as he speaks.

'I had planned to call you professionals together, but...' his Adam's apple frantically rises and falls.

'Maybe I have not gathered my sheep as well as I should have...' he says, his voice trailing off.

The Land Surveyor interrupts: 'We used to sit like this in 1976 with the likes of Wa Thuo and other Kigumo professionals. We would plan the development of the constituency, and we would consult with each other when there were jobs,' he says, voice dripping with nostalgia. There is a brief pause; the Bishop has received many a barb in previous meetings but today his past misdeeds have been forgotten – the last few weeks have seen the rise of a common enemy. Mr. Chair broaches the subject of violence once more.

'Back to Resolution 1. We will not allow violence in this campaign.' He calls for further suggestions on how to resolve the crisis.

The lady from the Coffee Board has a baby face with pouty pink lips and sunken coconut eyes that do not betray her age or her senior position. Her shapely manicured hands move in soft waves as she speaks. She is wearing a bohemian crocheted sweater and matching woolen hat. She calls for the distribution of pamphlets instructing people what qualities to look for in a leader. The waiter keeps reappearing and is waved away again.

'That person must be: 1. A GOOD LISTENER 2. SOMEONE WITH A CLEAN RECORD 3. A LEADER WHO HAS THE PEOPLE'S INTEREST AT HEART,' she says, reading from a notebook.

'Our people should not be bought cheap. We need to tell our people that this time we do not want a rich man. You know, Kibaki has given us money through CDF, the Women's Fund, the Youth Fund, etcetera, and so we want ... you know, someone who can manage it.'

The Enemy, 'Jamleck Kamau,' has not been mentioned in name so far. If anyone were to bring it up it would be her. She has often sworn that Jamleck will not to get to Parliament.

'He will never crap in the House,' she tells everyone who will listen. She has toured churches all over the constituency, addressed women, poured money into Jamleck's opponents' camps and set up a group of election strategy professionals to out-think and out-maneuver him. Jamleck is her ex-husband.

Another aspirant, a United Nations technocrat for the last seven years, hoarsely asks to be excused for his voice, the effect of a dusty campaign trail. He stands up, yanking his khaki trouser from between his fat thighs. His matching khaki jacket has as many pockets as a magician's coat, all of them stuffed with campaign materials, business cards, notebooks and money. He scoffs that discussing Kigumo's violence in an abstract and general way is a waste of time; they all know who is behind it.

Everybody nods in agreement: 'Mmhh!'

'This known man...' he says, and removes his beret and places it on the table, 'has been tearing up our posters and giving money to our young men so they can beat other contestants up. Mheshimiwa ... si you were attacked the other day?' he says to Bishop.

'Mmhh.'

Bishop tells how his cars have been stoned, his supporters slashed, and how The Enemy rigged him out openly during the party nominations. His 10-year record of bad governance is momentarily forgotten.

'The offenders were arrested and put in, but were drinking at the shopping centre the next day,' he says.

The only female aspirant arrives. Though born in Kigumo, she is married in Nyeri and practising law in the US, a hard sell. Kigumo voters find it hard to vote for a woman, let alone one they have already 'sold.' Her posters bear rudely scrawled messages: 'Go vie in your husband's home.' The campaign has made her face permanently taut, her lips are always pursed together even when she is smiling. She waves hello, pockets both her hands into the black leather jacket she is wearing and sits down. Coffee board lady places her fork and knife on the plate, stretches a hand behind the two men beside her and shakes Madam aspiring MP's hand.

'Jamleck has a security firm. He's been misusing our sons there, paying them peanuts and treating them harshly,' someone says.

The group have a secret weapon in Jamleck's ex-chief campaigner who has defected to KDI.

'In Kigumo, we do not want the poritics of thagare ene more,' he now says in heavily Kenyanized English. He is the very picture of Muranga street-smart in his Stetson godpapa hat, his perpetual dashes outside to take a call from his cell phone, even if everyone else has theirs switched off. He specializes in jumping campaign ship during the elections. He speaks with his hands and enunciates his words carefully, promising revelations of all secrets.

'Can I tero you a secret? Jamreck... is... a... coward. Money is his shield. Ask me, I have been with him for years. He... is... very... fearful.' Then he sits, satisfied that he has convinced all present that the enemy is not a formidable one.

Another woman shoots up. She is the wife on another aspirant, an older man who is quiet and dignified to a fault. 'Oh yes! In 2002, when he rigged my husband out, I walked up to him and told him you are very evil!' she says, wagging her index finger in the air for effect. Being her husband's mouthpiece in a chauvinistic space probably does more damage than good to his popularity.

'Jamleck trembled like a leaf. Coward!' she sits as everyone nods in agreement.

'Mmhh.'

Chefman, the young aspirant, is clearly agitated. 'Yes, I don't know why you fear him. You talk tough here, but when you meet him on the ground you shake his hand as if you are friends. Me? I tell him off!' Unlike his political father, the current President, this young Turk's speech is pacey and his plea like a war cry. He calls for a public thrashing of Jamleck, and joint rallies to give The Enemy a dressing-down. 'When our people see that the rest of us cannot share a platform with him, they will see him for the selfish man he is,' he argues.

'Mmhh.'

Mr. Gitu then speaks. His voice is quiet. 'One man cannot match 14 of us. Let all us aspirants sign a letter to the Electoral Commission of Kenya denouncing this violent man.' The group loves this last suggestion, and the lawyer is asked to draft a letter *in situ*. The tightlipped lady suggests that elders drawn from different parts of the constituency should sign the letter as well. SMSs are also to be sent out to constituents, telling them that Jamleck is a crook.

'I don't know why we are pretending. *Dawa ya moto ni moto*,' says Njiiri, a friend of Kigumo, but also in the campaign for Honorable Kihara. *Let's fight fire with fire*. Both hands firmly grip the table: 'We have sued Jamleck before – he loves that because he has bought off the police and the administration.' His protruding eyes survey the awkward silence as he waits for approval. 'Let us tear his posters and beat up his people as well!' An uneasy grin spreads over his face. Everyone starts talking all at once - the idea is eventually discarded. The meeting ends three hours later than scheduled. There are uneasy compromises even as the aspirants steal side-long glances at each other. Days later they will be smearing each other's names on the campaign trail. The meeting is considered a success.

HE WHO BLOWS THE HORN MUST WATER HIS THROAT (Coro maai)

3 p.m, Sunday, December 23, 2007.

Kangari town, a sprawling trade centre in the upper part of Kigumo, is abuzz. Residents are out in numbers to get a first-hand experience of Jamleck

Kamau's famed *muugithi* roadshow. Four days to the elections, Jamleck's campaign is at fever pitch. A large roadshow truck is crowded with people in PNU merchandise: T-shirts, bandanas, caps, all printed *Kibaki Tena* and *Jamleck for Kigumo*. A crowd of women standing next to one of the four-wheel drive campaign vehicles break into a scuffle over the blue and red headscarves being handed out and now flying in to the air.

'This one has taken two! I want the red one printed with Jamu's face!' The whole crowd seems to be in uniform; the black, green, blue and red T-shirts that have just been distributed are everywhere.

Banners of Jamleck hang high up; traffic is at a standstill, blocked by curious mobs who were promised Uhuru Kenyatta as the main act. The latter did not pitch up. Instead, Macang'i the comedian and current Riverwood film star, has been offered as a stand-in. The show starts, and Lucy wa Ngunjiri, leading presenter at Kameme FM, comes forward to pray and anoint the King whom God has chosen. The crowd falls over itself cheering. Kameme FM airwaves have been awash with Jamleck's pleas for votes: *'People of Kigumo: Do not listen to those enemies of development who say I do not like peace. I ask you to vote for me. Vote for development. This is your MP for Kigumo starting the 27th December.'* He has become Kigumo's first political celebrity. All the vernacular FM stations: Coro FM, Inooro FM, Kameme FM, Bahasha FM, powerful in the extreme in rural areas, have begged the people of Mumbi's house, the Kikuyu, to come out in large numbers and vote against the Luo. Accusations are also hurled between candidates. Kameme FM, Jamleck's mouthpiece, accuses Mrs. Gitu , headmistress of Nginda Girls Secondary School, of using the school van to ferry her husband's political supporters. They have urged the government to come down on civil servants who misuse public resources. When confronted, Mrs. Gitu burst out laughing: 'Those are my husband's opponents' hate campaign gimmicks. I was ferrying my furniture home.'

'Jamu is on top here. Kijana na Kibaki!' says a middle aged man caught up in the youthful excitement of the campaigns.

'Have you heard him speak. *Ngai!* This time, our MP will be Waziri. Minister. Straight. *Ma.' I swear.*

Bars and restaurants are central to the campaign. Many eat and drink on Jamleck's bill. For men, beer buys their votes. Women exchange theirs for *lesos* and blankets. Teetotallers guzzle crazy-hot cups of tea served in a kettle with a sufuria to cool it in, fleshy mandazi or potato samosas. The long benches spanning two tables each are packed – when one person wants to leave all 10 on his side have to stand up. Old men play checkers with bottle tops.

Kangari town is built on an embankment atop a near-upright slope, with its upper line of shops, butcheries, tailors, cafes, bars, Safaricom stands, Agrovet shops, and more bars and butcheries, seemingly poised to fall off the edge. The roadside groceries run along the road, an organic scene in vivid colour – the bright red heaps of the tomatoes, orange carrots, deep green bunches of *sukumawiki*, the brilliant white *nduma*, arum lilies, scraped and piled into clusters and the sunny inside of sample oranges sliced for display. From the upper line of shops, the people seem like an army of ants scuttling from morsel to morsel. Kangari also hosts the Kenya Women's Finance Trust and Family Bank, through which the Women's Fund is channeled.

Meanwhile in Kigumo, the ECK is distributing pamphlets and books at its offices to teach people to refuse to be bought and to vote wisely. The call for good leaders has been relentless this election, with civil society and ECK taking the lead. Chagua Amani Zuia Noma, Vijana Tugutuke, When You Vote, Think ...

Further down the road is the populous Kirere shopping centre and what is becoming a Central Province financial fixture, Equity Bank. At the famed Muthithi Market, one can buy anything from a bleating goat to a giant bunch of bananas or a sack of maize, any of which will be readily loaded for you onto a matatu. Sugar cane vendors chop cane into cubes at the matatu terminus, rush to the vehicles, baring their characteristic Kikuyu-brown teeth as they thrust their wares at passengers. Beans are sold in rows and rows of Kimbo tins, bars of soap are strewn all over, *mitumba* and fake human hair. Shop façades and walls are plastered everywhere by low-end companies, NGOs and CBO's. Tusker, Safaricom, Omo, Fanta, Uraia, 'Because citizens have rights' also colour the walls. Market stalls are shaded with flaps of plastic on stick frames, all bending and blowing in the wind.

December 29th, 2008. Results have been announced. From Heho shopping centre, the dirt road to the left leads to the home of Mr. Gitu, the aspiring MP. Two arcs of ornate stone funnel into an elaborate black metal gate. From the gate, a sloping murram driveway with a flailing remnant of kei apple hedge on the flanks seems to lead to nothing but an iron sheet pit latrine, a generator room screened with concrete ventilation blocks. A cattle shed can be observed from behind a mound of chopped wood.

Leading up to the house is a thick circular mound of shrubs in the middle

with pine, rose plants, bougainvillea, Kikuyu grass, ferns and the cactii. The large house is caressed by a twirling money plant from bottom to top at the chimney; a hundred species of flowers line the plinth of the house. Age, or neglect, shows in the tilting wooden fence and eroded embankment and the ant-eaten climbers. A leaking drainpipe leaves a green streak of slime on the wall. There is an air of genteel regression. Good times are on the wane.

On the back porch, a clay pot of *githeri* boils on an open fire under the chimney. Inside, there is a corridor that leads through to the dining room, with yellow-flowered curtains that belong to a sunnier time and a more sophisticated space. Six young people shuffle cards and play drafts.

There is a spacious sitting room farther on, where a once-glazed parquet floor shows the effects of the elections campaign; it is scratched by tens of campaigners shoes, and on it lies a solitary filter-less cigarette butt. Dragged stool legs have also left their mark. Underneath the dust and the yellow woolen doilies are expensive couches. On the wall, a sign with the words *No Politics, Please*, in half-jest, has recently been taped to cover the first word.

Mrs. Gitu draws the curtains with hard yanks. She is angry. On-the-war-path angry. *Six years of my husband's life and his pension, of taking people's kids to college, getting ID cards for the youth, attending endless harambees and funerals*, she thinks. Then with her hands flying in every direction, she erupts: 'Now, I can eat with my family without feeling guilty. If that is what our people have done to us after all we have done for them. Even if I see them dying and hungry like worms, I will not feel obliged to help. Let them go to Jamleck who gave them money. Even my own brothers and sisters! And when a child gets sick in the middle of the night, they come running here ... Mrs. Gitu, please nye nye nye. They have chosen money. Let us remain poor. That is what they want.' Her husband has lost.

Mrs. Gitu had invested, prepared, packaged and presented her husband to the people of Kigumo, especially to the marginalized eastern lowlands where he comes from.

'B, you must be arresting with your first sentence and pause when you sense you are starting to lose the audience. And you must finish with people begging for more,' she kept on instructing her husband, reading from the bestseller, *The Art of Public Speaking*. 'Stop clearing your throat, dragging your speech and interjecting the flow with mmms and aaaahs ...' She calls her husband B, which stands for Bethuel.

Months on the campaign trail are over just like that. She is annoyed but not completely shocked. Her husband, the most stubborn man she has ever met, will move through a wall if it costs him his life. She has often had to cry to God for strength. *God give me a sign. Will he make it through?* 'God tried to warn me, but I wouldn't listen,' she laughs remembering when, at one stage, how her husband fell into a ditch after her prayers. She can't believe that her husband garnered only 1546 votes. The four lines across her forehead have deepened in five months, but her characteristic spurts of hilarity persist.

On the eve of Christmas 2007, just before the real king was born, Mrs. Gitu, nee Cecilia Wanjiku, but of course called wa Gitu after getting married, rounded up her brood in the sitting room for a Christmas sermon. It was 11.30 p.m., two days to the polls; the campaign team was anxious and tired but hopeful that the people would reward their strenuous two months of campaigning with victory for Mr. Gitu. Mrs. Gitu stretched her hand to hold the Bible away from her and read through the bottom of her spectacles.

'Micah 5:2: A small village Bethlehem, *just like Heho*, one of thousands, *among Kangari and Kinyona and Kiqumo*, shall produce a ruler in Israel, *shall produce the MP for Kigumo*.' Her right index finger poked in the air, her voice loud but deliberately slow. She had believed that her husband would be the next MP. The elders in Muthithi location had asked candidates to step down in his favour, endorsing him as their candidate of choice. He had escaped death after eating poisoned *njahi* at a restaurant while on the campaign trail. The election was just the final hurdle, she thought.

She knew that any campaign without money was bound to fail. And they didn't have much of it. *He's the conscientious one, I'm the rabble-rouser,* she'd think. So while on the campaign trail, she smoothed over his weaknesses and broadcasted his strengths. In a tie and dye trouser suit, she would walk her size-20 funneled hips up a platform and let rip, her chocolate face looking tiny on top of her body.

'Better your brother, though he is dry, than a stranger who is drenched,' she declared. 'Would you rather that my husband looted the public coffers to give you money? He has been in the bank 30 years and has never been implicated with embezzling funds. We have finished our work, our children are grown up. We are now waiting for you to commission us to serve you.'

'Our people, we want to remove the thorn in your heel. Do you see that children in the west get the bursary fund while our children drop out of school? Do you see that they have computer colleges for their youth while ours are recruited into Mungiki? Our men drink due to frustration. The CDF

fund builds a school in the west, while in the east, what do we get? A well ...
which does not get the jerry can off our women's back, because you still have
to walk four kilometers to the nearest water hole.' Mrs. Gitu is the chairlady
of Maendeleo ya Wanawake in the district.

'Allow me to speak the truth; cutting with words is not like cutting with
a...'

'... knife.' The audience completed.

'Our people, I want you to say enough is e...'

'... 'nough.'

'Ciaigana ni ciaigana. Poverty has no...'

'... roots.'

'They call us *tu*-people, small people of the East. Because we sell our
votes to the westerners for a measly Ksh100. It's time we had an MP from the
East!'

Everyone would nod in agreement. Or so it seemed. One crowd larger
than all the votes that her husband eventually received. She would then give
every group Ksh 2000 before moving on to another, and another.

Kigumo constituency is also called Metumi, from the phrase *metumi
ndigi maguru* - 'those that tie their legs with ropes.' People from Metumi
were, and still are, so fond of the local brew that they tie up their trousers at
the hem so that when a man got drunk and defecated, he would keep the shit
to himself. Had they kept to *muratina*, the traditional swig, and the same
sense of humour about themselves, 24 residents of Kigumo constituency
would not have lost their sight after knocking back *chang'aa* laced with
methanol in 1998.

Think of Kigumo constituency as a badly matched suit made of two
distinct pieces: the lowlands and the highlands; east and west. The East,
made up of Muthithi and Kahumbu, is the proverbial eyesore. Shopping
centres are littered everywhere, half-complete, ghostly buildings. Roadside
advertisements are weathered away like broken windows. Road reserves are
planted with Napier grass up to just a metre from the tarmac. The topography
is unchanging – there are thousands of vertical shreds of land planted with
coarse patches of coffee, trees, bananas, maize and beans baked at 30 degrees
centigrade on sallow slopes. The landscape is littered with bleeding tin roofs
on huts that grow out of the soil, throwbacks to a past decade. Only churches
are built of concrete. Even drought resistant crops like coffee, sorghum,
cassava and pigeon peas have vanished from the landscape.

By contrast, the rolling Western highlands of Kinyona and Kangari locations are coloured luscious green with tea like a royal dress worn over supple skin, bathed in 2780mm rainfall every year at cool highland temperatures. These highlands are the land of milk and money: high grade dairy cows love the fresh air too. The Githumu K.C.C plant is a case in point. Kigumo constituency is crowned by the Aberdares, with the heavily forested Kinyona location at the western edge rising 2950 metres on the slopes of the Nyandarua Range. The only thread that runs the length of the constituency, uniting the East and the West, is the main road built by one of the many sleepy members of parliament through the Kirinyaga Construction Company, notorious for leaving bad roads worse.

In the East, the phrase *coro maai* became popular. Gitu's campaign manager would explain: 'the horn blower needs to walk around with water because he would get thirsty from blowing for so long. So they expect you to give them money if they are to campaign for you.' But Mrs. Gitu is peeved. *What bad values have we taught our children?*

Coro maai! all would call when asked during the rallies to 'Vote Gitu! He is a man who unlike many is not a stranger … He has been with you for the last five years … As a former banker he will manage your funds … And like President Mwai Kibaki, he's a man of few words, a leader, not just a politician … Gitu Juu! Mundu No Gitu!'

Coro maai! the young men would shrug before returning to camp outside the shops. Mrs. Gitu remembers all this.

Loud gospel ringtones would rent the air - Lois Kim's song *Ndi ihenyai-ini, I'm in a race, just about to touch the finish line*, a favourite with the team. There are none of those Nokia default tones here in the sticks. *Shags.* In the phone-charging cubicle at Heho shopping centre, where people pay Shs 15 for a full battery, Ruth Wamuyu, Kamande wa Kiioi, and Mike Murimi would all be going off at different times. Even in this day of *umeme pamoja*, when installing electicity only costs Shs 35,000 per household, half the constituency has no electricity. But this has provided a business opportunity to young men with car batteries.

On the line is a polling agent who is asking for a pay raise. Some candidates, he says, are paying Shs 1000. Campaigning is all about money. That is something she learnt way back when they were going around the constituency with a red Toyota Corolla 110 and the blue 1200 Datsun pickup, both battered by potholes and dirt roads. The 10-member team was forced to travel in a black Pajero donated by a friend for the campaigns. *Where would we be without friends and family?* She would say a silent prayer after each miracle, like the time a friend loaned them Shs 300,000.

'My husband cannot borrow. He is a man. So I have done all the scrounging. After this, I don't want to hear the word loan again,' she would lament.

Passing by people walking, she would order the driver: 'Hoot at them and wave,' then erupt in a guffaw over how glossy their faces looked, how their new clothes were stiff with starch, because it was pay day for them and they would have suckled the aspirants dry.

Peeeeeep! Peeep!

'Mundu no Gitu!' the people shouted back, after making sure that was what the posters on the car said. A few minutes later, they would hail: 'Mundu no Jamleck!' or 'Mundu no Chefman!' just as readily. They played every candidate up, having them believe that they supported him, that there was no need to preach to the converted. In village-speak, *siasa*, politics, is an open hotel for people to eat in.

Even after it all ended, Mrs. Gitu could not stand the name Jamleck mentioned in her presence. In her house on the day the results were announced she relaxed back on her couch and thought about all that had transpired. 'Our people have voted a thug into parliament. Even if they didn't want my husband, they should have voted for someone else, not Jamleck,' she decided. She remembered addressing a church with the same sentiments in late October. Now, Jamleck was chest-thumping on national television after the American and British governments blacklisted him for allegedly inciting post-election violence. He boasted that he does not fear them, had no plans of visiting their countries anyway.

On the night of December 14th, 2007, when most people were watching the nine o clock news, thugs walked into Mr. Gitu's house wielding pistols, guns, knives and pangas.

'We do not want grey hairs in parliament,' they warned, threatening to kill Mr. Gitu. Two women were raped, and property stolen.

'Muici uri hunyu arindagira uri maguta.' *The scruffy thief masks the well-groomed one* was Mrs. Gitu's reaction when she got back home. She happened to be away that evening.

Later, sitting in that same living room with all the memories, she burst into song, dancing with her youngest in the sitting room, their hands lifted up in full view of everyone, thanking God for saving her: 'Tha ciaku ituuraga tene na tene ee.' *Your mercies are forever.*

THE FIRE OF THE MWANGI GENERATION DOES NOT BURN TWICE
(Wa mwangi ndutoogaga meri)

By the time one meets Jamleck Irungu Kamau for the first time, they already feel they know him. That is if they've been spending time in Kigumo. You see him in the eyes of people who have met him, you hear him in the post mortem village gossip, or you catch a whiff of him at the merry-go-round, where he has donated headscarves for women. Like the nettle that grows wild all over Muranga District, he stings and leaves people to spread the itch.

On the morning results were announced, everyone in trading centres was looking for the Daily Nation. Pages were split in mid-air. People knotted in groups, discussing rumoured outcomes, re-living campaign experiences as they waited for returning officers to call the crowds to order. Then, an unruly agent, loud with bloodshot eyes, scuttled from group to group shouting: 'Jamleck for Kigumo!' His yelling was drowned in the sea of voices.

At Kigumo Bendera High School hall, polling agents had spent two punishing days and nights waiting for the outcome. At the front, on the raised podium, black plastic ballot boxes were stacked to the ceiling, partly masking green, yellow, blue, white manilla papers scribbled with names of candidates and corresponding votes taped to the wall. Some of the officials were now asleep, others lazily computing and compiling, others staring into space, the space manned by three police guns. Thirty or so GSU servicemen in their black raincoats swung their clubs, as if getting them nimbled up in case there were problems. The country was pulled taut by rumours that results from Central Province were being doctored overnight. Even with the Parliamentary results announced, things would have snapped – in a civil war kind of way.

'Now Jamu will grow fat. Give him five months and he'll have a belly,' says a girl with a piercing voice, perched on a table at the polling station, her fist raised and clenched into five years.

'Some people just can't grow fat. Kwani hasn't Kihara been there 10 years?' This is from a lady whose purple skirt peeks out from under a black woolen shawl.

'Wait and see. I swear, some people will go to hospital. All the money they have poured? Like Wa Gitu; he came to our polling station at Heho last night as we were counting. You know that's his home centre. He heard Jamleck, Jamleck, Jamleck and he almost fell. *Ma!' I swear*. It is unclear whether her words are sad or happy because her head is shaking in sorrow while her mouth breaks into a wan smile.

'An elephant is never buried with its tusks,' the girl with the shrill voice continues. 'We ate a lot of money, and we never voted for many,' she giggles, rolling her hips around the table, her form rippling in the tight faded blue *mitumba* jeans that must have been handed down by a college girl in the US.

'I hear Jamu spent 10 million,' says a preacher in pleated billowing nylon trousers, a flowered shirt, and a striped office jacket.

'Ma ya Ngai?' *You swear by God?*

'A thousand, a thousand. Everyone was given. Just last night and this morning before people voted.'

'He will make that back in a year. CDF will be his pocket money. And aren't they paid millions ... that will be nothing to him ... ' says the preacher.

'*Tamaka,* I don't know why Jamu was under attack from all the other candidates. *Ma* he has no quarrel with anyone. You should hear him address people. Like on Sunday at Kangari? He did not insult anyone,' says the lady in a purple suit. She was Jamleck's agent at the Muthithi polling station. She is dark and has a cotton wool voice, her freshly plaited corn rows label her a teacher, or maybe she has come into some money recently.

'People say he's a thug; a drug dealer.'

Jamleck's agent readily responds; the timbre of her voice changes, and stings.

'Jamu does not sell drugs to anyone, and even if he does, he does not force it into their mouths.

Where do you think the other candidates get their wealth from? Tell me that.'

'Ai! They didn't know they were campaigning for him by fighting him. Like Inooro [FM] said he fought physically with Chefman this week on Monday. Jamu cannot ...' the young girl is cut short and lowers the hand stretched to drive the point home.

'Chefman is very violent. Let him grow up another five years. We'll vote for him next time.' It's Muturi, the pastor, again.

'Who?!' This is said in chorus, meaning 'Never!'

'So you people are happy that Jamu is the new MP?'

'Ngai, Jamu, the things he will do for us? He's known by even Uhuru and Ruto,' says the agent. Four months later, when the cabinet is announced, Jamleck is the first MP on the screens, promising the coming of a grand opposition.

Jamleck's two handlers enter the hall in long black jackets with white print on their backs, 'Jamleck for Kigumo.' Like curious birds, eyes dart toward the door as quiet descends. Then Jamleck walks in, gap-in-front-teeth-first. His face is dark and angular, 40-something. His tall frame compensates for the small belly, which is quite modest for a Kenyan politician's. He's wearing a black suit and a white T-shirt. The hall catches fire when he roars out, '*Simba*' – Lion – and he follows with a loud, syncopated belly laugh. The air crackles with claps and laughter and cheers, adding fuel to his fire. He shakes everybody's hand, Thank-You's all around. Everybody struggles to shake his hand and congratulate him. Amidst the hugs and kisses, he remains upright, his head turning to the right, then straight ahead, then to the left in calculated angles. He has two women in tow, both with fresh powdered faces, painted lips and shaped eyebrows – their eyes, unlike Jamleck's, have bags underneath them. The light one is dressed in a fitting long maroon kitenge dress with gold embroidery and sports a shy smile, presumably his wife; the other woman, whose face is the colour of Kenyan clay, wears a knee-length skirt, her handbag is clutched under her arm like she's walking down Tom Mboya Street. Most likely a donor.

When it was all over, Jamleck won by 29,000 votes, leaving the other 14 candidates to split the remaining 24,000 votes. Hon Kihara would later write in response: 'The story of Kigumo is long and inexplicable. Like a fairy tale. I leave them to their God for judgement.'

The Kikuyu saying goes: 'The fire of the Mwangi generation does not burn twice. It is time for the Irungu generation to rule.' It might be no coincidence that the outgoing MP is Kihara Mwangi, while the incoming one is Jamleck Irungu Kamau.

Millicent Muthoni trained as an architect at the University of Nairobi before becoming a full time writer and part time actress. In addition to various creative writing projects (some of them read on the BBC), she is a columnist with the Standard newspaper and can often be seen both on and off stage at the Phoenix Theatre in Nairobi.

VICTORIA RISING

Tim Querengesser

The places where men gather to drink have rules. Like cigarette butts crushed into the bar floor, a pact is embedded in imbibing males. There are stiff codes of conduct, speech, admission and status. There is an unwritten list of insults that will bring laughs and others that will start fights. How one should talk to, and then about a woman when she leaves is well understood. Which football club is considered best is without question.

African Pub had lost these codes. Sure, there was still an Arsenal banner hanging above the red vinyl chairs made sticky from too many spilled Tuskers. There were still regulars, like Nixon, a 20-something maize-stalk of a man with big cartoon eyes, who was always at the bar wearing a baggy t-shirt, beer in hand. Cigarettes were still sold by the individual stick rather than the pack, a nod to the hand-to-mouth clientele. If you ordered anything to eat other than *sukuma* and *ugali* – say beef stew and chapatti – Carol, the pear-bottomed waitress, would still drag her flip-flops loudly in protest as she walked down the street to fetch it somewhere else. It was where the bar met the street that rules were being rewritten. Old social boundaries were meaningless now, regardless of whether you were trying to remember or forget them – like borders on a map suddenly made obsolete by a victorious battle. Once-excluded people knew it. Men with bodies stinking of sweat would arrive on the patio without worry, hawking under-roasted peanuts, fake gold watches or unfashionable leather belts. Prostitutes as young as 15 lurked around the bar fishing for clients before the sun had a chance to set. And if any of us drinkers let our concentration slip, one of the teen boys with a glue bottle at his lips, hovering near the bar as if in an orbit, would suddenly be sitting beside us eyeing our food, beer, cigarettes or pant pockets like cunning vultures. The riots were behind it all. Mobs had reduced large swaths of the downtown to ashes in early January after the election results were announced. Hundreds of Kikuyus, Kisiis, Indians and other groups fled the city. Now that the smoke had settled, those still in Kisumu were changing, too. Rich and poor, powerful and powerless, old and young – all these divisions were no longer enforced. A new rule in Kisumu was becoming clear on the patio of African Pub. The guarded status that once separated the civilized few from the unlucky and unwashed many had been bridged, or lost, depending on your point of view. Sure, it was the impoverished youth who looted, displaced, burned and faced the police bullets. But the distinguished leaders of the community, like so many of the *wazees* sitting with me on the patio, had turned their heads at the right moment and let it happen. Fueled by vengeance for their poverty and a touch of ethnic hatred, caged residents had been let out of their slum and had burned down much of the city after stealing what they could carry and forcing the unwanted out. It was the spectacle the *wazees* had hoped would happen. But with Kisumu scorched, the world watching anxiously and much of the country following the lead like so many dominoes, one got the sense those formerly above rock bottom wanted the hierarchy to come back. The youth were emboldened, though. They weren't interested in normal returning.

I met Patrick at African Pub. His massive black eyes, which sat above cheekbones that poked out of his face like angry elbows, pierced right through you. 'Drunks don't eat *sukuma*,' he barked when I offered to buy him and his friend, Amos, some food in exchange for stories. 'Drunks drink Tusker.' Nixon laughed to calm the mood while the *wazees* just drank without lifting their eyes. I had asked him to find me a looter to interview. To do this, Nixon turned his head to the street, leaned back in his plastic chair and summoned some glue sniffers. Within three minutes, Patrick and Amos were standing on the patio. Kisumu had become a walking army of former looters looking to sell interviews about their adventures to lazy journalists. At first, I wasn't sure if the pair had actually been part of the mob or simply hungry kids willing to indict themselves in print for food. The way Patrick swaggered convinced me that they were legit. His muscular chest, visible through his unbuttoned dress shirt, guided him like a compass. He refused to talk. Instead, he loudly chewed miraa and peanuts, glaring at me as if I was a devil. Then he got up and paced the patio like a guard dog sniffing its territory. Tonight, he said in his manner, without words, his poison wasn't going to be the industrial strength glue his friends were sniffing. It was to be Tusker like all the older, richer patrons at African Pub. Understand, *mzungu*? The pair were both 23 and clearly needed one another. They had been living together under verandas for shelter since the riots. Amos was shorter and less muscular than Patrick, but he had a permanent, slightly dopey smile and manner that made him tolerable in larger doses. He told me he had lived on a small plot owned by a Kisii man that had been burned by the mob. All he had managed to steal in the madness was a case of soda. 'I felt I should have a share while the people were looting,' he said. He later admitted he never drank a sip of it before it was destroyed by the flames along with his house. What, exactly, had he hoped for, by participating in the destruction of his city? 'When I came to town and found people looting, I felt like I should do what everyone else was doing,' he said. 'I was affected by the election. I voted for ODM, so when

things went the other way, it affected me, too. I didn't have any bitterness towards them (tribes that were pushed out). I was just looting because other people were looting.' Amos said the police had beaten him during the riots. He had battle wounds to prove it. Even weeks later, his face still had a long, fresh scar, beginning an inch below his left eye and running down his cheek to his lower jaw. He had papers from his hospital visit that he showed me. He then took off his red baseball hat gently, as he did most things, to show me the scars on his head, pointing at them with his fingers. I saw his hands. His right was covered with purple scabs ('From breaking glass windows,' offered Nixon, trying to make the boy seem tough) and his left hung like the rest of the arm it was attached to, limp and lifeless. 'I'm very desperate. I can't fend for myself because of my injuries. Now I have to live in the streets. I can't carry metal to make money; I can't carry the load because I got clobbered.' Patrick and Amos were scraping by but they were still moving. So many others who had participated weren't. I tried to find the family of a boy who was shot near the Kondele slum, just outside the downtown core. They had left the city to put him in the ground that day. The police, it later emerged from sources as reliable as Human Rights Watch, had taken sides during the violence. Protesters and looters in Kisumu had been shot by police using live ammunition, in what many believe was a shoot-to-kill policy. Human Rights Watch estimates 44 bodies with gunshot wounds were brought to the morgues in and around Kisumu by January 11.

I spoke with one woman who saw the boy – whose death was captured by television cameras and flashed around the world – shot to death in front of her charcoal stand. He was just playing, she said, putting his hands up to his face as if to say 'nyah-nyah' when the officer fired his rifle.

It was a game, then. One that could end in death – yours or someone else's – or in pockets filled with new stuff as the whites inside the broad smiles and wild eyes of those around you lit fading light. It was a game played by boys wanting to be men. And whatever frustrations these boys, like Amos and Patrick, had shouldered before the election – anger for being poor, slow, unloved, beaten, illiterate, underpaid – found catharsis in the mobs. Patrick stood, up as if saying 'Enough!' He pushed back his plastic chair with the backs of his knees, making a loud 'brrrrt.' It was time to show the patio, and me, how he drank beer. Like a man. He slapped the bottle from the table and in one jagged motion shoved it up to his lips while he cocked his head back. Shaken too quickly, the beer foamed. Creamy suds rolled down his cheeks as he gulped back half the bottle with too much bravado. Amos giggled, as the *wazees* ever so subtly shuddered. I lit a cigarette.

My part-time smoking habit has a rhythm. I smoke when I travel or when I detach from regular life. Surrounded by order I exercise and try to eat well. When I don't know what comes next, I smoke. On trips to Kisumu I chain-smoked. My first visit there, after the election riots, had been the surreal terminus of a dizzying road trip through the Rift Valley. In Turbo, I met a 70-something woman in a displacement camp who had fled her farm with only her life for the third time since the 1960s. In Burnt Forest, a similarly aged woman with a kind smile named Theresa was now living in the twisted metal of an SUV at a police station with two children. In Molo, a Kalenjin boy with the right side of his face ripped open to reveal its softer insides, like a smashed grape, sat on the steps of the over-run hospital. The flight into the Rift from Nairobi had been like a reconnaissance mission inspecting a recent war. Shambas smoked as far as I could see. Fields were blackened. Crops destroyed. Smoke hung in the valley. The emotions worked on me. Then my in-flight snack – crackers and orange juice – arrived. We landed in Eldoret beside a burnt field, and then the war film stopped being something I watched and started being something that ached inside me.

I arrived in Kisumu two days after the road trip in the Rift. Perhaps I was hoping the city would show some regret for what I had seen. None was apparent. I left, and came back two weeks later with higher expectations. A big chip was growing on my shoulder, my grudge building thanks to a continual increase in the numbers of people dying or displaced for a pair of politicians who clearly didn't mind. To me, Kisumu was the brand these other places were now copying, the headwaters of the grief.   As a journalist, I didn't want to admit it, but all I was looking for was shame. A few hands in the air begging for forgiveness from God, perhaps, or some honest man to peer into a gutted building and say, 'Fuck, we really screwed up. We burned down our own city.' Good sense said shame should be here. Civility demanded it. On Oginga Odinga Road, the main asphalt strip that meanders downhill past Central Square, where people talk politics under trees and an oversized Raila sign, and on to the Winam Gulf, where water hyacinth had trapped fishing boats like a storm without warning, altars for absolution were still everywhere. The burnt C.G. Panjani electronics store, the ashes of the Ukwala Supermarket (the owner of which told me he had lost 200 million shillings in the blaze), the chic Swan Centre, where men polished the beige stone floors to a mirror finish beside shops that still stood smashed and empty – all stood at the ready. Shame, though, had gone out of fashion. The teenagers on the streets moved like dogs suddenly cut from their leash. Most others were smug that they weren't responsible for the fires but secretly quite fine with what had been torched. Unwanted or resented residents had been killed or banished. Frightened Indian business owners were erecting steel bunkers around themselves. Those remaining compensated for this by going blind, forgetting the parts of themselves that at one point might have given a damn. It felt like the opening scene of a bad post-apocalypse movie when I bumped into Chalis. Tall, lanky, with cropped salt-and-pepper hair, he had a face that was gaunt with age that accentuated expressions around his mouth. He reclined in a chair in front of C.G. Panjani, the place he was guarding as an askari, on the mostly empty Oginga Odinga Road. His posture showed the deficiencies of his pants – two sizes too small in the leg and at least as many sizes too big in the waist. One of his socks was neon green, the other navy blue. His shoes looked to be cardboard imitations of leather. An authentic Armageddon look, I thought, if I'd ever seen one. 'What are you guarding?' Chalis just smiled, showing me his few remaining yellow teeth.

He pointed at my pack of cigarettes to ask for one. I obliged. Intrigued, I kept asking why he was guarding a place with only ashes left inside. 'There's nothing there,' I said. 'Yeah, there's some tables,' Chalis replied. He pointed a mile-long index finger at two wood tables sitting by where the store window once was. We looked at each other and started to laugh; Chalis even let out a wet hack as he exhaled smoke and giggled at the same time. His shirt was undone and I could see his ribcage move beneath his taught skin. He was right. There were *some* tables left. In the absence of morality, pride remained. Normal was a moving target. As bad as it was, Kisumu was better than the rest of the Rift Valley, where property and lives were still going up in smoke. Nobody was dying in Kisumu anymore. And the fires were out, for now at least. Was the fact it could have been worse enough to forgive the place for its lack of concern? When a city explodes with ethnic rage, is it inevitable that such events must quickly be forgotten, buried like secrets and ignored in order for life to carry on? Were people in Kisumu dunking their heads in the sand in the hope for peace? Or were they complicit, just refusing to deal with it?

So many bitter questions. I knew where I had to go for answers: Central Square. Under the big Raila sign, where the men gather every day to talk politics but do it in whispers. No one is listening but it just feels right, since, it seems, some in Kisumu are permanently plotting. I wanted an audience so I joined the scrum. Ernest Matengo sat alone, dressed in crisply pressed green trousers and a striped golf shirt. He also wore a baseball hat, in the way that rich people often do to make themselves look more casual. He said he was 47 and worked as a civil servant in Kisumu. He had moved here 12 years ago from a small town in the Rift and had raised a small family. 'This' was about a history of hunger, marginalization, a lack of land and economic servitude, he said – the 'this' always accompanied by a subtle swing of his hand in the direction of a burnt shop near Central Square. You couldn't have stopped 'this,' considering what happened after the election, he argued. 'This' was a story that had been put on its course long ago. 'Those who have problems with others, this was their wrath,' Ernest continued, wrapping a bow around the thought. 'The few people who were punished here were punished because their relations with the common man were not good.' Delivered with eloquence, Ernest still pushed the go-to argument in

Kisumu. It went something like this. During Kenya's early days, the Kikuyus and Luos had dominated politics. Founding president Jomo Kenyatta shot to the top with support from the Luo. Then Tom Mboya, one of their own, was assassinated in a suspected Kikuyu conspiracy. Riots broke out. But the Luo didn't kill anyone. Then former vice-president, Oginga Odinga, was pushed out of Kenyatta's cabinet. Bitterness set in. Then land in the Rift was handed to Kikuyu farmers in questionable schemes. Then came Kikuyus with money, starting businesses, keeping the locals poor. Anger and rage took root. The rift between the two tribes was created. The election malfeasance simply flicked a switch to 'On.' History can be interpreted in different ways. This reading, one that downplayed the choice people made to destroy their city and instead highlighted the inertia and inevitability of it all, worked well for the residents of post-election Kisumu. The narrative was one of a people patiently waiting for a turn in the limelight, only to have that turn repeatedly stolen. Justice in this story had to be served, whether by the courts or by the hands of the vigilante mob. Suspected conspirators had to be ejected. Kisumu had been victimized and its response was unquestionably just. No shame required. Victimhood has its privileges. This blanket of don't-ask, don't-tell spread to the kids who had destroyed the town and left many of their compatriots without jobs. They were, after all, acting for those who didn't want to get involved. Unsurprisingly, they had bigger ideals in their hearts, according to Ernest. 'We have talked to our youth and told them, 'Fine, you rioted against the system but the system used the situation against you,'" he said. 'Their point was never made. Before they aired their views there was teargas everywhere. It was the police who caused the damage, not the public.' I lit another cigarette.

Lake Victoria points at Kisumu from the centre of Africa like a finger issuing a challenge. Lined with rows of drab, concrete warehouse-style stores offset only by a pleasant park and leafy suburbs near the water, the city is an efficient servant of the lake, a depot where things don't arrive but move through on their way somewhere else, by boat, rail, or road. People in Kisumu are psychologically tuned to this movement. If the city hums they buzz happily. If it slows they sit on the street, bitter. If it falls still they start plotting. The soil is fertile in the hills of the Rift Valley that hold the city like a cupped hand. At the start of World War I, Nyanza province, which

Kisumu heads, was the most productive in all of British East Africa. The lake provides a reliable bounty of tilapia, and more recently, Nile perch. During the boom days, exports of food and manufactured goods from here and the rest of Kenya were sent west, across the lake, to millions in central Africa or north along the rail to Kampala, while in return the same places sent goods southeast through Kisumu, by the lake and the tracks, on to Mombasa and the rest of the world. But Kisumu is as cursed by its geography as it is blessed. What was once a vibrant lake port town has slowly been suffocated, cut off from the power that slowly shifted toward the centre, to Nairobi. Kisumu became the battlefield for a proxy war. This is the seat of power of the Luo and it has suffered as a result. The militant locals blame the long-ruling Kikuyu elite for enslaving them. The water hyacinth choking the Winam Gulf and rusting industry beside it are seen as so many lost battles, staring the residents daily in the face. As such it was their own home – Kisumu – that needed to be destroyed, to send a message to Nairobi and the world, they said. Zach, a hustler I met on a later trip, when the streets squirmed and danced with the friendly, happy life I had known in the city previously, as if a great amnesia had taken root, had thanked me for my 'help' as a foreign journalist. 'We needed the world to see Kisumu go up in flames,' he said. 'We needed that pressure from you guys to be put on the government. We were willing to keep it up for a month if we needed to.'

At the Central Police station, I joined 56 men and women who were camping in a parking lot. Some took to the shade offered by a large tree while others sat inside crashed matatus. A man wearing pink pants with a streak of white ugali stuck in his black hair cooked over one of three small fires.

At first, Arthur Wawera and James Mwaura were a bit suspicious of me. The mood was definitely in the air. Less than 10 feet away, a group of a dozen teenage Luo boys sat with foreboding silence on a smashed Peugeot 504, eyeing the older Gikiuyus. Nodding towards them, I asked James if they have been worried by the presence of boys who weeks earlier had likely sought to hurt them and steal their property. With his back to them, he said no.

Arthur was small, a stereotypical Kikuyu – at least in comparison to the Luos, who appear to be raised on a regimen of protein and weight lifting. He wore a soiled white shirt that his tiny shoulders hid within, but had a friendly, inviting face and inquisitive eyes. Arthur's grandfather had been born in

Kisumu, as had he. The mob had arrived at his house with pangas and rungas, he said. His family fled for their lives and came to the police station.

'They said we Kikuyus supported President Kibaki, but we even voted for Raila,' he said. 'They don't care. That is an excuse they are using to take our things. They want us to leave this town, leave it for the Luos.' James was becoming interested in the conversation. 'We have been staying with them; we are friends with them. The only problem is that Raila is a Luo and Kibaki is a Kikuyu.' He told me one child belonging to a member of the displaced group had been stoned while fleeing, sending him to hospital. He didn't know the fate of mother, father and siblings. They were in Molo, where the fighting was entering a meaner second phase. 'If Kibaki is president there is nothing we're getting. There's no difference. They're just benefiting themselves,' he said. He told me he dared not leave the police station and try to track down his family. 'If they see that you're a Kikuyu, they'll kill you.' It wasn't overblown. Nixon, barfly and fix-it man at the African Pub, had looked over his shoulders the first time we met before he revealed a big secret. There was a Kikuyu woman with an eight-year-old daughter that had arrived looking for help one evening. He had taken her into the back of the pub 'on humanitarian grounds,' and offered her a place to sleep. Landlords with Kikuyu tenants who weren't pushed out by the mobs, were now asking them to leave in order to protect their buildings from targeted arson, he said. He asked me to contact the United Nations to find the woman shelter.

Now, as Amos and Patrick left African Pub, Nixon told me more about the riots. 'They called it ODM shopping,' he mused, giggling at the slogan. The mob had rolled through the shops in an organized way. To those who participated, rising up against an election result they considered doctored appeared to be a free hand to loot stores owned by 'outsiders' (Indians), burn shops they resented (book stores, pharmacies, doctor offices), torch homes and businesses of those they hated (Kikuyu, Kisii) and take as many phones as their pockets could hold (Nokia, Motorola). To those that had been attacked, this threat was evident well in advance. Many had chosen to support Odinga and ODM as a result. It was a survival tactic – a political stance they found difficult to prove when the mobs arrived at their doorsteps hungry for blood and treasure – but one that underlined what few found words to express in the days following Kenya's violence. The world shuddered as its African sweetheart descended into 'ethnic violence' like so many of its screwed up neighbours. But in the end, it was politics masquerading as ethnicity. The hatreds were based on access to power, not skin shades or the shape of noses. The retribution for this, though, was delivered in the same way that it was in Rwanda and Burundi: pangas and flames.

'This is political,' said Joyce Wanjala, the 42-year-old owner of Tazama Hotel, one of a dozen or so open-air *samaki* restaurants that hug the shore of Lake Victoria. In the restaurant, a few customers licked their fingers in the mid-morning pall of post-elections Kisumu. Nothing much to do but eat and talk. Outside, beside the lake, Joyce, a pretty, round faced woman with soft features and plush looking hair, gathered her two daughters and picked an appropriate backdrop to talk to me: the hyacinth. The girls, both in their 20s, giggled at their defiant mother. She loved hyperbole. And she was full of the victimhood and denial fueling much of Kisumu now and was in a feisty mood. On who destroyed the city: 'At no point did any local boy start any fire'; on the future: 'I will die if people behind me can have democracy'; on the situation for her daughters: 'I'm damn sad. The next minute it will be my daughter being raped in the hands of a Ugandan.' She told me she had personally seen Ugandan soldiers, hiding in the bushes mere metres from where we talked. More giggles from the girls, both pretty like their mother. It was hard to argue with Joyce's main point, though. Behind her, as far as the eye could see, the hyacinth, which looked like an overgrown green lawn from the ground and a huge green-egg omelet from the air, had choked Winam Gulf and destroyed two-thirds of her business. 'If this was happening in Central, I can assure you, it wouldn't be there for long,' she said. The hyacinth was a living metaphor of neglect. The only power that could do anything was the government. While it was green, Kisumu residents viewed the hyacinth as just another coat of rust. All of the industries – the mills, the brewery, the molasses plant, the textile factories – were dead from government neglect, said Joyce. 'And you can see with your own eyes that fishing ... it's dead.' She refused to view the aftermath of the riots morally, or as anything other than simple political rivalries. 'Once Kibaki's out, I know it's hard to believe, but together we'll build the nation. With Kibaki in power, it will continue to be burned and Kisumu will be history. With Kibaki we are already finished, so it's the same thing,' she said.

Joel Waswa and Shem Ngoko appeared to be wasting time together near a wall on a dead street in the industrial area of Kisumu. As I introduced myself, a thoughtless kid lit a trash fire in a gutter and we moved to get away from the smoke. 'People are so scared because they know, maybe, it could happen again,' said Joel, a fat-lipped parking attendant holding tickets he said he wasn't interested in writing anymore. They represented the government, a four-letter word nowadays. He was short and thick and bounced on the balls of his feet, never really making eye contact but always keeping involved in the conversation. 'Our brothers and sisters are missing jobs. They are crying,' interjected Shem, a 40-year-old with eyes so glazed they looked like he hadn't closed them in days. He was tall and muscular, with a shaved head and a goatee. He wore a red Celtel shirt that looked like he had slept in it. 'I know they have promoted robbery and looting.' Shem said the 'they,' and I was suddenly awakened. I had assumed the two were friends. But like a photograph, my introduction had captured them together – a moment in time that they were now trying to navigate. It wasn't necessary but I asked anyway: what tribes are you from? 'I'm Luo,' said Joel. 'Kisii,' said Shem. Shem's family had fled to Kisii. All of his tools from his welding business were stolen and his house was burned by the mobs. He was broke. As cars drove past he held his hands out hoping to get a few coins. He couldn't afford a bus ticket to Kisii to re-unite with his family. His diabetic mother was running out of insulin, he added. He had come to Kisumu 20 years ago with nothing. Now he was hoping to leave in the same state. Joel could sense the mood of the conversation shifting, perhaps seeing my eyes surveying him. 'Was this man responsible?' was probably written brightly across my face. 'We are not angry with them,' he said abruptly. 'We are just angry with the president. They just revenged on them to try to see if he [Kibaki] would step down. If they are angry, they [the mobs] just come and worsen the situation. You realize after that you have done a bad thing.' It wasn't clear whether this was a slip of the tongue or a bit of guilt coming out. I asked. Joel said he was at home during the riots. Sensing the situation could get worse, I shook their hands and said it was time for me to go. After they let go of my hands, Joel and Shem grabbed each other's and shook as well. 'Are you guys friends?' I asked, hopefully. 'We are not friends,' said Joel. 'We are just looking how to be friends.'

The aftermath of the mobs had created an undeniable beauty in some places. Outside looted pen stores sat piles of colourful plastic – red, blue, green, yellow, purple – as well as piles of cool sea-blue glass and the red brown of tire chords that were rusting. The smell was different; it hung in the throat. From the restaurant in the New Victoria Hotel, a place that once had splendor to match its name but had now fallen into slow decline, the smell of smoke from a pen shop burned kitty corner to the entrance mixed with the smell of grease. Dinner was served to guests starting at 8 p.m. The choices were chips, chips with chicken, or chips with masala. All deep fried. One of the Yemenese owners brought out my plate of chips and slapped a bottle of ketchup in front of me. I noticed I was not the only one in the room, which feels like you are sitting at the bottom of a swimming pool with its curtained windows and 20-foot high ceiling.'You know what's wrong with Africans?' he said, getting me to turn around. 'We don't think. Will Raila make the bus arrive on time or my life different in any way? No. Does he even know the difference between bitumen and asphalt, even though he got an engineering degree and was roads minister? No. We pushed out all the Kikuyu, the business-minded people, and now we are starving. How stupid.' He was eating chips like me. He said he was Luo and had grown up in Kisumu but was now leaving. He'd had enough. All anyone cared about now was politics, and all that was doing was destroying the city. 'I'm going to the United Kingdom. This city is full of idiots.' As he said this, the Yemenese owner of the hotel, a fat teddy bear of a man, ran in giggling. A friend had just gotten him what he'd been after for weeks and he couldn't wait to put it up. As the man, wearing a black shirt and with graying hair, paid his bill and returned to his room, the hotel owner pasted up his prize: a near-life-size poster of a smiling, smug-looking Najib Balala, surrounded in ODM orange.

Tim Querengesser *is a Canadian journalist. He spent eight months in Kenya before, during and after the December 27 election, which he covered extensively for the* Daily Nation, Ottawa Citizen, *and other publications. He is now somewhere else in the world.*

Reasons
Gathondu Mwangi

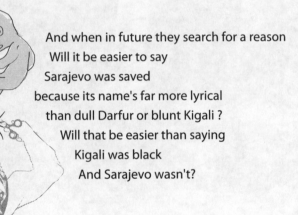

And when in future they search for a reason
Will it be easier to say
Sarajevo was saved
because its name's far more lyrical
than dull Darfur or blunt Kigali ?
Will that be easier than saying
Kigali was black
And Sarajevo wasn't?

Gathondu Mwangi is a Kenyan living, working, and studying in Johannesburg. When he's not ducking and diving, he's scribbling and shooting.

That Girl Died of Democracy
Wilson Wahome Kiriungi

That little girl died of democracy,
You can tell by the way she lay in death.
Yellow crayon fell out of her pocket
As they loaded her body onto the trailer with the rest.
School opens in a few weeks;
But her friends dispersed like pollen in the wind.
If from the other side she could only take a peek,
And behold the sight of the forlorn mass exodus,
She might just be glad that she had to take leave
From this uncouth abode that's supposed to be nesting us.
For as much as she longed to show off her new clothes,
And tell her school friends about places that she went
Or even how uncle Ben sucked Spaghetti up his nose,
Her words would only have echoed through the charred wasteland;
For her friends, either dispersed like pollen in the wind…
Or like herself, they all died of democracy.

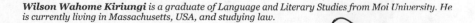

Wilson Wahome Kiriungi is a graduate of Language and Literary Studies from Moi University. He is currently living in Massachusetts, USA, and studying law.

An Exile's New Home
Alison Ojany Owuor

I'm an inhabitant of this land.
He is not,
Herding together,
leading his kin in repetitive exercises of thumb printing and signature.
Their eyes broadcast what mouths fail to utter,
Wearing pain like garments made for the living dead.
They wear it well.
A multitude of mangled souls each carrying the others grief.
Their feet don't touch the ground.
It isn't allowed.
Memories are greedy and hoard their dreams and nightmares.
They had declared everyone's blood but their own poison,
The worms in the soil being the only benefactor of their feuds.
Who will benefit from our wars?
I move closer to the exiled one,
Realising, … I'm standing nearest to myself.

Alison Owuor is a published poet and a regular performer at various Kwani? forums.

New Speeches
Alison Ojany Owuor

Paranoiac statements mating with words that provoke hope in our spirits,
Absorbed as a nation, encouraged to separate
Schizophrenic.

Sanity never questionable in war.
I'm not envious of my neighbor who speaks the distant tongue.
We are allotted the same proportion of madness.

We retaliate for the dead. eye for an eye.
A blind nation.

The new speeches.
They are written, reactions unrehearsed though predictable.
We remember the old ones though,
When some fought in forests and others, with words.
Reclaiming what was taken an interloping guest
Respect, contempt, it didn't matter what they felt ,we won. they lost.

Four decades is a long time.
Fight goes on. who wins this time?

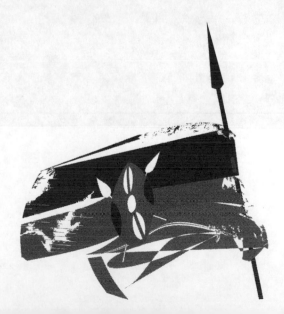

RIFT VALLEY

**James Mwangi, resident of IDP camp at Nakuru
Showground**

Where were you living before you came to this camp?
I was living at Kaptembo. It is an estate and shopping centre
on the outskirts of Nakuru town. The word kaptembo means
elephant in Kalenjin, but the official name as it appears on our
business licences and permits is Kipsigis-Tugen Farm.

What kind of business did you have?
I had a retail shop, and I also sold charcoal.

From a kiosk?

It was in a brick building. I had rented five rooms in a compound that had 33 rooms. I lived with my family in one room and used another as a retail outlet for things like cooking oil, flour, charcoal and other such things that my neighbours needed to buy. As for the other three rooms, one was my equipment store where I kept my three *mikokotenis* (hand carts) and five bicycles, the other was my main store where I kept sackfuls of charcoal, and the last was where I stored the tins I used for measuring out charcoal for retail. I had all these things, but when I left all I had was this Bible. And now I am living in a tent.

Were you born in Kaptembo?

No. I was born in Olenguruone where, according to my grandmother, our family moved to and has lived since 1943. But I moved to Nakuru after our family was evicted in the tribal clashes of 1992.

What happened in 1992?

I had just finished my A- levels in 1987 and been farming for a few years when at about four p.m. one Sunday in 1992 the Kalenjins came and burnt our houses. We were out in the field playing football and never had time to go back and save any of our things. At that time we did not know what was going on, but those who had been at home when the houses were set on fire came and told us that it was the Kalenjins and they had started fighting us. We ran for safety.

I walked for over 60 kilometers from Olenguruone to Molo town. There were many of us running and we took shelter at the Molo stadium. There were very many displaced people there from other areas and settlements around Molo, but there was no organised plan for moving them to safety even though we were fearful that the Kalenjins were going to come after us there. Later on, we – my mother, my seven siblings and I – got a lift into Nakuru town where we took shelter at Christ the King Church for six months. We did not know anyone in Nakuru then but we figured that it would be safe.

How did you adjust to your new life?

It was hard with all of us living there so I started to look for something to do. I found work as a casual worker at construction sites and eventually managed to save 1600 shillings. I figured it was not safe to stay there (at the church compound) with my mother and sisters, so I rented a house in Kaptembo where the rent was 250 shillings a month. At that time I had nothing- no clothes, household goods and such things- and after I bought a few basic things, I realised that I was only left with 300 shillings, which after the rent was paid would leave me with only 50 shillings. I approached my landlord, Baba Jesse, and told him: I have only 300 shillings. If I pay you the rent, I will remain with only 50 shillings and I have no job and no food, how will I be able to pay you for next month's rent? I gave him my national identity card, my driver's licence and my school living certificate, and he told me to use the 300 shillings wisely so that I could pay him two months' rent the next month. Three hundred shillings is the money I used as capital to start a new life, earning a livelihood through selling vegetables in Kaptembo.

What was your average day like?

I used to wake up at 5 am and walk to Kabarak about 20 kilometres away to buy milk from the farmers. In December of 1993 I married my wife, Esther Wagithi, and she is the one I left the milk with for sale before walking to the market in Nakuru town to buy vegetables for resale at Kaptembo. Once I got back home from the market, I would take a rest until four p.m. when I would walk to Kabarak and back again.

How were you received by your new community?

They welcomed me warmly in Kaptembo. Even though I was a Kikuyu, I spoke fluent Kipsigis, and the Kalenjin always told me that I was one of them. I was also always with them politically. In 2002 when President Moi endorsed Uhuru Kenyatta as his successor, the Kalenjins embraced him and so did I, while other Kikuyus voted for Kibaki. In 2005, I went against what was perceived as the Kikuyu line and voted 'no' in the Referendum on a new constitution. It really earned me the love of the Kalenjin.

In the run up to the 2007 General Election, no one threatened me; this while all around me Kikuyus were being told that they would have to leave Kaptembo whether Kibaki won the election or not.

On Sunday, December 30th 2007, I opened my shop and went about my business as usual. I figured that I would not be affected. In the afternoon, I started to see houses go up in flames, but I was told that no one would touch me. As all the Kikuyus started to run out of Kaptembo, I decided to stay and I received protection from even the Kalenjin elders who I knew were complicit in the organisation of the arsons and evictions.

Besides, as a businessman with five bicycles and three *mikokotenis* that I used to deliver charcoal with, I had hired some Kisiis, Luos and Kalenjins.

So how did you end up in this IDP camp?

When the chaos started, I moved my family to Kiambu where my wife's people are. I know these people (the Kalenjin), when they say 'no' they mean 'yes.' I have lived with them for so long... I knew I was their target.

On January 24th, I received a call from my brother who had abandoned his *kinyozi* (barbershop) in Kaptembo and gone into exile in the Langa Langa area of Nakuru. He told me that he had overheard that Githima (a predominantly Kikuyu village next to Kaptembo) would be set on fire.

The next day, I went on with my business and closed the shop at nine in the evening. As I sat in my room reading the Bible, I heard a group of people on the road outside, but I did not mind them. They were speaking in Kiswahili. At about 11, I heard a Kalenjin war cry and went to peep through the fence. I saw over 2000 warriors.

The warriors uprooted the wooden fence to the compound I lived in and used the timber to barricade the main road, even though the distance between the compound and the Kaptembo police station is only about 100 meters. They lit a massive fire right there in the middle of the road.

The warriors outside were attacking Githima village. It was clear that the group was multiethnic because their commander spoke Kiswahili.

At around midnight, wounded attackers began to return from Githima complaining that they had been stoned by the villagers. All this time I was restless; walking from one room to the next peeping at them and looking for a place to hide and hoping for an escape plan. It was at this point that I heard someone say: 'Hii plot si ni ya yule Kikuyu anauzanga makaa...? situchome.../ Is this not the plot that belongs to that Kikuyu that sells charcoal...? Let's burn it...!'

They uprooted the verandah's support pillars and tried to use them as fuel to set the place on fire. They kept trying to do it for about seven times, but every time they were at it, they were called on to provide back-up to the group in Githima. In the end, they decided to let the place stand for another day with the intent of using it as storage space for what they would loot in Githima.

The attacks lasted all night and at six a.m., Githima fell. But the raiders continued to barricade the road and at some point the police even came to sit by the fire saying: 'Nyinyi chomeni lakini mtuachie kitu kidogo.../ Just burn the houses but remember to give us something small...'

By two p.m., I had become very tired. I walked to Room Eight, which was my living room, to draw water but I was too exhausted and scared to drink it. I wanted to change clothes but I just could not. I took my Bible and decided to move to Room 33, the charcoal store which faced the street for a peep. As I stepped out, I came face to face with four warriors armed with bows and arrows relaxing inside the compound. When they saw me they armed their bows, and at that moment I decided to walk towards them and on to the street. I walked past them and they did nothing and I walked into the street where I found another 100 warriors lying about.

On the street, I also saw three or four women who were my neighbours, carrying loot back from Githima. 'We James unaenda wapi, si ufungue hizi nyumba tuweke hizi vitu.' (James where are you going? Just open these rooms we store these things.)

'Unaona yule mzee,' I told them while pointing with my Bible at no one in particular, 'nataka kumpatia hiki kitabu, narudi.' (See that man over there, I want to give him this book and then I will be back.)

I kept walking, saying the same thing to anyone who asked me where I was going. After walking for about 500 meters, without being attacked, I saw a *mzungu* pressman. As I approached him, suddenly the warriors started to run after me. At this moment, two police cars, a Landcruiser and a lorry filled with armed-policemen, drove up (from the direction of Nakuru town) and parked 50 meters away. I ran towards them.

'What tribe are you?' they asked me. 'Do not dare come back here,' they warned me, helping me into their lorry. On one side of the road, where they were parked, was Githima all burnt up. On the other side a huge group of warriors, about 1000, was staring at us. One officer complained, 'we cannot work here. If Githima is on fire and you can see the attackers are getting reinforcements, how can we just keep shooting in the air?' The police left the scene with me in their lorry. They dropped me up the road at Eveready, where a lot of displaced people were gathered planning a return to their homes to salvage their things, but they had been deterred by the road block. I walked to the show-ground.

Do you plan to go back to your home?

This time round I am not going back. I feel like this is something that will keep happening to me; like if I go back and start all over anew, they will come and take it all again. Fifteen years ago my mother, a single mother of eight, was kicked out of Olenguruone but she returned. Now she is back camping at Molo stadium... Me, if there was somewhere else I can go, to Kakuma or something, I would go, but I cannot go back to Molo or Kaptembo.

On May 14th, the Rift Valley Provincial Commissioner came to this camp and tried to convince people to return home. The meeting was abandoned because the IDPs demanded compensation before they would return home, while the government was adamant that compensation would only happen after their return. But one thing the PC said was that there is a difference between *amani* (peace) and *usalama* (security). He said that the government could only provide security.

NEEMA IDP Widows' Group at Nakuru Showground IDP Camp; Mary Wakio Kamau (Secretary) & Helen Kerubo (Chairman)

Were you born in the Rift Valley, Mary?

I am not sure, but I was born in 1973 and I know that my parents moved to the Rift Valley in the 1970s. I grew up in Nandi Hills and did all my schooling there. I attended Kibwori Estates Primary School, where I sat my KCSE in 1990 and joined Samoei Secondary School. I managed to only attend Form one and two before dropping out of secondary school for lack of school fees. It is at that point, while still a teenager, that I started working as a tea picker in Kibwori Estates.

Did your parents buy land in the Rift Valley before they moved there?
No, my parents moved to Nandi Hills in the Rift Valley to work. My father was a supervisor at Kibwori Estates, a private tea farm, while my mother was a matron at Kapsimotwa Boarding School.

Do you have any children of your own now?
I have one daughter who was born in 1993 when I was still at my parents'. Currently she is enrolled at St. Mary's Academy, a day school here in Nakuru. She has not settled well in school because she is living here in the camp, and she is constantly being sent home for lack of school fees. Most of the parents here are not working, they are just idle; money is hard to come by.

Helen Kerubo: Our children are having it hard at school now; they are being discriminated against so much. Not only are school fees a problem, but they are feeling shunned by the other students. I do not have any children of school-going age myself, but I have a boy and a girl who have special needs. My son who is 22 years old has a heart problem and needs specialised medical care and drugs every now and then which I can not afford. Right now he is out at Nakuru town trying to find some work. My daughter, on the other hand, is deaf and dumb. She has finished school at Kuja Special School in Nyanza but is not employed. At the moment she has gone to the District Commissioner's office to seek any assistance that she can get from there. The children just wake up in the morning and go out into town to do this and that, search for *kibarua* (manual labour) because they cannot just stay here doing nothing.

Helen, how did you become a widow?
My husband was killed in the land clashes of 1992. We were living in Molo, and even after he was killed and we were evicted, we still went back. But this time round we are saying: enough is enough, we are not going back to Molo. I lived in Molo for over 35 years. I did not own the farm I lived on. It was given to me by my relatives who are well off, but I call it my own because I have lived there for so long. I used to grow wheat and maize and was also working as a home-based care-giver to support

myself, my children and two others who had been left under my care when their parents died.

What are conditions like in this camp?

A lot of us mothers in this camp are sick, but there is nothing we can do about it. Personally, I developed diabetes and high blood pressure after my husband was killed. We live under so much stress and when we find ourselves in this camp, with no means to earning a living, our health condition just gets worse. We cannot afford medicine.

But the government is saying that you have to go back home; what will you do?

HK: We are not willing to go back to those places we were evicted from. What we want as NEEMA IDP widows is a place in Nakuru town where we can start income generating activities. We do not want to keep crying every now and then that we are in need. We want to stick together as a group and live in this one place where we can support ourselves and our children.

How was NEEMA formed?

MK: We did not know each other before we came to this camp. Everyone came from everywhere and we all met here, but we have become friends. At the beginning there were 50 of us, but the group has now grown to 80. That was back in February and we began meeting and discussing our common problems and what we could do to resolve them. Helen wrote a proposal and during one of our meetings, our members accepted it as a good mission statement and vision for our future lives.

At one point, the Nakuru District Social Services officer came to speak to us. She told us what we needed to do to have our organisation registered. She asked us to send minutes of our meetings to her together with our list of officials and 500 shillings as registration fees. We organised ourselves and elected a core team with a chairman, a secretary and the treasurer, Veronica Njeri. We also elected representatives from each of the seven districts from which our members hail to join the steering committee. We did not have the money for the registration fees but fortunately, a pastor who has been ministering in this camp came to our assistance. She gave us 1000 shillings to pay the registration fee and open a bank account. So now we are just looking for well-wishers.

Mwangi Njoroge, an IDP returning to Kondoo Farm outside Burnt Forest.

How old are you, and when did you come to the Rift Valley?

I am 80 years old now. I have been living in the Rift Valley since 1944. That was the year when my parents moved to this area from Gatundu in Kiambu district in search of work on the colonists' farms. They first went all the way to Nandi and then came to this area and started to work on a farm across the road, owned by a *mzungu* called Bwana Tom. I was a young boy then.

When I grew older, I started working at Bwana Tom's farm and then moved to this one. At that time, this farm was owned by another *mzungu* called Big Shaw. I was his overseer.

How did you end up owning land here?

After independence, Big Shaw left and this farm was taken over by the government through a company called the Central Agricultural Board (CAB). In Big Shaw's days, this land was all under wheat and he also reared cattle. When the government took over, they started to breed a huge number of sheep which they would buy from the Keringet area of Molo. That is how this farm came to be known as Kondoo (sheep) farm.

Then around 1966 or 67, the CAB began to subdivide the farm into five-acre plots. The people who had been working for Big Shaw and living as squatters on the farm had continued to work for the CAB, and they were the ones to whom the land was allocated.

Did tribe affect how the land was portioned out?

No. People from different tribes worked here. There were Luhyas, Luos, Nandis, Kisiis, and others, and they were all given plots of an equal size. What happened is that there was a ballot process and you got the plot that you picked without even having to choose who your neighbour was; no sections were marked out for specific ethnic groups. I got plot Seven.

Everyone received a five-acre plot for farming and a small plot in the shopping centre. Of course some people have since sold their plots, and others like me, subdivided them and gave sections to their children. So here where we have been brought back to is the shopping centre and this plot we are standing on belongs to me. I used to run a soup restaurant here before the clashes and would come here everyday and return to the farm house in the evening.

Do you have a title deed?

Yes I do but those came very recently even though I cannot recall exactly when and, as a matter of fact, most people do not have them. The thing is that my title deed got burnt when my house was set on fire after the elections. You know, most of us took away nothing. We ran off with just the clothes on our backs. But I believe that just because my title deed was burnt down here does not mean that it was burnt up there (in government records).

Do you know who burnt your houses?

Yes we do. We know these people. They are here now. Some of them have been coming here to give us their apologies while others like that one there (points) just come here to taunt us and listen to what we are saying and planning. You see that one there, the drunk one in a blue coat, he is one of the really bad ones – the ones who were organising it all.

And what do you feel about them?

What can one do? If we fail to forgive them, then what? In life, there never really is a need to carry anger and hurt towards the other person in your heart. We have to forgive them, and we will.

Do you think you will be attacked again?

That we cannot tell. Here, at this point, only God will be able to take care of us. In 1992 and 1994, they attacked us but it was nothing like this time. But we mean to return and that is why we are here.

The government moved us to our shopping centre last week, but no one has gone back to their farms yet. There is nothing there. We have no houses, no seeds and no food, so we do not know how we will go back there. We are willing to move but we are waiting for a more concrete statement from the government on security and how we will be assisted to rebuild what we have lost. The government has built a new police station but we are still waiting for the help they said they would send towards tilling and replanting our farms.

Charles Matathia *lives in Nairobi, and is currently studying for a Masters in Criminology and Social Order.*

KIAMBIU/ EASTLEIGH

Shukri Guracha, married; mother of two

How were you affected by the elections?

My house burnt down after it caught fire from a neighboring bar.

Do you know who burnt your house down?

You can't know who started the fire. You can't!

What happened on the day of the elections?

We woke up and people had lined up at the polling station. Voting went on well. Out of the blue, the violence started about three days later when

235

it was announced who had won. Some people were in their houses and some were outside. We never thought that the outcome would be like this.

Do you know the people who were involved in the violence?
They are neighbors, they are people we know. We could see them that night running around, so we know them, it's just that we can't say anything.

Do you think life in Kiambiu can be the same as before?
It is very hard to understand the heart of man, but from the outside people seem to be fine. You can find that the same person who burnt your kiosk still comes there to eat.

Do you ever talk about politics these days?
I don't bother with politics; I have my life to worry about. I am a Borana, and my house and restaurant were burnt. I am neither a Kikuyu nor a Luo. If the neighboring bar was not set ablaze then my hotel would not have caught fire. The bar belonged to a Kikuyu, and I am from Moyale. I don't see why I was involved in all this.

Victoria Akinyi

How were the elections conducted here in Kiambiu?
Whenever the politicians came, one after the other with different views, all aiming to get ministerial posts, we would receive them irrespective of their political parties.

What was the actual voting day like?
People came out in large numbers. We voted for change with one mind, but instead of that we found ourselves in grief and sorrow and death. It has brought hatred amongst us to this day. The plot in which I stay has that hatred because there are Kikuyu, Luo and Luhya. At times the Kikuyu speak harshly, but when I am in their presence they don't talk because I understand their language. They call out and say '*Jaluo, Jaluo ...*'

How did the violence affect you personally?
I lost my belongings: chairs, cooker, and cutlery. But I thank God for life

because I came here to the chief's camp to hide with my children. The looters probably thought I had a television set in my house. They just took the little that I had but since they left me alive I didn't worry.

Do you think anything was accomplished by the violence?
I don't think so because it has caused the deaths of many people. Hatred amongst neighbors is still a problem and I don't know when it will ever end. People have not been cooperative; if one wants to buy something from someone who is not of their tribe, the person thinks twice before selling. It reaches a point where they have what you want to buy, but they tell you it is not there. Even when you can see it, they say that someone has already paid for it. Most Kikuyus houses on this side [of the chief's camp] were burnt.

When they see a a Luo buying from a Kikuyu they ask, *why are you buying PNU items?* They even beat people up. I have many T-shirts from both parties but can't wear them in an area which does not relate to each respective party. I have come to realize that we are fighting ourselves for no reason. The leaders are not fighting and the people who complain most are the Luos. When they see one of their own wearing a T-shirt from another party they tell them, 'remove it and stop shaming us.'

I am a Luo married to a Kikuyu so most of the Luos accused me of betraying them, even threatening to lynch my husband.

Now that the leaders have struck a peace deal do you think that spirit will trickle down to Kiambiu?
Yes! They agree that they need to go to the grassroots and tell their people what steps to take to live in peace. But if we continue to interact with them only through the media, it won't help.

Vincent Ochieng Odhiambo

How was your average day before the elections?
I would wake up and go to work with the Child Rescue Team and later try to approach aspiring councilors to get money from them.

What was the ethnic composition of your neighborhood?

237

It was a mixture. Youth from all tribes would come together and plan where they would go to get campaign money. Whatever we got would be shared out equally amongst us.

What happened on the day when results were announced?
That's the day when the fights began, because the results did not reflect the voice of the majority. That is when things went sour, and I immediately began to hear people saying it had been waiting to happen. On that day many houses were burnt and some people were killed.

Do you think this violence was necessary?
I think it is advantageous because it has made people become aware and know their real neighbors and understand their environment.

Do you talk about politics at home or in the streets?
Now people can talk about it because peace has returned. A lot has been achieved, though the leaders remain selfish.

Would you vote again?
Yes! I am a Kenyan... I must vote, for it is my right.

Christine Auma

What happened here when the results of the elections were announced?
The day people voted, I went with my husband to visit a friend of ours. We came back in the evening to find people gathered, waiting for the results. The next day my husband went to work on the night shift. He had a feeling that if something bad was announced there would be problems. He worked as a guard, so I cooked for him early so that if anything should happen it would find him at work. I also left the house and just a few steps away, the area was on fire, so I went back to check on my child.

People were armed with clubs and pangas, and my husband had to come back because the roads were blocked. My neighbors came and we sat together. The next day I told him that because of my pregnancy I couldn't live at home. We took our things to the chief's camp and planned to stay the night, but even there people were fighting. I decided to go to my uncle in Jericho, but the road there was blocked. I decided to go to my friend in Dandora. We could hear gunshots as we went. My husband tried to go back but he couldn't make it to the house because of the commotion. We didn't leave anyone in charge of our belongings so our wooden door was broken. Our neighbors were mostly Kikuyu, who left immediately after the elections so no one was around. It was like they knew. They are back now, and they do not talk to us.

Did you see any benefits come out of the fighting?
There can't be any.

Joyce Akinyi Omondi is a student at Nairobi University. A poet and short story writer, she has been published in Journalist *(A magazine for the University's School of Journalism) and* The Ghetto Storm.

"**DANDORA**

"

240

Alvando Msamani, electronics salesman

How do you explain everything that happened after the elections?
I won't blame the politicians. I think we are the ones that were influenced by immature politics. We spend most of our lives listening to every word of those politicians. That's why we are suffering, especially the middle class and poor people. The rich from Westlands, Lavington, Runda are very safe.

Do you think violence is necessary?
When needed. If you feel deprived of your rights and want to be heard, you can use violence.

Joan Adhiambo, mother of six

How many of your neighbors came from a different tribe before the election?
The majority were Luos, Luhyas and Kikuyus.

Has this changed since December?
They haven't changed. They are still the same.

Do you think the violence was necessary?
I don't see the reason. What for?

But what if people are fighting for their rights?
They are their rights, but for people like me who are poor, there is no need for violence.

Were the leaders fighting for your rights?
Yes, but let the truth be told: at no time is violence necessary.

Who do you blame for all the violence that happened?
Of course Kivuitu. Who else? If he would have stood for the truth, all this chaos wouldn't have occurred.

Mama Owiti, Kiosk owner

How did the elections affect you?
Everything was fine until we voted. Since then, all jobs have really been affected, and business has been crippled. The stock in my shop has gone down since consumer prices shot up. My customers now pay double for everything. This election hurt me and my marriage. My husband and I were supporting different presidential candidates. After the results the inevitable happened and we parted.

Why do you think the violence erupted?
It is all these leaders. All was well, then the leaders started the hate campaigns, making us fight one another; now we have destroyed all that we built...

How has the violence affected your neighborhood?
The numbers of orphans has increased tremendously because many parents died during the elections. Some children come here asking me to give them food because they don't know where their parents are. I asked one why he was alone and he said 'Baba was beaten by youths and he died.'

What should be done to avoid this scenario in the future?
There is no way to prevent this since a seed has been planted, and in the next elections the harvest will be plentiful violence.

Beatrice Adhiambo, 18, unemployed graduate

What was an average day like before the December election?
It was unlike any other Christmas: there was tension and noise, it was chaotic. I did not enjoy my Christmas.

And after the election?
Even walking alone was scary. People were suspiciously staring at each other. You didn't know who was who. The first question from a stranger was, 'From which tribe do you come?'

And what about your neighbors?
In the plot where I live, we hid members from different communities who

were unwanted in this place. Others used to come and bang on our doors, asking, 'What community are you from?' But we didn't fight with our neighbors. We protected them.

Three young men chewing khat in an alleyway near Joy Villa Primary School, Dandora Phase V

Do you guys feel the violence was necessary?
(First boy): The way it started was okay. But the way it escalated, things turning worse, stealing became part of it... It was crazy...

(Second boy): Yes... It is true!

Were there people who benefited?
(All three in unison): Yes... Yes.

(First boy): You see, when unwanted communities were chased from their premises, people started fighting for the small plots and small business premises they left behind.

How has this violence affected the youth?
(Second boy): It has affected the youth a lot. You want money to pay for your house, but there are no jobs, and leaders are hustling for their stomachs only.

(Third boy): They put their interests first ...

Did the violence affect you personally?
(First boy): It has affected me a lot ... you know, there are no jobs, my friends have died. The one I used to share a house with, he was stabbed in the stomach and died.

Why do you think all this happened?
(Third boy): These things happened because of the truth. People were fighting for their rights. If all things had gone straight, we wouldn't have witnessed all this chaos...

Do the youth have a reason to indulge in crime?
(First boy): That's the way things are right now...a guy is broke and needs

to pay the rent; he needs to eat; maybe he has a ghetto girl in the crib, and she has to eat and dress...

Has the price of khat been affected by all this?
(Second boy): Yes, because of the transport.

How much is one kilogram retailing for?
(Second boy): before it was 500 shillings, but now it costs anything from 600 to 800.

Lillian (withheld her last name), a Form Four student at Good Shepherd Secondary School.

Has the violence affected your education?
Early in the year we missed classes very often - and we have a syllabus we are following so we are very much behind. You would come to school, the screams would start and they would send us home; many lessons were lost.

Whose fault do you think it was?
I don't blame anyone. I know there are patriotic and peace-loving people in Kenya and many people were fighting for their rights. But others were fighting for fun. For many this was also an income-generating thing. They were making money, breaking into shops and ransacking everything. I saw that with my own eyes.

Did poverty have a role in the violence?
In a very big way. You will discover that at least 80 percent of the demonstrators were fighting for economic gain, and the remaining 20 were fighting for their rights.

Why do you think all this happened?
I blame the Electoral Commission of Kenya, and even PNU – people were not happy with the results. There was a high level of corruption. These leaders tell us to shun corruption and yet they are the most corrupt people in Kenya.

Were any of your teachers affected by the skirmishes?
There is one new teacher - I think he is a Kikuyu, and was chased from

Mathare. The students now call him Mr. Displaced. He knows that people call him that. Sometimes we make jokes telling students to bring small things like salt and sugar for him.

Do you know anyone who died in the violence?
Yes, my neighbor. He was burnt to death, and he was only 18 years old. His name was Brian. I don't even know how they recognized his face.

Brian Onyango, father of three and kiosk owner

What went wrong with the election?
The election was unfair and the electoral commission deserves a reshuffle. I am Luo and we had to demonstrate because it was our right to do so.

Do you think tribalism helps in any way?
Tribalism is bad. People should open their eyes because such things are bad. We should not let them happen again. If another election is conducted in the same way and we kill each other again, don't you see that we will be tied to tribalism like slaves?

Did you take part in the violence?
People like us are always on the forefront when such things happen. Let me ask you, can you watch someone stealing your cows and then pretend that nothing really happened? Can you? That was the case during that period. Kikuyus wanted everything, but their plots were taken by Luos here in Phase IV.

Do you think that violence helps?
Yes and no. You know, mass action works miracles; anything can be done. But at the same time people lose their lives, and it is bad when such things happen. But sometimes we must demonstrate when need arises, and this time we really had to demonstrate.

Daniel (withheld his last name), father of two, born and raised in Dandora

What happened during the election?

I voted but things turned out the wrong way. Although the person I voted for won the election, I really regret it. I should not have voted because of everything that followed. I hate to say it, but the election caused violence and the merciless killings.

What was it that made people start killing each other?

This violence was caused by the politicians. They are the ones who are responsible for whatever happened. They initiated violence; they made us fight each other, and they used us I was on the frontline fighting, I threw stones and that makes me a fool.

Mwani Mahugu *is a writer, poet and musician who grew up in Dandora.*

Interview with

MATHARE LANDLORDS

*From an interview with Peter Mwangi, Chairman of the Mathare
Landlords United Association, conducted by Samuel Munene*

[Peter Kihara Mwangi, 48, owns a 24-room compound in Mathare. Until
2008, he occupied four rooms himself and charged an average of 2000
shillings rent for the rest. When the post-election violence began he was
warned by a tenant that he was about to be attacked, and fled with his wife to
safety.]

Where did you run to when you heard it wasn't safe to stay at home?
   I went to a friend's place in Mwiki. The next day when I went back I tried
   to access my house, but in vain.

What happened? Were you chased away?

Tenants from the Luo tribe in Mathare teamed up with the invading gangs who were also largely Luo.The residents, our tenants, were not beating or threatening the landlords, but they could pinpoint us to the gangs, thus we were marked. This was understandable considering that they had been told they would be paying half of the previous rent amount, or very little.

For instance at one time I tried to approach my house, but saw six men armed with pangas forming a net around me. Of course I ran away. Some of the landlords were not so lucky and were beaten.

Did you report this to the police?

Yes, and when we did they told us to go report in Othaya; *'Kazi iendelee Othaya,'* they used to say. That was how bad it was. After we realized that the government was not coming to our aid, I mobilized about 20 other landlords and started brainstorming on how to save our houses, the source of our livelihood. That was the genesis of the Mathare Landlords United Association.

Did you landlords know each other before this, or have some form of organization?

We knew each other, since when we came to Mathare North it was a plain area, very poorly developed and so we got to know each other as we built our houses. We didn't have any formal organization though, other than informal welfare organizations. The violence served to bring us closer.

So what happened after you mobilized some of your fellow landlords?

At that time the country seemed to run on jungle law. And we planned to use the same jungle law to solve our problems, I mean if someone approaches you with a sword you don't expect to use a Bible against him. We started raising money with the purpose of retaliating.

How did you plan to retaliate?

We were planning to call men to come help us. Hope you know what that means. The same way they chased us, the same way were we going to chase them away.

What happened next?

First although we were bitter with what happened to us, a number of the landlords and myself were a bit apprehensive of what would happen if we went ahead and used violence to evict the illegal tenants. At that time the government was fragile, anything of the magnitude we were planning in Mathare would be enough to trigger chaos in other parts of Nairobi and the country in general; so we moved a little bit slowly, raising funds, contacting the gangs for hire, while hoping a peaceful solution would be found.

Around the same time, an organization known as the Kenya Veterans for Peace (KVP) heard wind that we were looking for mercenaries to help us achieve our goals. They contacted me and said they would help at no cost. They came in the nick of time. We had gangs ready, we just needed some logistics. Some little funds were needed, and we were trying to lobby politicians for some cash and good will.

I called a meeting with the landlords and told them KVP, whose coordinator Mathenge had contacted me, had offered to help free of charge. KVP came with a completely different solution from what we were expecting; they said they would negotiate between us and the illegal occupants. Our members were hostile, they wanted to hear nothing to do with negotiations and reconciliation. Some were even about to beat us, the officials, saying we were traitors.

Somehow we prevailed upon them to reason. Mathare North was ours, and there was no need to shed blood and destroy our property.

What did the KVP do?

They urged us to seek help from the government; they introduced us to some senior government officials. We talked with the DO, who started taking some action. The DO was known as Kamau.

What action did the DO take?

The DO worked with some other government authorities and came and arrested 150 illegal occupants. It was in the newspapers.

How were the occupants identified?

It was known that Mathare Area 2 all the way to the border with Baba Ndogo was a no-go zone for landlords and the Kikuyu. Even the DO was stoned. He had been ordered by the DC to go remove all campaign posters or materials displayed in public, and when he tried to remove posters belonging to Raila some group threw stones at him. It was easy to identify the illegal occupants.

150 people were arrested; what happened then?

After they were arrested we, as landlords, made a police statement which was to be used in court. Unfortunately these Luo gangs kidnapped one of our committee members together with his daughter. They threatened to kill him and the daughter if the arrested illegal occupants were not released.

Did the kidnappers or the kidnapped committee member communicate the demands to you?

No at all. And that made us very angry, because we had said we were ready to die to achieve our goals. You see they released him but held on to the daughter, who was to be released once all the arrested 150 occupants were set free; if that didn't happen, the daughter would be killed. It was upon him to use his connections to make sure they were released. But instead of coming to inform us what had happened he succumbed to the demands of the gangs.

What was the alternative? What would you have done?

He could have informed us, and somehow we could have found a solution, never mind how.

So what did he do?

The kidnapped committee member is vey rich, he has about seven flats, almost all fully occupied. The gangs had invaded some of his houses. He had already promised to donate a million shillings to boost our mercenary kitty.

So he announced to the media that those arrested were his legal tenants and have done no wrong. He then lobbied the police and they were let to go, and so was his daughter. The gangs returned to the houses and declared there was nothing the landlords could do to them.

We excommunicated the said committee member because we felt he was a traitor.

Where did things go from there?

The DO and government official who were helping us were very angry.

They had tried to assist but one of our members had let us down. The members on the one hand were burning inside, the diplomatic way was taking too long to bear fruit and they wanted us to forget it and use 'the other method.' KVP approached again, pleading with us to be a little bit patient.

The DO also urged us to be patient and he tried to get another solution.

The situation is still very tense. Some of the landlords are able to access their houses but when they demand rent, the occupants say they don't have money, or tell them to wait a little bit longer and many other excuses. And if you threaten to evict them, they report to the gangs and the situation becomes worse. They are using water and electricity, not paying rent and the landlord is expected to shoulder that entire burden. We are waiting for the government.

What do you want the government to do?
The government should give notice to the illegal occupants to vacate the houses. We built these houses with our sweat, nobody gave us the houses. To make it worse, the administration on the ground is biased.

How so?
The chief and sub-chief are Luo. What do you expect? We want a neutral administration on the ground, otherwise the current administration tends to favor, or rather are afraid of, the gangs. The government should come in and build a link between the landlords and tenants.

Previously, how were you communicating with tenants?
A tenant is someone like you, also the landlord. We can talk and agree on terms. But now there is a ditch between us. The government, the president and the prime minister and MP should come and talk to the people here.

Mathare North belongs to which constituency?
Kasarani.

Have you tried to seek audience with your MP?
There is no way. Since she was elected she has never come to Mathare, and there is no way you can tell me she doesn't know what has been happening here. We have no channels to communicate with her. It seems

she is also biased.

What about the councilor?
We have not seen him. Just like the MP, he disappeared after the elections.

What happens when you report to the chief?
Well, the chief listens very keenly and promises to take action, but she never does. For instance there is a man known as Okello who forcefully takes your materials when you repair your house. We have reported several times to the chief and no action has been taken. The gangs have started demanding money from tenants for 'security.' The sub chief knows this so well.

What exactly should the chief do once you report?
Once I report, the chief should inform the sub-chief, who will take his wingers to go evict the person. Unfortunately the wingers are from one tribe and some of them are involved in the gangs. So there is nothing that will happen.

How long has the-sub chief been in office?
He is relatively new, because Mathare North is a new sub-location, created sometime last year. But he knows this area very well. The chief is in charge of Baba Ndogo location. We don't know the chief very well, I have lived here for so long but she does not involve the landlords in any of her meetings or activities.

To be realistic houses in Mathare North are largely owned by members of one tribe, the Kikuyu, but the tenants are mainly Luo.The chief forms all residential and administrative committees using tenants and ignoring landlords. The landlords are being sidelined and yet we are the investors, we own Mathare North and we would be the last people to want this place to go down. The government should give us enough security.

Is it true that some of the gangs are demanding cash from the landlords in exchange for returning their property?
Yes, the same gang stealing building materials is the same gang doing this. They have started seeing signs that the landlords might eventually come back, and so as an exit strategy they demand between shs 6000 and 10,000 shillings as payment – 'for taking care of your house ,' they say,

yet for the whole of that period they have been 'protecting' your house you haven't received even a single cent in rent.

Interestingly the gangs are not residents of Mathare North. They are from Baba Ndogo and Ngu Nyumu, but they collude with the rogue tenants.

Why are so many of the landlords in Mathare North Kikuyu?
Kikuyus like investing. When the city council was distributing these plots, it gave to all tribes. But most members of the other tribes sold their plots to the Kikuyu, who saved and built these houses. It's not that we were given free of charge. There are still a relatively large number of the landlords who are from other tribes.

Were landlords of other tribes, say Luo, also affected? Were their houses invaded by illegal tenants?
Some were affected, but not in the same way as the Kikuyu. The gangs have a soft spot for their own.

Is local government doing anything about all this?
The DO and DC are working hard. The chief is changing her attitude. We hope she changes completely. At one time I had asked her to help me evict the illegal tenants, and she asked me, 'do you want me to carry them on my back?'

We complained to the administration and maybe that's why she is changing.

Not all the landlords are willing to speak publicly about the situation – are they afraid of repercussions?
Yes there are some landlords who are still traumatized and they fear if they come out openly they may be harmed by the gangs. They just need assurance and counseling.

Are there non-Kikuyus in your organization?
Yes, but not Luo. Luhya, Kamba, many others; we have over 150 members.

What is the way forward?
The government should come and assist. We have restrained from acting violently. Mathare North seems like it is ignored, or no one knows what is happening. They could start with a police post. The government should

also hold a meeting with Mathare tenants and landlords, especially the Luo, who are the majority of tenants. We are for dialogue, but the government should make the dialogue work. The gangs are thieves and we have lowered ourselves enough to talk with them. The government should come in.

The Mungiki have been very active in other parts of Mathare, is their presence being felt in Mathare North?

The Mungiki has not been felt here, however, they are making inroads. They have started asking people in Area One for security fees. You can imagine what will happen when they meet with the Luo gangs.

Did your tenants complain about the cost of rent before the election?

Yes, people complain. The tenant has the freedom to choose where to live. Like in Mathare North, rent ranges from as low as Shillings 1000 to 5000. Furthermore, tenants and landlords talk and negotiate. It would be foolhardy to say all this invasion is because of high rent.

Is it safe for you to go to your house today?

Yes, I have been lucky and the illegal tenants moved from my house. Somehow the gangs have also kept away. There are still some tenants who are not paying rent, but I am trying to talk to them.

Samuel Munene *is a young Nairobi poet, short story writer, and contributor to Kwani? as well as various literary online magazines. He holds an economics degree from the University of Nairobi, and currently earns a living as a freelance writer.*

Interview with KENYA VETERANS for PEACE

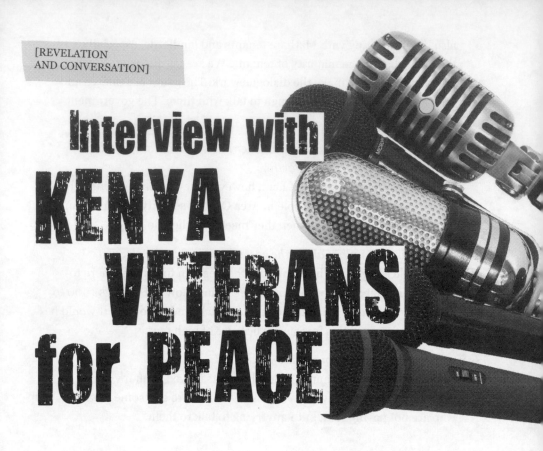

From an interview with Rev. John Mathenge, founder of the Kenyan Veteran's For Peace, conducted by Samuel Munene.

Could you start by talking briefly about your background?

My name is Reverend John Mwangi Mathenge. I was born in 1948, in Laikipia District. I Joined school in 1956 and completed my O-levels in 1969. I joined the army in the early 1970s and completed 22 years of service. I was a member of the military intelligence services; I attended several courses: communications, intelligence collection, analysis and dissemination.

I am an opinion leader in Laikipia West, where I come from. I also ventured in politics as a member of KANU in Laikipia West constituency.

I wanted to unite the people of different tribes in the area. I also was the national coordinator for *jua kali* exhibitions. I have gone to China and various countries in the world.

When did you form Kenya Veterans For Peace?

It was founded in early February this year. I got the vision to start the organization in early January when the violence erupted. I thought about the retired security agents, because these are the people used or misused in the violence and have been used before. As you know, the retired officers get a minimum pension. A person may work for 30 years and earn 2000 shillings per month, and the gratuity he gets is about 300,000 shillings, which he or she uses to buy land or some other fixed asset

They are also not accepted by the community because they are the first suspects in crime. Politicians hire them to mobilize the youth, criminals too, to train them how to use firearms. We cannot deny you are used.

From your brochure you say its an organization for 'junior officers.' Why the insistence on junior officers?

In Kenya there are various classes of security officers; those who are rich and high-ranking in the military. These live well and have no problems. Then there are the juniors, who are considered primitive and only know how to say *afande*. From the rank of major and below, these are the people who are badly misused. The first group of founders was about 14 people. Today we have 790 registered members. Our target is 30,000 members. We only register those who agree with our vision, which is peace. We are apolitical, non-religious and also not a bureau where retired soldiers come expecting jobs. We are also not a union, where people dismissed or retired from service come and air their problems.

I have seen some of your members; they look pretty young, like they are yet to get to the retirement age, can you comment on that?

Once you join the forces, especially in Kenya, you are prone to many problems: Witch-hunting, crime, etcetera. You may have worked for several years and just one day you are dismissed from the forces. The police force are especially under tough conditions getting them into problems, so there are some who leave the forces prematurely. These are the most potent.

How do you actually mobilize ex-officers to join KVP?

I contacted those I knew and sold my vision. They contacted their friends and so and so on. Security officers know each other, and there is a retired security officer in every village.

How do you actualize your vision of achieving peace?

Most of the retirees were in peace-keeping missions, sometimes in places where they could not communicate with the locals on basis of language or culture. But somehow they were able to break such barriers. We wanted to use such techniques. We are in a very good position to talk to the people, considering that we, the people with the expertise, have come together irrespective of tribe. This should be an inspiration to people.

There are places which are very hostile, where even the police cannot penetrate. But the ex-security officers who are almost in every corner of the country can assist the police in such areas.

Are you based only in Nairobi?

We have members from all provinces, though Nairobi is the capital and many of the members are located here. We want first want to actualize our vision in Nairobi, and then it will be easier to diffuse it in other parts of the country. We don't want to look like a militia group or compete with the established authority.

We want to create an organization through which even serving soldiers can look forward to their retirement. Here in Kenya we have a use and dump policy regarding the security forces. And when you dump them you are dumping poison. These people have to survive; they have families to feed; they want to live well, and what do they have? A skill, a dangerous skill.

What have you achieved so far?

We have been recognized internationally, but our government is yet to fully accept our role, say only for the Nairobi provincial commissioner. There are some people who I may call senior citizens and some are not happy with an organization such as ours.

We have achieved:

1. Mediatating between the landlords and illegal occupants in Mathare.

We were able to talk to 397 illegal occupants and landlords and they just quit peacefully. This was a time bomb

2. We are able to establish the real and fake internally displaced people. Using our experience in intelligence we able to know who are the real and illegal IDPs. We have been working with the provincial administration on this

3. We have been able to counsel some of them who have agreed to go back to their homes.

I am trying to get at how this actually happens on the ground. Take for instance the case you mention in Mathare: Did you just approach the illegal occupants? Or did the landlords approach you, or how did it happen?
It was through intelligence that we learned that the landlords were contributing 10,000 shillings to hire gangs to go burn and evict the illegal occupants. We contacted the landlords and persuaded them against it, telling them to give us some time. We try solve the problem peacefully. We tactfully approached the illegal occupants, combining reason and some forceful words, and we have been relatively successful. In those places where houses were occupied by members of particular tribes, we use those of our members from that tribe. This creates confidence which we exploit to hammer reason into the illegal occupants.

We also started talking to the gangs who have brought these people. We have had several meetings with the gangs that were acting as the illegal landlords. They are very appreciative of our efforts, and their only worry is what will happen next, once they stop collecting the rent ... we showed them the way, proposing alternatives and the response was good. At the last meeting we had about 47 gang members, and they were really happy. We are approaching some organizations to see how they can integrate the gangs back into society as useful citizens.

Where does KVP get its money from?
We have never had a penny from any organization. It was only Ambassador Bethuel Kiplagat who gave us 10,000 shillings, and then there was Deka Ibrahim, the chairman of CCP [CONCERNED CITIZENS FOR PEACE] who gave about 20,000. We have approached many organizations to fund us, but it has never translated to actual cash. They

appreciate our activities, but they say we have no money.

Which organizations have you approached?

Peace Net, Oxfam, Keeps, Civil World. It is only the Universal Peace Federation which has given us sponsorship by offering to train our members on peace. We contribute money from our pockets.

What about the government?

We have talked with Director of Settlement Mr.Ndolo, and he told us the ministry does not have money to sponsor the group or organization. But once they get money they will assist us.

How are you organized internally?

We have the executive board, the secretariat. The executive board plans and schedules meetings, looking for resources, etcetera. We have coordinators in every district. They arrange activities at the district level. We have division coordinators and groups in community policing. We have contributed greatly in reducing crime. We have engaged the carjackers, petrol bomb experts, mobilizers of violence... the government should come and support this initiative.

How do you get along with the police?

We have a good relationship with the police. We sometimes arrest criminals and take them to the police. Our relationship is cordial and informal. We have tried to invite the commissioner of police to meet with us, but he has ignored us. This however does not discourage us, and we soldier on.

But isn't there a potential for conflict with the police, in the event that they see you as trying to do their job for them?

Whatever we do, we act peacefully and harmoniously. We believe that someone, somewhere will recognize and understand. Peace is crucial, and that's our vision. I wonder why someone should think an organization promoting peace is negative.

Most of our members are very street smart. They have worked or been involved in crime, and these are the people who will help curb crime.

So you don't think the authorities will feel threatened by KVP?

Not really. We are just being realistic. Of course, there are those who might think we are undermining their authority. But that's petty.

What is KVP most in need of?
We need resources. If we are able to get some way to keep our members busy, so that they are not idle and tempted to engage in crime. Perhaps the government should establish a fund for veterans. We also want to approach the Kenya Armed Forces Comrades' Organization [KAFCO]. This organization gets about 100 million per year. Where does then money go?

You said earlier that many veterans are misused. How does that happen?
It's very easy to misuse a retired security agent. During the 1991-92 clamour for multiparty-ism, I was misused by the opposition in that time. I was used to mobilize people to riot, loot shops and fight with the police. I was also involved in the clashes in the Rift Valley. We were being paid 5000 to 7000 shillings per day, and we very happy. Then I defected to KANU in December, 1992, after surrendering a G3 rifle and some ammunition I had. I met President Moi when I was a Kanu activist in Laikipia. We are still friends.

Have you seen him since starting KVP?
Not yet, but I plan to meet him eventually.

Do you work with any politicians at all?
No. But we plan to.

Do you have an office?
No, we work from hotels and the streets. But we are trying to fundraise and get an office.

Your target is to attract 30,000 members. What would motivate an ex-security officer to join KVP when they could make more money in crime?
It starts with a personal conviction, to realize that peace in the country is good for everyone. Only the grace of God can make one realize this. Generally, it's very hard to convince people to join us, and we don't do that. We want people to join because they believe in our vision.

BLUE eyed dolls

Sitawa Namwalie

PART ONE: BLUE-EYED DOLLS

There are dolls in my past, two of them. I found them lurking menacingly in my subconscious as a grown-up, like sentinels to my past. Those dolls had made their journey to Africa to unsettle an unsuspecting black-eyed girl. They reminded me of those Hollywood movies in which children's beloved toys turn into monsters and pursue their child owners in the darkness of night. Both dolls were blond and blue-eyed.

'Kinky-haired babe, think again.'

That's what they said to me in their silence. These dolls revealed the texture of my hair. I was kinky-haired. My hair grew in tight little corkscrews. It certainly was not blond. One time I got to experience what it was like to have a mane of hanging, swinging blond hair. It was quite by accident. I was helping my mother husk green maize cobs. I looked at the silky blond tussles and gathered a handful and put them on my head. My mother laughed with me as she swung golden locks out of my eyes like a white girl.

But let's tell the stories of those dolls.

I was six years old when I first saw a real live doll. It belonged to the little blond girl, Susan, in my new class in standard one in K primary school. I wanted that doll. Its eyes blinked and it cried, 'Mama, Mama.' I had to know why and how. Where did the sound come from? So I took it home with me that day. Technically, I stole the doll; I went into Susan's school bag without permission, I took it without telling her, and I took it home. I didn't tell my mother that I had it either.

The next day I handed it back to Susan with a calm, 'Here is your toll.' Heavy mother tongue interference in evidence. I was an earnest little girl simply returning the tools of a successful scientific experiment to a fellow avid researcher. Where I come from the 'T' sound becomes a 'D' and vice versa. P and B are also interchanged. We have real problems with 'W,' interestingly, because when you think about it, it is pronounced with a series of 'Ds and Bs'. I was yet to acquire the posh English accent I have today, that always makes foreigners ask me where I went to school. Usually, they mean, 'Clearly you are one of the privileged ones, you went to school in Britain!'

Innocent of the consequences of my actions, I was surprised when Susan burst into tears clutching her doll and ran away.

I did not expect the trouble that followed. I remember standing with many tall white adults looking down on me with opprobrium. I was in discomfort. I was being accused of being a thief, lectured to as if I were a half-wit. My mother was there, as was a weeping, golden-haired Susan, clutching the hand of her mother. 'Never steal again,' the headmaster Mr. Asher sternly warned me. I couldn't understand them. What were they on about? Couldn't they understand that I could not be a thief? I only took the doll to find out how it could cry, how its legs and arms could move like that, whether it was real, how it could exist. The thoughts stayed in my head, unspoken. I stood silent, looking from face to face, overwhelmed.

Can you imagine my horror when I met Susan in first form in my new secondary school? The first thing she said to me was,

'I hope you won't steal anything from me again.'

No send-up. We were still too young to know irony or sarcasm, described by my secondary school teacher, Mrs. Hopkins, as 'the lowest form of wit.'

'No, I won't,' I assured her.

I was relieved when she left that school shortly afterwards.

The second doll appeared on the first day of primary school. It was only three years after independence and the *mzungus* who had not already fled were still making plans to leave the country. African children of the soon-to-be bourgeoisie were taking over the *mzungus'* places in schools whilst their parents took over their jobs, homes, businesses and farms. The *mzungus* fleeing from Kenya made it unnecessary for Africans to get nasty by forcibly taking back their land, as the Zimbabweans did in later years. Still there were incidents that I overheard the grown-ups talk about.

A *mzungu* or *muhindi* had had their land or home taken away by the newly prominent African or a minister who could not be refused. There was always a sense of victory and sometimes a mumbled 'serves them right.' We didn't talk about this covert stealing in public. In that uniquely Kenyan way, we swept that uncomfortable thing under the carpet, consigning it to our burgeoning basket of dirty little secrets that we hoped to ignore into oblivion. Each generation has added its own to the growing festering heap; now there are so many that we don't know what to do.

'When you get there give this package to Diana. Don't open it, it's her birthday party and this is her present,' my mother instructed with a worried expression on her face.

'*Mai*, what is a birthday? What's a present and what's in here?' I asked, holding up the pretty box.

Questions tripped off my tongue. I was intrigued by all the secrecy and the encounter with so many new things at once, things I did not know, words I was hearing for the first time, birthday, party, present. And at the center of the mystery, a shiny box wrapped in beautiful paper of so many colours. That was not all. My sister and I wore new dresses, shoes and socks, and our hair was combed back and tied with blue ribbons. I was in high spirits.

In the back of my mind, I still found room to explore jealous thoughts.

'Why is my mother giving things to other children?' I wondered, 'She has never given me anything like this.'

My mother's voice disturbed my train of thought to answer my questions.

'A birthday is the day you were born. And a party is to celebrate it,' she answered.

I looked at her with even more questions, but her patience had run out. Now she shouted,

'Just take it to Diana and don't open it. It is not yours!'

I cringed as I always did when she got that way, knowing that I couldn't ask anything more and wouldn't get any more answers to the teeming questions in my mind. I wished that

Papa was with me now. He always patiently answered my questions long after my mother would have stopped.

We got into the car and drove the short distance to Diana's house.

I didn't know it then but Diana and her family were playing an important role in teaching many emerging Luhyia families in the 1960s how to step into the shoes of the *mzungus*. My first birthday party had to be hers. Her family was the first one in our circle to embrace western style 'middle-classness' and all its trappings.

My family was slower on the uptake. We looked middle-class on the outside – we lived in the city in a four-bedroom house with a large compound, we had a car, and my brothers and sister went to the right school. But in our home we lived more like upcountry peasants. Numerous assorted relatives lived with us, relatives who had come to the city for their education. This meant space was always limited. For many years I did not have a bed of my own, sharing a bed with my sister and my room with more relatives.

For some reason when I was 11, my parents went into bourgeoisie overdrive. The impact on me was that I moved from sharing a bed with my sister to having my own bedroom. This was terrifying. I no longer had the safety of my sister and several cousins at night. I was later to find out in high school that many girls and their families from my social circle had a 'Diana experience' locked away in their past. Diana experiences included 'the first time I went to a birthday party and saw a birthday cake and ate too much and was sick;' 'the first time I saw Africans living in such a big double-storey house;' 'the first time I saw a small African girl sleeping by herself in her own bed and even worse in her own bedroom;' 'the first time I encountered store bought toys.'

We also learned about social hierarchy at Diana's. Of all the children in my life it was Diana that I preferred. I considered her to be my best friend. I know the conviction was not reciprocated. She had toys bought from shops, not made from sticks, old wires, cloth and paper stuck together with the imagination of children, the kind that I made with my brothers and sister. She was the source of my most intriguing discoveries and experiences about urban life. But I soon realized that I was only her very good friend when there were no other children around.

She had a friendship hierarchy, and I was at the bottom. The hierarchy went something like this. If I was alone, I could definitely count on being her best friend. If there was a coloured[1] child, I came second but still I was allowed to play. If there was a *mzungu* child, then I was relegated to a poor third, barely seen and vaguely tolerated. At Diana's, many future middle-class kids started to learn life's more dubious lessons. In our small close-knit society Diana loomed large.

Diana was busy when we arrived, so my sister and I decided to open the birthday present ourselves. The package revealed a doll. A beautiful doll with blond hair and blue eyes. I stood transfixed with emotion. Shock, envy, recriminations against my mother.

'How could she?' I thought.

I had dreamed forever about a doll like this, after I had seen one on television. I had asked my mother to buy me one and she said she could not afford it. I shook it and the doll's eyes blinked. It was wearing a short yellow dress that barely covered its bloomers. It was a baby doll with fat thighs and arms. All I could think of was it should have been mine. So how come my mother had bought the doll for Diana? I was filled with anger and it took me a while to hear Diana, who had discovered that I had opened her present.

'Give me my doll,' she shouted, 'it's my present.'

I looked at her with determination. I was not going to let her have it.

'No it's mine,' I shouted back. 'My *Mai* bought it; it's mine.'

She quickly took hold of the doll's head and yanked it hard away from me. The head came off in her hands. The sudden momentum sent her backwards. She fell onto her back and screamed piercingly as she lay on the ground.

---

1 Racially mixed person

I let go of the rest of the decapitated doll in horror and pulled my sister away from the scene of the beheading.

'Now you've done it,' my sister said. '*Mai* is really going to smack you.'

'Shut up, you,' I hissed back. 'She won't if you don't tell her.'

But it was already too late. Adults and children were running to Diana's rescue.

PART 2: KENYATTA AND ME

I had four encounters with Jomo Kenyatta, the first president of Kenya. I was a schoolchild the first time. Our school had been chosen to stand by the roadside waving little flags to welcome a visiting president. As the car with the two old men inside passed by, I looked directly at Kenyatta. It was as if I had entered a vortex, spinning faster and faster to the beginning of time, the point of the very creation of the universe. I saw stars being born, others dying, explosions of light and fire and . . . With all my will power I forced myself to draw back from the abyss. I turned away from the eyes and stepped back to hide behind another child, confused and afraid at what I had seen. I never talked of the experience for fear of being considered insane.

The second time, I was 16 years old, seeing my world around me emerge and become real. One of the things that I had begun to notice was that Kenyatta made the same speech year after year. In fact he made the same speech several times a year and people got excited each time. The soaring words were more than mere speeches, and always began with,

'*Ndugu zanguni*! . . . .' In between there were references to the fight for independence and a few insults thrown in. My favourite was a reference to the nation's enemies being shown '*Chamta makuni*!' The ending was the Hindu word *harambee* to which the crowds answered with a resounding 'Heee!'

I brought this fact to my father's attention and he cautioned me against disrespecting our nation's Founding Father.

'But Dad' I protested, 'it's true. He always says the same thing. I bet he has been making the same speech since independence 10 years ago. Why does he do that? Doesn't he have anything else to say? And what's even worse, why do people go to hear him say the same thing time and time again. Don't they get bored? Or are they just crazy?' I asked scornfully.

'Now *Kukhu*, you know he is our president. Don't say things like that,' my father said with a twinkle in his eye that told me that he was amused and just going through the motions of managing my curiosity.

'He is a great man. He did great things for this country.'

'Ten years of the same speech?' I said, dismissing Kenyatta with the certainty and cynicism of a 16-year old.

When, on the next National Day, my father asked whether I would go with him to the celebrations in Uhuru Park, I was reluctant. I only went because I would get to wear my beautiful new green dress. Also there was a high chance I would be on TV and the whole nation would see how lovely I looked.

We arrived at Uhuru Park and were led to the VIP pavilion by a soldier who marched ahead of us and stopped abruptly at our designated seats.

'Good beginning,' I thought, as I tried to act as if I'd been born with soldiers marching before me. I looked up at the cameras and tried to look much older than my 16 years, hoping that they were focusing on me.

On the day I went to Uhuru Park with my father, Jomo Kenyatta arrived with his young and elegantly dressed wife in tow. As he started to make his speech with the same words he always used, I prepared myself to be bored.

Instead, I was mesmerized.

I was transported into a trance-like state, to a new realm of existence, where anything was possible. His words were conveyed to me not only through sound but also on the backs of waves that seemed to emanate from the presence that Kenyatta had become. I had heard of the word 'charisma,' and now I could touch it, feel it pulsating from a being. I imagined that I could see it and I was lost. I wanted to follow Kenyatta to fight wars; for him I would conquer the enemy, slay them with swords in epic battles.

And then the speech ended, and the familiar closing resounded through us all.

'Harambee!'

'Heeeee!'

The third time I encountered Kenyatta was six years later. I was on the tennis team representing Kenya in the second All Africa Games in 1978. And as tradition demanded, the Kenyan team went to see the president State House and to depart with words of wisdom from him.

The Kenyan national team numbered about 120 sportsmen and women, including officials and coaches. We traveled in one bus to Nakuru Town and arrived shortly before midday. Officials met us and ushered us into the reception area that had been designed to recreate a traditional Gikuyu dwelling place. It was named *Thingira wa Iregi*. Soon Kenyatta arrived surrounded by faces familiar from television and the newspapers.

He began to address us.

The mesmerizing charismatic man of a few years ago had disappeared and so had the frightening one of my childhood encounter. He seemed lost in some fog. I had heard it whispered that he was senile. A few minutes into his speech it became clear that he did not know who we were or where he was. He seemed to be addressing real warriors setting off to do battle with the *wa coloni*; he exhorted the imaginary warriors to fight for the land they had lost to the white man and not stop until the *mzungu* was driven off the land and into the sea.

There were several girls from my school on the team. We all sat together and giggled as we watched the aides make vain attempts to steer the old man back on message. He veered off again and again, encouraging imaginary battle-ready warriors. 45 minutes later the aides managed to head him off and stop him. But not before he had repeated himself and repeated himself and addressed many groups of warriors, none of whom were present.

The fourth time I met him was only one month after the third time. The team he had sent off to fight his imaginary battles had heeded him and returned triumphant. We had won more medals than we had ever won or were ever going to win again for a long time.

The vice-president passed around the customary gourd of *mursik*, a traditional fermented milk that I usually loved when I visited my grandmother. When it came to my turn I held the gourd to my lips and pretended to sip it, too cool to drink *mursik* in front of my friends who had already sneered at the prospect of being subjected to such *mshamba* stuff in the full glare of television cameras.

Two days later, Kenyatta was dead.

PART 3: OUT OF AMERICA, OR HOW I BECAME A MARXIST

I went to study in the US in the 1980s. Before the first year was over, I had imbibed the paranoid conspiracy theories of my new Marxist circle and lost my African ease. Late one night I turned on the television to find the President of the United States of America, Ronald Reagan, ranting and raving in the most alarming manner about the 'evil empire.' He was referring to the former Soviet Union, America's then mortal enemy country of Cold War days. (And you thought 'axis of evil' was original?)

There is a moment in the deep night when reality becomes suspended, and we become susceptible to our original lurking primeval selves. In this night moment, assorted distorted demons and night creatures with names like *linani,* banshees, ghosts and ghouls rule as reality twists and turns changing shape and resonance. The howl of a dog becomes that of a were-wolf. On the Kenyan coast, that night moment brings with it all manner of djins and mermaids prowling in their woman shape to steal the souls of men. Mating cats evoke the screams of damned souls burning in a Christian hell. It is easy to believe the bizarre. (I am setting up my excuse for what happened next.)

It was at such a moment in the night that I found Reagan's ranting so aggressive that as I listened I became convinced that I had only missed the first part of his speech, in which he had finally gone over the edge and declared war on the Soviet Union. I went to bed that night terrified, in the grip of my imaginary world war. Before I fell into erratic sleep, I obsessed about how I would not be able to get out of the US before the actual war started, and that I would die alone in a foreign land. The next morning I was relieved and abashed to find that all was normal and there was no sign of impending war.

Twenty years later as I watched the elections that brought George Bush Jr, another dumb, dumb US president, into power. I realized that my vantage point with its emphasis on linear 'development' or *maendeleo* had warped my thinking.

Until that instant, I had thought development also brings highly enlightened people who would not lie about the presence of weapons of mass destruction to bring pain and destruction to innocent women and children many miles away in another country.

Before I went to America I was a student of the biological sciences at the University of Nairobi. Someone had put the University of Nairobi on the then outskirts of town. But it had not been far enough. By the 1970s, the outskirts were already part of the central business district and students could make their grievances felt by pelting the central business district with sticks and stones. It was a rioting students' paradise. During my time, there were numerous riots, demonstrations and campaigns many with echoes of Marxism or some left- leaning ideology with slogans like 'Down with the bourgeoisie, the proletariat rule!' shouted by students as they battled the police in the streets.

Somehow throughout these riots I remained largely innocent of any ideological infection. This is incredibly surprising to me now because we were sent home on at least four occasions over the three years of our studies for some issue with ideological overtones. In total, we spent about seven months at home. The male students had to report to their local chief every week but the women were not taken as a threat, so we did not have to report.

The only time I was absolutely certain about what we were striking for was the time we went on strike over food. We were all tired of the strange cuisine. The final provocation came when even the minced meat had weevils in it. For those of you who do not know what weevils are, these creatures are a type of beetle. For those of you who may not know this, never having been exposed to the wonderful world of entomology, here are some facts to fascinate.

Beetles, the family of *Coleoptera*, had over 300,000 species in 1980. Weevils, *Curculionidae* had 65,000 species in the same year. I am sure many more have been discovered since I studied entomology. The thing is, they are all vegetarian, so they will infest beans, legumes, rice, maize, but none feed on meat. I could never get it: how did the weevils get into the minced meat? We joked that the university kitchens must have used them to season the minced meat: a delicate flavouring.

It was always those unserious art students at main campus who started the riots. We science students with our 36 hour-a-week schedules – not much reduced from our secondary school schedules – had no time for such frivolous pursuits. Also we had no ideology to spur us to action and were so out of touch with current issues that we had no idea that our politicians were up to no good and that we should care. No science lecturer was ever caught in the political crosshairs during my time at the university.

The arts students had plenty of time with their eight-hour-a-week lecture schedule that we sneered at, ideologies such as Marxism, political issues that they cared about and lecturers with a death wish to egg them on. So what would happen is that the arts students had to threaten us to get us to join their strikes. When a strike started we would be the first target and rather then face the wrath of our fellow students, we joined in. Soon we were caught up in the excitement of the moment and forgot our original reluctance.

We were to be seen wearing jeans and sneakers, running around town being chased by police, stoning unsuspecting motorists in an orgy of anarchy that was surprisingly heady even when the threatened dire consequences were that we would be beaten or raped by the police and the paramilitary (at this time they still did not use live ammunition) and expelled wherever you had reached in your education, whether you were in your first year or just about to graduate. I took part in the running around town part. I didn't want to take part in the stoning of motorists in case one of them was my mother or father or one of their friends.

So what about the Marxism? I know that many people will find it surprising that I became a Marxist in the US, but it was common knowledge back then that you were likely to become a Marxist or at the very least end up leaning way to the left if you did your studies in the US. The reverse held true if you went to study in the USSR; you turned irrevocably capitalist and probably ended up holding some extreme right-wing perspectives as well. Certainly I found many of my friends and relatives who went to study in the USSR ideologically bereft. For both groups it was shopping that did it. According to my friends who went to the USSR the empty shelves turned them to the right.

In the US, the shopping experience couldn't have been more different. Walk into any supermarket in the US and there were shelves and shelves of different detergents. Twenty different brands of dog food. Try buying toothpaste and you had to choose from a row of 30 brands. I was confused about what parameters to base my choice and offended at the waste. As a consumer I had to ask myself why would I need 30 varieties of toothpaste to choose from?

What's funny is that back home the thought of such a long list of western goodies had always sounded delicious. Back then western goodies were in short supply, and some were not available in real time. You did not expect to keep up with trends in music or fashion in real time, for example. There was a genuine difference between the Third and First world, largely based on time. This time difference meant that at home there was a premium to being ahead of the pack.

I still remember the cachet of being one of the first to own those skintight Jordache jeans that were not going to hit the Nairobi streets for another two years. The first to wear the latest lip gloss, the really glossy kind; this particular trend might become extinguished before its existence is even heard of in Nairobi, and there I was wearing it because I had made a trip to New York City. With some of these more transient trends there was always the danger that no one ever got to even hear about it and to decide that it was a 'must have' fashion item. The extreme Third World trendoid ran the risk of simply looking strange and eccentric rather than enviably trendy. Sometimes I thought that it would have been useful to wear a

T-shirt reading, 'This thing that I am wearing really is the latest trend in London, New York, Milan.'

The road to my becoming a Marxist was littered with hardship though, and I almost didn't make it.

First, it was clear that I had a problem. I was the problem.

I arrived in America in the dead of winter never having experienced winter in my life. I also went to a Marxist university only having been vaguely aware of this ideology or the concept of ideologies for that matter, so I was green on many fronts. If my father had known, and then been able to believe, that he was sending me to America to a Marxist university, would he have walked me to the door of the airport with such pride, giving me one of his gems to take with me? I repeated it later to my new boyfriend, starry eyed, in a 'behold the wisdom of my father, I want to share it with you' moment, only to find that it was Confucius who originated it? You can guess the one, 'A journey of a thousand miles begins with one step.' I remember laughing and not being embarrassed by the busting of my father's 'original' gem. You must understand that I had once believed my father could speak Russian.

When I stepped into the graduate class at C University I was the first African for over 10 years. And I was the first African woman in more years than that. I am Kenyan, which back then had a baffling specialness. I still remember the whispers as I walked by fellow students in my first few weeks. Later when I made friends I found out that my arrival had been announced and was anticipated, 'Class, we will have a real Kenyan woman.' I was used to being taken for granted at home. For a while I basked in this adulation. Soon enough it was rudely interrupted, apparently it came to everyone's attention that I was bourgeois. According to the Marxists, this made me a criminal. It was my political class in Africa that kept the peasants trodden down, whilst my economic class exploited the workers. I was held personally culpable for the ills of the continent. I kid you not, when the lecturers talked about the problem of the bourgeoisie and petty bourgeoisie presented in Africa, my fellow classmates turned round and looked at me with accusation in their eyes.

It gets worse: I had servants. This particular thing was treated like some sort of character flaw. A friend of mine captures the dangers of being found out as an employer of servants by left-leaning elements in the US at that time. She was doing the bleeding heart liberal thing, *à la* the Third World, working in one of those poorly paid jobs learning at the feet of some feminist guru. One day she was called into the boardroom where the head feminists were meeting. The interrogation revolved around questions of whether she had servants at home. She turned red (she is a Kenyan of a hue that can blush) and fidgeted violently, giving her discomfort away. She realized she was on the horns of a dilemma. What was she to do? If she admitted that she had servants she could be fired. But she realized her behaviour had given her away so an outright lie was out of the question. So she chose to limit the potential damage by making a partial admission.

'Yes, we have servants,' she admitted with her fingers crossed, 'But only part-time.' Many years later we roared with laughter at how much we lay down at the feet of little tyrants just because they were supposed to be ideologically sound.

I would have chewed razorblades before I admitted this back then, but the logic of my fellow students escaped me; still, I was intimidated into silence.

This is what I would have told them had I been able to speak up: 'Any African attending university is by definition no longer a peasant, a worker or a proletariat even if they are a direct descendent of any of these preferred classes. A real worker is out there being just that a worker, not attending graduate school in the USA. Not all Africans are guilty of oppressing their brothers and sisters back home. Heck, Africans have the right to be not poor, peasants or workers. We can be anything.'

This is what has always been so intriguing for me. The attitudes of my fellow students were not strange. Africans are allowed only to be poor; it seems to me that the logic that follows is that then they can be saved or rescued from their conditions by kindly westerners. There is no place for Africans who can look after themselves in the psyche of the west. And interestingly, there appears to be no scenario for what happens when the 'helping' has worked. The logic seems to suggest that for Africans there must be no rainbow.

In 1982, an attempted coup in my country met with all-round gloating. A fellow student whom I considered a friend broke the news of the coup with words to this effect:

'You Kenyans have been the darlings of the west and now, finally, you have fallen!'

He was not simply being mean; he was just being a Marxist. Others joined in, expressing joy at the collapse of this false citadel that was often touted as a capitalist success story by the west, much to the chagrin of the leftist elements in the same west. Today, that Kenya seems too good to be true. A few years earlier, in 1975, a World Bank report noted, 'Kenya is now in the second year of its second decade as an independent nation. Behind it lies a record of sustained growth in production and income that has rarely been surpassed by countries in Kenya's stage of development.'

Some of the statistics that offended people are these:

In 1975, Kenya had 27 percent of the population living below the poverty line. GDP grew at a rate of 6.6 percent. It is true that by 1982 things were beginning to collapse as the post-Kenyatta regime that we like to call the 'Moi error' began to slash at the progress made in the first decade of the country's existence.

Today Kenya is very different; the same statistics reveal a country deeply mired in poverty. Poverty levels are at 57 percent, while the economic growth rate reached a low of 1.1 percent from 1997 to 2002. Although it is doing much better now, it is literally digging itself out from a deep hole. Is Kenya today a Marxist's wet dream? I don't know. All I can say is that it is uncomfortable to live in the midst of all this poverty. And now many years later we know that extreme poverty does not a revolution make. It can just as easily lead to a total implosion as a country sinks into civil war or worse.

STORY FOUR: HAIR AND THE FEMINIST HEAD

Of all the ideologies I picked up the most incompatible with my country was my hard-core feminism. It was not just any ordinary feminism, but one that looked for converts with the fanaticism of a born again Christian from the American Bible Belt out to capture souls in Africa. And I never missed a chance to advance my mission. I was a one-woman missionary determined to be martyred at the altar of feminism.

Red bull statements that would spur me into action were endless. 'Oh you know, women are like that' or 'Oh you know, women are their own worst enemy.' My country back then was still so innocent that it did not know that it should hide its chauvinism from view, at least in public. There were many sexist and misogynist statements said in my hearing by men and women on a daily basis.

Just so that there would be no room for speculation, I would declare my feminism openly on introduction. It wasn't quite, 'Hi, my name is Sitawa, and I am a rabid feminist who is vigilant and looking for opportunities to spring into action in defense of women everywhere by lecturing you into submission for any anti-woman statement that I may detect.' But it might as well have been. How I actually introduced myself was 'Hello, my name is Sitawa, and I am a feminist,' I said, looking them straight in the eye, daring them to make a joke of my declaration.

Just in case you might be misled into thinking that there was any irony here and maybe laugh out loud because you found the introduction funny, the clothing and demeanor completed the picture. I wore a uniform of black jeans, shapeless t-shirts and sneakers, the drab universal uniform of feminists, at least in the USA. 'Appreciate my mind, not my behind' is what I meant to say with my whole presentation to protect myself from another little habit I had picked up from the US: an aversion to unsolicited male attention.

All my friends were innocent. After I had lectured three or four of them for half an hour each on separate occasions, I soon found myself alone. I wore my aloneness like a badge of honour, seeing it as the inevitable the price paid by any champion of a cause who sticks their neck out – Nelson Mandela, say, who was still in prison on Robben Island, or Ghandi. Thank goodness I had seen the film 'The Loneliness of the Long Distance Runner.' I could use the image conjured by the title to console myself when I felt like giving up.

In an act of rebellion against my society, I smoked openly, even in front of my father. This particular statement was especially effective in establishing my rebel credentials to no one in particular. When my friends gasped and questioned this particular act as going too far, I had another lecture prepared for them. 'My up-country aunts,' I would say from my imaginary soap box, 'they smoke and drink, so why shouldn't I?' This was actually true. In the western part of Kenya women can smoke cigarettes. Some of my aunts smoke cigarettes, but with the lit end in their mouths. I have never seen a man smoke like this and I don't know why. I have one particular aunt who is hard-smoking and hard-drinking, who has always gone drinking with her husband, so I just don't understand the sanctions levied against the so-called modern African woman, that is, a woman in the city.

I have long since quit all those habits I picked up from America. I gave up picking on everybody around me because I realized that I had mistaken being constantly angry and fighting with people who did not agree with my opinion or with championing a cause. Besides, it was alienating and exhausting, and no one wanted to hang out with me because I was so intense and boring. When my friends could talk to me again, they told me that they had run away from me because I was just plain boring.

Where I am today can best be explained by my relationship with my hair. Freedom to be is after all what this long journey has been about. Emerging from the tyranny of my ideas about hair has been a wonderful journey of self-discovery and revelation. I don't have to have the right hair or long hair or straight hair. I wear my hair short and shorn. I look best when there is but a hint of hair on my head. It ceased to be my crowning glory long ago. Instead what you get is an uncompromising presence. I am not hiding, or softened in any way. Deal with that!

But there was a time when I wanted hair, when I thought I needed hair, and I finally got it. It was 1983, and I finally had hair, long hair.

Hair, I thought, would stop the gnawing self-doubt, the feeling of smallness, which had to be covered up by excessive accomplishment. I would finally be beautiful.

More hair would give me mystery. Think of those Hollywood screen sirens who peeked mysteriously from behind a curtain of hair – Mae West saying, 'Is that a gun in your pocket or are you just pleased to see me?' I wanted to be that way.

So there I was in America with long hair. A long harsh winter had grown my hair to shoulder length; that was the key variable. I had kept it in braids for eight months, and now I was ready for the chemical relaxer. It was going to be long and straight.

I did my research meticulously. Which was the best saloon to go to get the best treatment? I walked up to many black girls on campus and asked them this question and they all said go downtown to saloon X and ask for Tommy. He's the best.

One Saturday morning I walked downtown and placed my large afro into Tommy's capable hands. Tommy started to do his magic. The chemical relaxer was supposed to stay on my hair for 20 minutes. But after five minutes my scalp was burning, it was on fire. I called out to Tommy, 'My head's on fire, I can't take it any more – get if off,' I insisted when he tried to fob me off. A look of alarm passed over his face as he realized I was serious. 'It shouldn't be burning after such a short time', he said. 'You're an African.' But he washed off the chemical.

The hair was a disaster. It was still on my head, it hadn't fallen off, and it was very straight. Tommy looked shocked when he saw it.

'But I thought you had coarse hair because you are an

African. All Africans have coarse hair so I used the strongest relaxer that we have. It doesn't look good,' he said. 'It will have no body. I have to cut it to give it some body.' My hair is fine and soft, but Tommy didn't feel it or see it that way. The real texture of my hair was hidden by his African-American prejudices.

I looked at him in horror. What was he telling me! When I am shocked I become very quiet. I am not a shouter. I don't get abusive, and I don't stand up for myself, nor do I demand to see the manger or demand my rights or my money back. I just quit and feel really, really bad, all the time wishing I could scream at Tommy.

I managed to get out of that saloon after paying that man $30 dollars for ruining my dream, and I walked out in a daze with sparse limp hair that made me look like an orangutan. All the time I was wishing I could sue the saloon and Tommy. I knew I would make a lot of money. I walked round and round the mall not daring to look into any mirror like surfaces. Finally after a few tears I went back to campus.

Still, I had hair. It was over-processed and it would fall out soon, but meanwhile I had hair. I spent time looking in the mirror for that change in being that I thought would come with the hair, and there was nothing. I still saw myself as I had always seen my self. I still counted my flaws and wished that a miracle would wipe them away. Since the hair had proved not to be that miracle I clearly had to keep looking. But meanwhile, I took lots of photographs because you couldn't really see what a limp mess the hair was in a photograph.

Many years down the road I do sit in that miracle. What I found, what was revealed to me, were the essentials of being a human which comes with those same preoccupations of mine. Sometimes I have a general disgruntlement with my lot, and many times I am at ease and it's OK. Beyond styling options, my hair isn't an issue anymore, nor are any of the things about my body that preoccupied me in my callow youth – my height or lack thereof, for example. My job is to reveal the best in me by taking the attention off of my hair and going out and making a difference out there in the world with you. When I think about it, those flaws have never stopped me until I let them. I remember listening to a young woman talking on an FM radio station about how here life had been ruined because she had tiny boobs. She had fixated on the size of her breasts and had literally gone into hiding. She was in the process of throwing away her life because of something as irrelevant as that!

Is there a lesson in this? Yes, there is. And it isn't the one about how I will make sure that my daughter is proud of who she is. My daughter will go through all the steps and stages that are rightly hers in the process of growing up. She will have her fixations, her doubts about her hair or a body part that may not fit the bill in her own eyes. And she has a right to these doubts. What I give her is what my father and mother gave me: The space to explore her nonsense and to make mistakes, the strength to reach the other side of the road where all that stuff becomes insignificant. Where she can be proud of who she is on her own terms. That is the legacy I want to pass on to my daughter and my sons.

Sitawa Namwalie is a writer and a poet who lives and works in Nairobi. She is married and has three children. She has a BSc. in Botany and Zoology from the University of Nairobi and an MA in Environment from Clark University in Worcester Mass., USA.

REFLECTIONS

Father Healy

APRIL, 1994

On the afternoon of April 6, 1994 I was walking through the parking lot of St. Joseph's cathedral in downtown Dar es Salaam, Tanzania. A young Tanzanian boy ran by me shouting, 'They're coming, they're coming. Quick. Go to the front of the church.' Without knowing what was going on, I started running to Sokoine Drive, the highway named after former vice president Edward Sokoine, that is immediately in front of the cathedral bordering the harbor. Dar es Salaam, by the way, is Kiswahili for 'haven of peace' because the waterfront area is a natural harbor of the Indian Ocean – the name being one of the many ironies connected to this story.

And yes, they were coming. The presidents of different East and Central African countries had just finished an important summit meeting hosted by Tanzania to discuss peace and stability in the region. The motorcades of the presidents flashed by on their way to Dar es Salaam International Airport where the respective leaders would board their presidential jets to return to their home countries. Of course we cheered and waved as they sped by, hoping to get a glimpse of who was hidden behind those tinted glass windows. It was all over in a minute, and then we returned to our normal activities. I headed back to the Maryknoll Society House in the Oyster Bay area of Dar es Salaam not far from the residence of former president Julius Nyerere.

Early the next morning, April 7, 1994, I innocently drove to the campus of Dar es Salaam University to meet John Sivalon, a Maryknoll priest who taught sociology. We planned to visit several professors on the campus. John warned me ahead of time that the parking lot near his office building would be crowded, but that I would probably find an empty space. As it turned out, the parking lot was totally empty! Suddenly I had an eerie feeling. 'Strange,' I thought. I walked to John's office with hardly a person around. John himself was surprised that there were so few people on campus. He quickly inquired from a friend down the hall. We both were shocked to learn that President Ali Hassan Mwinyi had declared a national day of mourning in Tanzania. The presidents of Rwanda and Burundi had flown together from Dar es Salaam back to Rwanda; their plane was shot down approaching the capital Kigali, and both leaders were killed. So, no classes at the university.

And the rest is history. That fateful day, April 7, 1994 began 100 days of brutal and unrestrained genocide and violence. Hutu extremists butchered 800,000 Tutsis, Hutu moderates, and people of mixed ethnic blood.

Again and again and again I have reflected on the many associations with this particular month of April 1994. The British poet T.S. Eliot called April 'the cruelest month' because it is popularly known as the month that Jesus Christ died. During this very month African bishops of the Catholic Church were meeting in the historic First African Synod in Rome in 1994 to discuss topics such as the 'Church as Family' in Africa. At the end of April 1994 Nelson Mandela was preparing in 10 days time to be sworn in as the first black president of South Africa. How could so many momentous events happen in Africa at the very same time? Ironies abound.

OCTOBER, 1994

In October 1994 I joined another Maryknoll priest to travel to Rulenge Diocese in western Tanzania to study ways that Maryknoll missionaries could help in the refugee camps. We called our trip a 'Journey into the Heart of God's Suffering People.' I stood solemnly on Rusumo Bridge that connects Rwanda and Tanzania. After the Tutsi-dominated army took over Rwanda, 300,000 desperate Hutu refugees fled the persecution and crossed this bridge into Tanzania in a single day. Visiting the nearby Benaco refugee camp I wrote the following prose poem:

They came walking, walking.
They came walking, walking up the long, steep hill.
They came trudging, trudging.
They came trudging, trudging up the long, steep hill.
Loaded down with bundles of firewood on their heads
They came walking, walking.

Women, plenty of women, men, girls, boys
A long line of bewildered children.
An endless stream of weary humanity.
5 10 20 40 80 160 320...
And still they came.
They came walking, walking.

Then the pouring rain came.
In torrents, in sheets -- a cold, biting rain.
Still they came walking up the long, steep hill.
Balancing bundles of branches and heavy logs on their heads
Occasionally being blown across the wind-swept road.
They came walking, walking.

We watched warm and dry
Inside our Toyota pickup truck.
Peering out of rain-splashed windows.
Whipped by the wind, Hutu refugees slowly staggered by with
tired and pained faces.
Wet bits of clothing clinging to frail bodies
They came walking, walking.

We drove slowly for three kilometers down the long, steep hill.
During the biggest downpour
Forced to pull off the road and park.
After the heavy rain stopped
We drove slowly back up the long, steep hill.
They came walking, walking.

Some sat exhausted with their firewood by the side of the road.
Drenched and shivering.
Large tree limbs and logs left abandoned.
Others trudged ahead in a wet daze.
Still others reeled from fatigue.
They came walking, walking.

It was the road by the Benaco refugee camp.
Northwestern Tanzania.
Late October, 1994.
Overnight the second largest city in Tanzania.
Now 400,000 wet, shivering Hutu refugees from Rwanda.
GENOCIDAL WAR IS HELL!

APRIL, 2004

Once again by a strange coincidence I am in the compound of St. Joseph's cathedral in downtown Dar es Salaam. Suddenly the church bells peal out the 12 Noon Prayer. Stunned for a moment, I suddenly remember and turn to my Tanzanian companion and say, 'Let's observe one minute of silence.' Then we prayed together for Rwanda. The United Nations had designated today, April 7, 2004 as 'International Day of Reflection' for Rwanda, and the African country had asked other nations to observe memorial silences to commemorate the 10th anniversary of the terrible genocide. But apart from official ceremonies at United Nations offices, in major U.N. centres such as Nairobi and Geneva and at Rwandan embassies worldwide, there was no sign that the gesture was widely observed. How many people really observed one minute of silence on that day? Did you?

APRIL, 2007

Now move ahead three years in time until today, Sunday, April 15, 2007. Yes, April again. As William Shakespeare wrote: 'The wheel has come full circle.' But April doesn't have to be the cruelest month. It can be the kindest, gentlest month. It depends on us – you and me. Peace and justice and forgiveness and mercy and reconciliation can flow like a river throughout Rwanda, East Africa, the Horn of Africa, the continent of Africa, the whole world. We just have to imitate the Rwandan woman in the following true story that I collected after the genocide:

In a particular section of Kigali, Rwanda, where people from the Hutu and Tutsi ethnic groups lived together, the genocide began with a bloody vengeance. In one area, a Hutu man murdered his Tutsi neighbor. Some time later, after the Rwandan Patriotic Front had ended the killing and taken over government, local investigations of the atrocities started. The wife of the dead Tutsi man was asked to identify her husband's murderer. She refused, knowing that the Hutu man would be arrested, imprisoned, and probably killed. The woman preferred to remain silent to save another life.

'This is enough,' she said. 'The killing has to stop somewhere. One murder does not justify another killing. We have to break this cycle of violence and end this genocide.'

So she chose to forgive.

Reverend Timothy Healy is the president of Georgetown University in New York, and head of the New York Public Library. In between his religious and academic duties, he has lived and traveled extensively in Africa.

Spreading the Word

If there was ever any doubt, the 2007 General Election proved that media houses and book publishers aren't the only agents capable of reaching a large audience. In the build-up to and fallout from December 27, Kenyans made use of their cell phones, emails, and printers to deliver all manner of messages to neighbors, friends, and foes. Posters appeared on walls, pamphlets were dropped on doorsteps, text messages sent out by the thousand. Ranging from cries for help to calls for war, they all occupied a slippery space somewhere between public discourse and personal dialogue. The following sample presents only the tiniest fraction of those conversations; but it's enough to suggest that Kenya's darkest hour may also have been its most talkative.

People stranded at
kipkelion, mtalagon
in kericho district.
Plz evacuate no
food for 7 days.
08/01/2008, 18:34

Luos being given notice
to vacate kahawa west
Nairobi someone help
please. 08/01/2008,
11:29

Internly displaced
women n gals urgently
in need of sanitary
pads (ochiko nrb).
06/01/2008, 15:56

Please help people in
kajibora, hakuna polisi
wa kutosha, jana mama
wawili shot dead na
hakuna usalama. Help
them. use this no. from
violet. 06/01/2008,
14:53

THERE IS A GROUP OF
MORE THAN 1500 PPLE
CAMPING AT KUNYAK SEC.
SCHOOL, GIRMORIKORU WHO
BADLY NEED FOOD AND
SECURITY.

06/01/2008, 19:24

Here at mukinyai 30km
from Nakuru past Salgaa
people are burning
houses and killing
at this time. We need
urgent help. Please
help us. 06/01/2008,
17:35

A police station is
raided at kachipora
cherangany, where many
people have camped
please calling for
additional security.
06/01/2008, 13:56

Don't know where to start i pray for peace and unity in this country. GOD bless. 06/01/2008, 13:47

Kenyans are not being attacked by Ghosts in Rift Valley or Coast. Organised Gangs are on the prowl with their Generals busy inciting in safe bases. 06/01/2008, 13:19

294

I need help.
We r a
family of 7.
06/01/2008,
13:39

Losd n i av 2
stay indors
coz am kikuyu
n am scared if
they find out
they mght burn
me. Rght now
am living on
sugarless uji.
Am so scared
where i am. Thnx.
06/01/2008, 14:01

The insurgence
of refugees in
nakuru show ground
now poses to b
a threat within
that environment.
Please beef up
the security.
06/01/2008, 13:22

Hundreds of people
r unable to find
way out of Mugumo-
ini & Subukia farm
shopping centre
(Timboroa) refuge
camp 4 a wk now. Pls
help!
06/01/2008, 13:44

My name is mary. a mother
of three i had my cereal
shop in mathare north
area 1. it was raided
on 29 after election
after election whereby I
lost goods worth 4500.
06/01/2008, 13:47

O chomewa manyumba na
kuuwawa ni wa kabila za
kisii na kikuyu tafadhali
tafuteni msaada ya
transport na security
kuthibitisha madai haya
tafathali wapigie.
06/01/2008, 13:42

Please tell this pple
who r harrasing kikuyus
that hata sisi wengine
we voted 4 raila and its
unfair 2 kill us as they
cant know who voted 4
who.
06/01/2008, 13:44

This is getting too much. PANUA PANUA ndio Raila aingie kabisa aweze kupatia PNU mimba ili watoto waerevu wazaliwe baadala ya wale wapumbavu wanaokunia mavi ya kuku! (Open up so that Raila penetrates completely and Impregnates PNU so that clever children are born and not Stupid ones that go around defecating chicken feces)

The Odinga Destruction Mercenaries, today announced that its changing it's emblem from an Orange to a Condom. This is because it more accurately reflects its political stance: A condom allows for inflation, halts production, destroys the next generation, is intended to protect a bunch of pricks and gives you a sense of security while you are actually being screwed! Kazi iendelee!!!

Why you should be in ODM.ODM women scream YAWA, YAWA, YAWA in praise of Nyundo. While men in PNU are busy telling their wives to PANUA ,PANUA kazi iendelee. Women in ODM-K are so wet that their men keep asking wapi Wipper.

We, as the Gikuyu, Embu and Meru communities, possess six million votes. You want us to be ruled by an uncircumcised people [Luo people] and go back to the jobless corner? Come out in large numbers to re-elect President Mwai Kibaki so that the country is not ruled by an uncircumcised man who will make the Kikuyus wear shorts. Circulate this message to five or more members of the Gikuyu, Embu and Meru communities. Your vote is the one that will prevent us from going back to Egypt.

Gema twina kura 6 million mwaiga twathwo ni kihii na tucoke mung'etho? Umirai tucikirie Kibaki ciothe bururi ndugathwo nikihii gia gutuma twikire inyatha na kunina indo citu ciothe. Tambia ndeto ino kuri andu 50 a gema kana makiria. Kura yaku niyo ikugiria bururi witu ucoke Misiri. Mwene Nyagah akurathime.
(GEMA we have 6 million votes, you have said we be ruled by an uncircumcised man we go back to poverty? We should all come out and vote for Kibaki so that we are not ruled by an uncircumcised man who will make us wear shorts and finish all our wealth. Send this to 50 or more people of GEMA. Your vote will ensure that our country does not go back to Misiri. May the Lord Bless you.)

For Jaramogi hated Kenyans that he gave his son Raila that whosoever believe in shall line in enternal slavery, hunger, diseases and die in pain. Look at Kibera , look at Ntanza; we do not need Kiberas and Nyanzas in Kenya!

May God protect you from all the harms of the devil, including diseases, thieves, fleas, ticks, weevils, lice, bedbugs, and especially, ODM

297

ALL LUOS AND KALENJINS
ARE OUR ENEMIES FOR
THEY ARE KILLING OUR
PEOPLE IN THE RIFT
VALLEY. THEY HAVE
48 HOURS TO VACATE
OUR LAND OR SWIM IN
THEIR OWN BLOOD. ALL
LANDLORDS HOUSING
THEM ARE ADVISED TO
OBEY THESE ORDERS
OR THEIR HOUSES WILL
COME DOWN BY FIRE.
MUNGISH [MUNGIKI]

FLYERS CIRCULATED DURING THE POST-ELECTIONS CRISIS

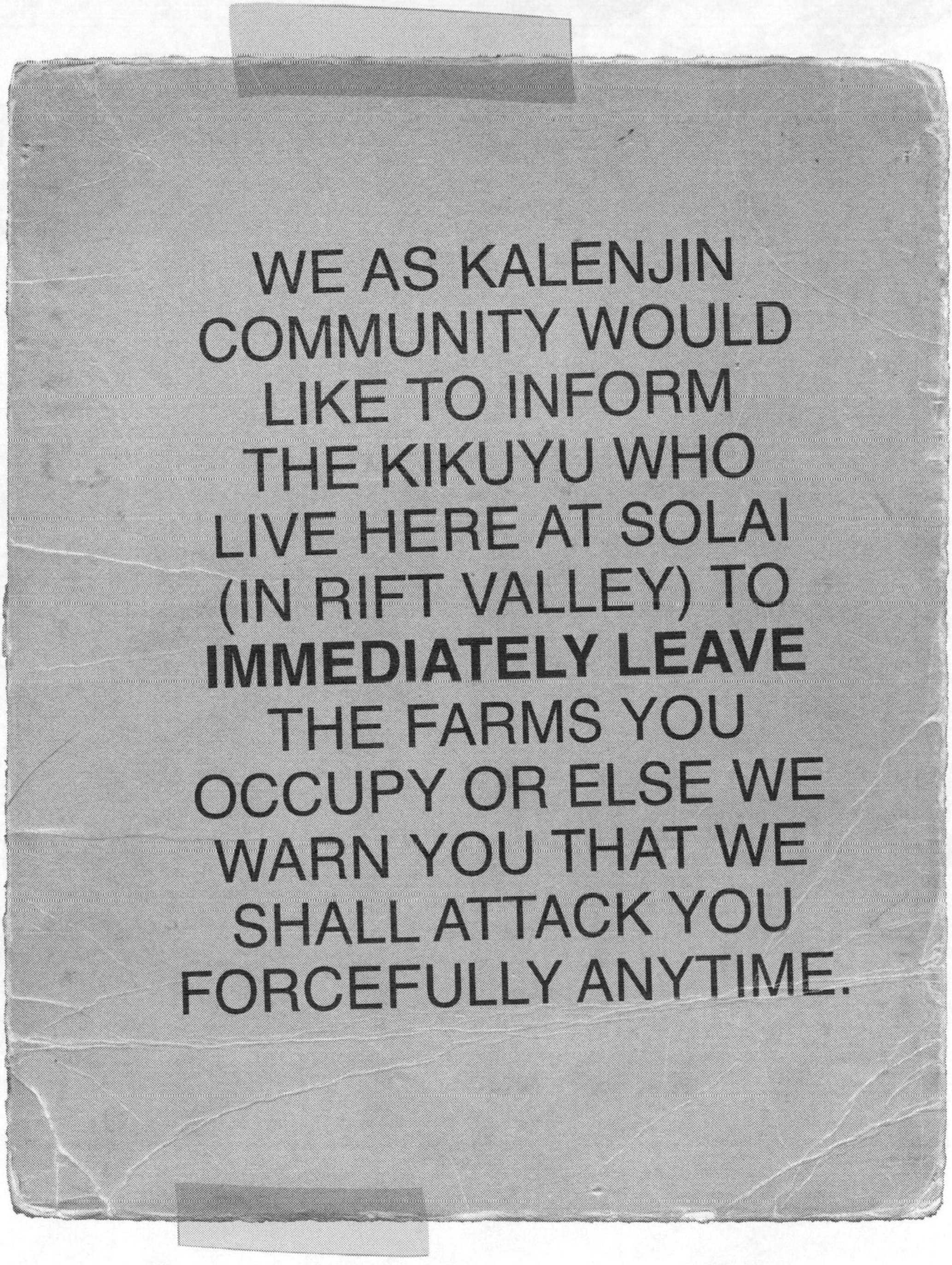

WE AS KALENJIN
COMMUNITY WOULD
LIKE TO INFORM
THE KIKUYU WHO
LIVE HERE AT SOLAI
(IN RIFT VALLEY) TO
IMMEDIATELY LEAVE
THE FARMS YOU
OCCUPY OR ELSE WE
WARN YOU THAT WE
SHALL ATTACK YOU
FORCEFULLY ANYTIME.

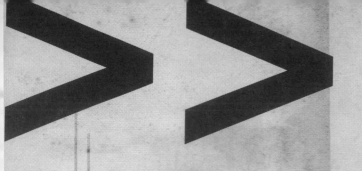

SUBJECT: ODM's form of Majimbo, Kenyans beware!!!!

What is being said: 10 Jimbos or regions will be crafted as per Bomas Draft

What is not being said: These are **actual tribal chiefdoms.** If you do not belong to the tribe of a particular Jimbo then you will not have any business dwelling there.
Tribal clashes will be the order of the day and they could start in Earnest on the day Raila is sworn in as president!

SUBJECT: Beware! Fake Penta-Goon Orange Juice

A container at the Mombasa port has been impounded, documentation shows it originates from America. The contents are an orange juice blend from DICK MORRIS & co. packed in 500ml and 30m sachets.Reliable lab-results state that Pentagoon Orange juice will:

-Retard speech and thinking
  -Cause rhetoric & euphoric behavior.
      -Make the consumer engage in in idle talk.
      -Create the illusion of an utopic country.

TETUTIET NEO NEBO ARAP MIBEI (RAILA) EN BIIK AB KUTIT

On 5th September 2007, Raila Odinga held a meeting on the 17th floor of the J. Edgar Hoover building, 935 Pennsylvania Avenue. NW, Washington DC. In the meeting, which was taped by the FBI, Raila told America officers that he would finish former president Moi, Ruto and other Kalenjins who had ruined Kenya as soon as he becomes president. The tapes are available

INTERNALLY MISPLACED

Wambui Mwangi

Despite his anxiety, Margaret Dorobo's driver, Seth Karanja, is in a philosophical mood as he swings left off Ngong Road onto Elgeyo Marakwet. He is very tired, and resigned to it, because he expects fear to continue to keep him awake.

It is one of those warm days in Nairobi, beautiful and sunny, where from some angles, the light seems silver, and many drivers have their windows rolled down.

He checks the rearview mirror again. Nairobi traffic is an exponentially-calculated product of the state of Nairobi's roads. As he eases around a large pothole, the box in the boot of the car shifts slightly, but there is no time to stop and secure it. The potholes are almost alive, he thinks, in the way they grow. The jagged holes give birth to rounded but deeper adolescents, gradually develop into self-conscious trenches, and finally join together to become one full-fledged adult abyss.

A woman drives past: she is wearing a red top with thin straps drooping over her shoulders, and a baseball cap with "Yankees" written on it. Seth marks the angle of her cheekbone, the crease of her eye, the slope of her nostrils—something about the set of her lips reminds him of his niece, Wacera. She is probably one of us, he thinks. Or maybe not; it is so difficult to know these days.

Seth's secret favourite book of the Bible is the Song of Solomon. He enjoys, with a satisfying mixture of shame and virtuous diligence, all the talk of doe-eyed women and of pomegranate breasts, of dripping myrrh and of the stirring passion of the beloved's caress.

Madam is not in the car today, so Seth allows himself to pick his nose. His thoughts follow his finger around his nostrils, enjoying the voluptuous feel of stretching and probing the spongy inner surfaces. If pushed to it, he could explain why it is acceptable to pick his nose in front of his mother, but not in front of Madam, or why it is possible to pick his nose in Madam's car but never in Madam's house. He is sure that all behaviours have geographies and economies, that they have their own proper places and times, and that the wiping of foreheads, picking of noses, scratching of buttocks, cleaning of ears, or picking of teeth are actions to be indulged in only outside of the territory of his employer's gaze.

The order of eating and drinking in Madam's house is that Madam's Husband can have anything he wants. Madam can have anything Madam's Husband does not want. Then first the indoors staff (drivers first, although they work outside), and then the outdoors staff can have anything after that, if it is already open or in use and at least half-way consumed, and is not a specialty item like butter or Ribena or rice, and of course nothing like Madam's yoghurt – although wine has been subverted by Joshua into the exception to this rule – but if there are guests then they move to the top of the list, even above Madam's Husband.

The guests of Madam or of Madam's Husband can have anything they want, at any time, full time, anything at all, at all times. This is a rule of the house. Never question guests, never contradict them, never embarrass them, never see or hear anything that might cause them discomfort of any kind: this was hospitality of the old-fashioned and now-rare Kikuyu kind. Unless Madam's Husband asks you about the guest, and then you must remember everything, and you must repeat it in good language and clear speech, no stammering or hesitating or scratching your head, and then never bring it up again: but this happens only rarely.

With all the other worries he has, Seth muses, if he had been a drinking man he would have been an alcoholic by now: like Joshua, the cook at Madam's house, who has an elaborate relationship with Madam's liquor cabinet. Joshua is happiest when either cooking an unpronounceable European meal, or providing Saturday afternoon refreshments for Madam's women friends. This is not because of any pressing gourmet reasons or dictates of hospitality, but because in the first case, Joshua can demand wine for all his recipes, and in the second case, Madam's friends always ask for white wine. These sorts of occasions leave Joshua multiple opportunities for the covert slaking of his sadly expensive thirst. Unfortunately for Joshua, Madam's Husband most often asks for meals consisting of such components as *ugali* or *githeri*, and, even worse, Madam herself rarely entertains.

Sometimes, though, especially after he had consumed most of the liquid ingredients and all of the liquid leftovers of an especially French dinner, Joshua could be induced to break into weaving performances of *iskuti*, to which he would accompany himself by voice. Joshua had trained at Utalii College. He mentions this at least twice a week, as if it had been America or something, as if he had been rich and powerful there, but in any case Utalii is where he acquired his imprudent but powerful taste for wine. Between Joshua's Utalii memories and Madam's generosity, there are never any unfinished boxes of South African wine in Madam's house. Nothing left over; everything put to use, and eaten or drank.

Familiar amusement at Joshua's frailties is almost but not quite enough to lighten the dread weighing Seth's bowels down like a stone. The terrible conversation he had with Jackson this morning is now rancid in his mind. It had been very strange because Jackson, although always indefinably menacing, is usually very silent and polite. He intimidates mostly by withholding himself, so Seth had not known that Jackson had these thoughts brewing in his head. Usually, trying to read Jackson's thoughts is like trying to see the occupant of a car with tinted windows. You simply cannot tell, without a lot of strenuous effort, what is in there—it might be anyone at all.

This morning, Seth had only been cracking a Luo joke, but Jackson's surprisingly long answer had been as serious as his face. He had spoken with a flat passion worn drab and tattered at its edges. Seth had not really seen Jackson before—never really looked so as to see properly, putting effort into his vision, making his eyes strain to see deeper. What he had seen this morning had made his heart burrow deeper into his chest like a small creature hiding away from a sudden light.

Jackson definitely frightens Seth more than Madam's Husband. Madam's Husband is a very soft-spoken man; he orders his world through a whisper. He murmurs into the air, at no-one at all, and things mysteriously happen to his satisfaction, or else. Seth does not know, and never wants to know, or else what.

Yet, while Seth considers Madam's Husband a sort of major shareholder in the universe, one of those men who is sometimes obliged to share his castoffs, but never to divulge or explain his acts, he himself experiences Madam's Husband as an impending disastrous event, like a potential flood or a threatened famine, which requires a soothsayer to avert. *Mundu mugo*. Exactly. Luckily, Madam's Husband does not often speak to Seth, and Jackson does not often speak to anyone at all.

J ackson is Madam's Husband's driver. He is a very tall and gap-toothed compatriot from the lakeside region. Seth thinks of Luos in these elliptical turns because his fastidious mind prefers the scenic route, and also because he knows the power of names to summon daemons, and he is afraid. Jackson is only below Madam's husband in the domestic hierarchy. Jackson is tops, even more than Muthee. Muthee is so old, he really can't do much anymore, although he pretends to: laboriously moving brooms from one end of the house to another, and mops and buckets as well. He has his own broom, mop and bucket for this purpose; nobody else uses them, and if they go missing he gets terribly upset.

Jackson is really the main guy, the one who goes everywhere Madam's Husband goes. He has heard the business deals in the back of the car, he knows what's what, the big bucks, the payload. Jackson would have known which minister was getting fired, when; he knows what arrangements have been made. But does he say? Never.

Jackson has two cell phones. One line is just for Madam's Husband's use, direct; only he can call that line, and it has to be answered at once, at any time of the day or night, answered after only one ring, or else. Seth has heard Jackson answer Madam's Husband's phone calls many times at night from the bedroom next door. Jackson says "Yes, Sir," once, like that, as soon as he answers the phone, then he listens and says "Yes, Sir" again, and hangs up. That's all: two words, two times. Yes Sir and Yes Sir. Then Jackson hangs up, picks up the car keys, and leaves. He never reveals where he is going or, on his return, what he has seen. Jackson is always preoccupied, always absorbed in matters that he cannot and will not discuss.

Look where Anastasia's female foolishness had landed her now. Seth shrugs his shoulders, but instantly feels irresponsible. He should do something, but then again, what can he do? She is not the first girl to whom this has happened, although it is unfortunate that it has happened to his niece. Seth knows that the matter of his niece will soon require decisive action from him, and the knowledge fills him with a resentful but unfocused anger.

He fingers the knot of his uniform tie with one hand and tightens the cloth at his neck. At that moment, one of those pedestrians with a near-mystic faith in the driving skills of Nairobi drivers hurls himself jauntily into the road almost under Seth's wheels, causing Seth to tap the brakes sharply, rebukingly, once, and then gently once more to an abrupt but still-controlled stop. The pedestrian looks at him in calm surprise, as if possible dreadful injury to himself were a new idea. Seth wants to weep at his innocence, but a half second later, he is angry: who is this foolish boy who can still look like that in Nairobi after everything that has happened? Did he just land at JKIA today? It will not take him long to get that Jackson look in his eye. Yes, Seth thinks, if he was a drinking man, he would certainly have been an alcoholic twice over by now. In these times, only the mad can be said to be truly sane.

Seth slows down at the junction of Elgeyo Marakwet and Argwings Khodek, indicates right, and seeing a promising gap between a black

Audi and a black Toyota Starlet—one of those cars that Madam's friends' children seem to like - swings the green Mercedes into the lane of traffic on Argwings Khodek with a dignified haste. The treacle-line of cars moves in imperceptible inches forward, then suddenly speeds up for no reason at all, hiccups, and steadies out. Seth sighs as he upshifts hopefully and then morosely downshifts again. He slows down for a speed bump. There is a white Toyota Corolla behind him, and even before Seth has finished slowing down to negotiate the bump, the driver of the Corolla, a fat man in an unwisely-patterned orange shirt, is hooting impatiently at Seth to start moving faster. Seth waits two heartbeats before engaging first gear. He is that sort of person.

He never offers his hand first for shaking.

The man in the Corolla behind him hoots again, short sharp prods of sound which Seth largely ignores. As far as Seth is concerned, Nairobi drivers are always in a rush to get to unimportant places. They always behave as if at their destination there are lives waiting to be saved. The man in the orange shirt is in a hurry to buy a kilo of beef, Seth thinks, which this man will take to his wife, like a dog offering a dead rat to its owner, only to find that she has decided to cook chicken that day, and is anyway having an affair with the neighbour. Humph. People who think vast haste implies a matching importance.

Seth lets the turning signal noise click on and off three times at least, before turning the wheel. He understands that true importance lies in making people wait; in being able to move slowly and in knowing that you can retard all emotions to your speed. Rushing around implies a serious loss of control of your world.

A *matatu* blares past on the right, having edged out oncoming traffic. It elbows past him like a rugby player with the goal posts in sight, driving on the wrong side of the road, intimidating other drivers into collusion with it, and leaving, along with a cloud of diesel smoke, a faint suggestion of a defiant bass rhythm in its wake. Seth notes that the back left-hand corner of the *matatu* has a broken tail-light. A coil of panic slithers into Seth's belly. He belches deliberately, for distraction, and adjusts his hands on the wheel, his knuckles tight.

Seth's hands are set in the ten-to-two position on the wheel. They are chapped and the approximate shade of grey-brown of the bark of a certain kind of Jacaranda tree that lines Waiyaki Way. It is a colour that speaks of complicated lives, like the ones Nairobi jacaranda trees have had—troubled by blight and inattention, influenced in unnamed ways by forgotten white rulers, rescued for political reasons from being pulled out, like good molars threatened by a greedy dentist, then neglected again: an intermittent nurturing that has left them strangely resilient.

Seth has never known who Argwings Khodek was, or why he got a street, but before the thought has finished forming itself into a question, one of those disrespectful courier motorcyclists, with the metal box welded to the space behind his buttocks, chooses that moment to veer dangerously close to the side-mirror of Seth's car as he edges past. Seth is distressed, and hisses sharply. For that one yawning second he is very angry. The courier is a fast millimetre away from vehicular desecration, and further, he is guilty of overtaking on the left. That is the problem with this country, Seth says to himself; no discipline at all.

His niece had come to speak to him after being thrown out of her house. Anastasia had always been a somewhat unserious personality, lacking in gravity and moral platform.

—Uncle, my mother is not feeling so well, she had said, she is not feeling well in herself.

—What is it? he had asked, thinking perhaps it was his sister's old knee trouble flaring up again.

—No, it is--it is only her thoughts, Anastasia had replied, looking with concentration at the floor.

—What thoughts? Seth had asked. What thoughts are these that can make a person sick? What is she thinking of? How can thoughts make her sick?

This had been two months ago. Seth now knows that thoughts could make a person sick, because his own have had him retching every day for weeks. But he only throws up in the mornings and this has strangely made him feel much worse. This is a woman's rhythm. The mornings are the only time that he allows himself to feel cold panic, fear burning in his throat; his very ankles trembling. As soon as he finishes his morning preparation routine of putting on his uniform, he feels better. In his uniform he is soothed and symmetrical.

But at that time, at the time that Wacera had come to see him, he had not yet understood. He had asked her what her mother had been thinking about, to make herself sick in this way. This was the point at which his niece had been struck dumb yet curiously restless, and could only frown sorrowfully at her shoes. They had been green-coloured sandals, with a buckle on the side, and she had been shifting her foot from side to side as if admiring the silver square, as if trying to make the metal catch the light.

—No, it is – it is not that – it is not like that, she had murmured defensively to her feet.

—What is it, then? What are you trying to say?

It had taken him some time to winkle the problem out of the hole into which she had dug it. He had had to carefully tease it out of her, each strand of allusion and query spun thin and fragile, stretched to near-transparency. It had not been easy. He had advanced and she had retreated; when he had moved to the right, she had feinted left. He had shadow-boxed a question and she had deftly verbally ducked, all the while twisting her head sideways, placing her cheek on her shoulder, looking off to her side, like a wilted plant in a stiff breeze. Thrust, parry, thrust, deflect. Feint, dip, dodge, hedge, and then a tricky counterfeit: both Seth and his niece spoke Kikuyu with some skill. Her obliquely angled silhouette, turning and twisting away and then towards him, made her voice harder to understand, as if the wind whipping her body had snatched away her voice, as well. She had been trying to twist her torso into an even smaller target than her words.

In the end, it emerged that the man who had unpeeled Anastasia Wacera's virginity from her, removed it like a banana skin, had subsequently moved on to juicier fruits. She was called Anastasia when working but Wacera when she was being herself, or at home with the family. The man had been her employer, so she had lost her job as well. Her mother had told her to go away, to get out of her house and find someone else to keep her and her shameful, pulsing womb. She had said she did not want *mitumba* women in her house. No soiled secondhand goods under her roof: which was similar to what Anastasia's erstwhile employer had told her, as well, except that he had been less polite.

In any case, people like Anastasia's former employer went for fruit salads of the more exotic kind; they mixed bits of orange with slices of banana drenched in foreign drinks all at once, mixed them up promiscuously like that and then served them in little glass bowls. Seth had watched Joshua the cook make fruit salad uncountable times for Madam, Madam's Husband and their guests. But they only ate fruit salad after the main course. They only ate this after the real food, after the stomach-fillers had been consumed. Unless, of course, the fruit salad was for breakfast; then they ate it by itself.

After her rage had subsided, Anastasia's mother, Seth's sister, had called Seth to ask him to do something about the situation.

—You work for them, she said. Do something – talk to that man. Talk to him for us; you speak their language.

Seth had had to explain that this was impossible because Wacera's ex-boss, her sometime-lover, and the owner of her now-swelling waist, was the husband of Madam's friend. He was also a business colleague of Madam's Husband, and almost as rich as Madam's Husband himself.

Worse, he was a Meru, with a temper to match.

It was rumoured that he had once cut off a rival's head and kept it in a basket, in his garage. The story went that after three weeks had passed, he had woken up early one morning and taken the basket to the police chief's house, where over some coffee, fried eggs, arrowroots and stewed tomatoes, and an undisclosed amount of money, the crime had been attributed to a mysterious sect, and had attracted only a small paragraph in the national press.

Seth's sister had nevertheless insisted that he should use his privileged position in Madam's house to intercede, to trade on his long record of loyal service. He had not tried to explain, and she would not have understood, that he felt he was about to need, for other purposes, all the credit with Madam he had. If he was not mistaken about this morning's events, he wanted his credit with Madam to be full to the brim and overflowing.

Seth had felt very disappointed at Wacera's thoughtlessness in getting pregnant, at her lack of foresight. In addition to everything else, Wacera had been earmarked for a potential respectable marriage to the young gardener at Madam's house, one Samuel Njogu, and they had been on the verge of announcing their engagement. This would have kept the good jobs in Seth's family, and also added to the numbers of Seth's family on the spacious grounds of Madam's house. Why would Wacera be so careless as to let herself be robbed of her future like that? Lack of professionalism, that is the problem, Seth thinks; lack of professionalism and dangerous inattention.

Seth is a good driver, he knows. He is always ready at his station by the cars at seven o'clock every morning. All three of them, both of Madam's cars and Seth, are well-presented and gleaming, and he stays on call every day until midnight. He has perfected the art of waiting in garages and courtyards and parking lots, on lawns and behind kitchens and outside the gates. He knows kiosk owners from Runda to Karen to Ruiru, and all points in between. He has seen all of Nairobi's mansions and eaten their food, delicate party-fare smuggled outside by compliant housegirls, thimbleful of fine spirits for the alcohol-inclined, although drivers were a non-drinking lot, as a whole.

They made up for it by smoking copiously, feverishly, each hurried lungful anticipating being unfinished. They had to be in the car and ready to go at any time, to have previously reconnoitered the parking situation for instant extraction. It required a fine touch, being a personal driver. You had to know at what time Madam's goodbye meant really goodbye and not let's stand around outside and talk for another 20 minutes, for no reason at all. This was just a skill you had to pick up, a job requirement, knowing when all those farewells finally meant business, when Madam meant:

—Let's go, get us out of here; this woman is driving me crazy with her pointless chatter: put the windows up and let's go.

His salary went up every year, like clockwork, every year a decent raise, one new suit, and sometimes an additional hand-me down from Madam's husband, and a pair of good black shoes. He would be fine if everything carried on as expected. That was the problem, that and traffic. Seth did not know any more what to expect, what things were supposed to carry on as normal.

Seth had never been this close to death before, not death that mattered so much, so completely, death which changed everybody's life, without it mattering in the least who, exactly, had died.

As he passes the exit from Yaya Centre, Seth pauses to let a car join his lane, and recognises the blue Jaguar as belonging to one of Madam's friends. Madam's friend's husband has been dead for three years now: Seth is proud that after his unexpected demise, Madam had persuaded Madam's Husband to manage the finances of her friend. With all the businesses having had to close and the properties auctioned off, Madam's friend had been rescued in the nick of time by Madam's Husband. Still, proof of Madam's friend's bereavement, and her ensuing diminished means, could be found in the fact that Madam's friend was now forced to drive her own car herself. Another good job lost, thinks Seth—he had known her driver, now unemployed.

HE HAS PERFECTED THE ART OF WAITING

Although Madam's Husband habitually frightens Seth mute, Madam's Husband's unyielding certainty is certainly a source of comfort to everybody around him, although not so much these days to Madam herself, a worrying development.

When Madam's Husband had suggested to the air this morning that Seth, and not Jackson, run this errand, Seth had not even thought to question why. Madam herself had been nowhere in sight, and Seth's deeply inscribed terror of Madam's Husband had taken over his body and manoeuvred him like a puppet on a string. Seth had heard, as if from far away, his own voice saying an instant Yes, Sir as Madam's Husband's voice began its soft whispering, and then another Yes, Sir when the whispering stopped.

Seth slows down and stays back a respectfully courteous but precise three feet away from the bumper of Madam's friend's car, a cautious foot hovering over his brake pedal. He does not trust women drivers, not even Madam's friends. The brakes are working well, but the car still needs to go in for service very urgently. That Madam's car's regular servicing is now two weeks overdue, Seth is well aware, but he cannot book an appointment for the job while the missing mechanic is still absent. Fear of the discovery that would be caused by the sudden eruption of payments to D.T. Dobie from Madam has begun to grow panicked green shoots in Seth's heart. He feels one such tendril uncurling now, and stretching, as if reaching for the sun.

—I'll see you then, in January, Ezekiel, the mechanic had said. He had been wiping his hands on dirty piece of cloth as he spoke. His overalls were clean and ironed.

—There's a slot free on the fifth, at ten. Do you want to bring it in then? Seth had agreed that the fifth looked like a likely date, and they had said goodbye. That was the last Seth had seen of him.

Once, fetching the car from servicing at closing time some months ago, and with an hour to kill before Madam's earliest next summons, Seth had given Ezekiel a lift home in Madam's car. He had been feeling generous, and Ezekiel had not only done an excellent service job as usual, but had also ingeniously crafted some extremely plausible additions to their longstanding private arrangement. Just before they had reached the turn-off beyond which the laneways in Ezekiel's neighbourhood became too rutted, too narrow-dirty to be for Madam's car, they had slowed to greet Ezekiel's wife, Amasabeth, who had been out on an errand to the kiosk. She had been holding a small bunch of onions in her hand, two candles, three tomatoes and a box of matches.

—This is Mama-mtoto, Ezekiel had said, and to his wife: --Amasabeth, greet our visitor. He is one of my best clients. He is in charge of transportation for Mrs. Margaret Dorobo.

Seth had declined to stay for tea that day, but he had promised to one day come for a proper visit, on one of his days off. When Madam was next away, he would be back for a meal and a talk. He had waved goodbye and driven off, and had never been back again. And now Ezekiel is missing.

Seth nudges at this thought like a tongue worrying a swollen gum. He has been trying to call Ezekiel on his cell phone for two weeks now. He had first called on the fourth, wanting to suggest that they postpone the tentatively scheduled maintenance service for the fifth until things had cooled down a bit. There had been no answer. Seth had called a few more times, increasingly anxious. Madam had already asked him twice if it is was not yet time to take the car in, but that had been in December, before the other things had happened. She has not asked him since, but even so, Seth could not forever count on her strange mood making her forgetful. Finally, he had made a call to D.T. Dobie's customer service desk, pretending to be somebody else's driver who wanted to reach Ezekiel. The first time he had called, there had been no answer. Seth had not known whether Dobie were back at work then— some companies were still closed, even after all this time.

He had called again and this time a voice, with none of the dispassion normally displayed by corporate receptionists, had told him that they were very worried about Ezekiel as he was one of their best mechanics, and nobody had seen him since he had gone off to Nyanza for the holidays. Ezekiel had spoken to one of his colleagues from Kisumu town, so they knew he had definitely made it there, but since then nobody has heard of him at all. They cannot trace his wife, or his relatives, or his neighbours here in Kibera, and of course even in Nairobi it has been difficult to know anything with certainty at all. There is no news: he is just missing.

Seth values his soul's record book in heaven, where he is sure that the accounts are rigorous but above board: he is not a thief. The D.T. Dobie invoices he delivers to Madam, complete with the company's logo, are for the amount of the standard Dobie rates; sometimes even below. It is only that the mechanic, Ezekiel—who, let it be strictly noted, is after all employed at Dobie: this is a virtuous fact—has a duplicate invoice and receipt book, and Madam likes to pay in cash, which in this instance, is serendipitous. Madam gives him the brown manila envelope with cash in it, and he conscientiously returns to her the change and the receipts for the exact amounts.

Her domestic filing systems consist of neatly-stacked up and labelled cardboard boxes, full of brown manila envelopes. Madam, extracting the change and writing the amount on the front, puts this envelope and its associated invoices and receipts away in its appropriate box. Seth thinks that Madam uses these envelopes because she wants to categorise and store the essence of all the hands that touched them and all the relationships involved, perhaps for examination at another time.

The frugal beauty and simple seriousness of this arrangement appeals to Seth.

As long as Madam intends to pay a certain sum for certain services however, Seth sees no harm in combining his own interests with those of her well-maintained machine, for which he feels a strong sibling affection. He and the car are good allies, a good teaming up of well-oiled German parts and limbs, of fossil fuel and flesh.

With the amount of Madam's money that has been creatively adapted to new uses with Ezekiel's help, Seth has even managed, over the years, to afford small luxuries. He has a Nokia cell phone and has in fact just migrated to Safaricom's *Jambo* tariff. This has allowed him and his sister to discuss Wacera's fate in the odd moments when neither one of them is working, as for a reasonable amount of money and provided he keeps his conversations short, Seth can now afford to make phone calls at any time of the day or night, which is useful, especially with things being what they are these days.

The traffic finally starts to creep through the Hurlingham shopping centre. Further along, the walls of the Department of Defense barracks rise up, grey and grave, and begin their protective march alongside the rows of traffic. These walls are one of the only sizeable exterior vertical public surfaces in Nairobi which do not wear bedraggled garlands of last December's campaign posters, already now tattered and torn. Seth finds this reassuring. The lines of the wall's cement-blocks seem attentive, alert. It is clear to Seth that the wall itself is ready to defend this country with its stern, rough, concrete texture.

There is a line at the Barclay's ATM, across the way, at the Hurlingham Barclays Bank. The line stretches almost to the low retaining wall, against which a fat woman in a yellow boubou is leaning. She is so large that the voluminous garment only smooths over, but cannot blend, her prodigious bulging outline. She is sweating profusely in the sun, and the loose end of her headwrap is listing forlornly alongside her over-permed hair. Seth fancies that the blue Barclay's eagle is looking somewhat tense these days, as if it knows that its mechanised agents are not up to the job of dispensing enough cash to satisfy fear; they cannot calm hysteria. Their creativity stops at the ability to swallow disobedient debit cards, or delinquent ones. Those, the ATMs can battle: anything else is not on their job description.

In the next lane, a bicyclist suddenly swerves onto the hustling *matatu's* path, then wobbles away, weaves wildly, and finally falls. The cyclist is on his back in the road, looking dazed. His shoes have come off. He had been carrying some papers. They are scattered all over the road, crumpling and flattening under speeding tyres. A small gash is bleeding in the cyclist's head, over one of his eyes. The *matatu* has driven on. Seth sees a small tattered boy steal the cyclist's shoes and run away. A half-hearted crowd begins to gather, not so much to help the cyclist as to observe his fate. Nairobi is always ready for a spectacle, no matter how banal its ingredients—people will always gather for a free feast for their eyes.

At the Barclays, there is a commotion at the front of the line. A man is shouting angrily, his arms jerking though the air. Another man in a badly dry-cleaned black suit and carrying a battered leather briefcase looks at his watch, shakes his head in disgust and then, after an upward glance at the sun, strides around the corner to the bank itself. Next, a young woman in jeans steps out of line and, extracting her cell phone from her beaded bag, dials a number and starts to talk with an urgent tilt to her head. The line continues to fragment, one discrete person at a time. After watching three different people walk up to the computerised screen, punch a button, and then turn away in disgust, Seth deduces that the ATM has closed itself down, probably because it has run out of cash. The Barclays eagle definitely looks worried, Seth thinks, and snorts sardonically at himself, automatically slowing down as the brake lights in front of him gleam red. The vigilantly professional part of him has noticed that it is time to make a decision about what to do after Argwings Khodek. State House road will be jammed as usual, should he try to give Valley Road a chance? The problem is that this will bring him, or rather it will bring Madam's car, too near Uhuru Park, and Seth on principle always steers clear of places which threaten Madam's car. State House it is. As he turns left to go to Dennis Pritt and then State House road, Seth notices as he shift gears that there is a slight stickiness, a faint hitch, to the clutch.

Where is Ezekiel?

State House Road is a comforting stretch of tarmac, especially from the point of view of a professional driver. It is true that Bishop's Road has a sign that proclaims it the safest street in Nairobi, but faced with a choice between trusting in Israeli Embassy security and the security arrangements of the republic's president, Seth sees no choice at all. Israelis die all the time, as CNN has repeatedly shown, but no Kenyan president has ever been assassinated, and that is a fact. Terrorists always want to kill the Jews, but why would they turn their attention to Kikuyu gentlemen? Although, with these new things happening these days, who knows. Madam's friend had said, not 10 days ago, that she had cancelled her holiday planned for the Coast. Seth had been driving Madam and her friends back to their homes after a function. Madam had said to her friend, then, that she would not let fear dictate her actions, but, of course, that had been before everything else had happened. Besides, Seth argues eloquently to himself, do you mean to tell me that if Al Qaeda can bomb America, they will be defeated by Israelis here in Nairobi? Al Qaeda obviously has no quarrel with the Kenyan president. Seth, taking in State House's lawns, feels his head nod thrice, to agree.

Along this stretch of road, security and safety are a certainty, and a minimum decorum amongst drivers is expected. This certainty and decorum, of course, is only for some people; it can be quite bad for others. For example, Seth has heard about a person who had lost control of his car, right alongside State House, and inadvertently crashed into the presidential wall. It was rumoured that he had been drunk, but perhaps not Luo, and after the State House guards had shot him, the autopsy report had been lost. Even the car had been confiscated, as part of 'the evidence.' It was impossible to know if all this had happened because the unfortunate and possibly drunk man had been a compatriot from the lakeside region.

Despite himself, a hot, anonymous rage fills Seth.

—Burning and murdering and what have you, he thinks disjointedly. Running around with pangas like as if they think blood can be replaced in a body: as if people are like cars and have spare-tyre lives which they will use the next morning after their deaths. You can't just stop in the middle of having your throat cut, and, using some handy tools, just exchange your life for one with no puncture and better treads He has been told that socialism is able to excite and degrade the brain in this fashion. When Seth's friend Mwangi had told him about the driver who crashed into State House, he had added an editorial comment at the end.

—They can't even drive a car, much less anything else! Mwangi had said, clicking his tongue in disgust.

As he swings by the windows of State House Girls', Seth reviews again his own job performance, to check himself for fault and to marshal his thoughts in his mind in case Madam or Madam's Husband asks him to account for himself, which he is no longer sure he can do. Seth likes his place in the world, but its edges are getting fuzzy, dissolving away, and the more fragile it gets, the more he anxious he becomes, and the more appreciative of what is threatened by an unseen and ominous fugue.

The thing is about these *athungus*, and he means this not in the literal sense of "white people" but more neutrally of "rich employer": the thing is that if you play your cards right you become necessary for them, like a daily cup of tea. They forget how to drive and become afraid of traffic at night and before they know it, they cannot go anywhere without you.

He slows down for the left turn into Arboretum Drive, whose leafy shelter soothes almost as much as thoughts of Madam usually do. Madam only goes abroad once a year these days, if even that, and she mostly requires visits to hairdressers, weddings, charity events and her friends' houses. She does all the shopping herself though, she knows the prices of things, Madame does, she knows where all the shillings and cents in her house go, she has a grasp on things.

Seth is now behind a large Land Rover Discovery with red license plates. Seth has professional opinions on these machines: they are the only things he gets argumentative about. He has a small but surprisingly comprehensive collection of car manuals and car magazines The American four by fours are certainly roomy, he'll give you that. Some people are now using them more than the Mercedes. That, and having bodyguards, seems to be the new trend. Maybe because American cars encourage American behaviour? Seth thinks about this, about the various types of cars that Madam and Madam's husband's friends and business acquaintances drive. Yes, the American cars are encouraging strange behaviour. Although of course they are very nice and big, with all that fancy chrome and roll bars and extra lights.

If you drove the car of an important person or an important person's wife, the cars were guaranteed to be excellent, and to be of several German makes also, that or British, but definitely one or the other. German, and solid, or British and somewhat flashy and ponderous, but of course, as Seth knows, the Japanese or was it the Chinese have now taken over some of the British. The German four-wheel drive by Mercedes is a mistake, Seth thinks, it simply looks like a box of matches on wheels. He thinks the toy cars he used to play with in Mathare were like that, ugly angles and liable to overturn at any moment.

Seth's car magazines were always somewhat delayed, because he could only buy them from one special stall, and Madam's routes did not take him there often. They were second-hand, of course, the magazines, but still enough to keep him able to hold his own with other drivers when the need arose. The other drivers were often men like him, long-term employees with solid reputations. No beeping or honking, except when requested to do so. Just beep and let her know we are here, Madam will sometimes say, and he will beep. But at the gates of stranger's homes he does not beep unless told to by Madam; he flashes the headlights instead. If the watchman is even half-way decent at his job no noise is necessary at all, the gates will open and the car will glide silently on, as is right and proper.

One of Madam's friends' husbands had just purchased an Italian for himself. A Maserati; but he wouldn't let the driver drive the car for him, so what was the use of that? It was a nice car, no doubt about that, but drivers needed work. Seth has no use for the driverless rich, he finds them selfish, especially these young ones, who were buying their own cars now but not hiring drivers. Madam's Husband had a Hummer, which of course Jackson drove — he had had the first one in Nairobi. Seth had been allowed

SETH HAS NO USE FOR

THE DRIVERLESS RICH

to sit in it, once, when the household was asleep and he had given Jackson a whole packet of Sportsman cigarettes. Even Jackson had been impressed enough to show off.

Seth strongly disapproves of the new trend towards flying that the Nairobi rich have been exhibiting. Aeroplanes are nice, but what do you do for transport on the other side? Of course Seth flies where Margaret does, if it is in Kenya. She simply pays for him to accompany her, so she can have a driver when she lands. Except of course if it is a game drive: those are a completely different type of driver, more adventurous, but less well-paid, of course. They are paid to be slightly dashing, somewhat world-weary, dangerous even, they have to excite white tourists while delivering their practiced lectures. Seth has a professional regard but also a slight contempt for these drivers, they are good at what they do, admittedly, but why do it at all?

At a recent party by one of Madam's husband's friends, the drivers had gathered to ridicule one of their own, Muriuki, Winston, or William or something like that, who had been so stupid as to get drunk at a party his employers were attending. It is quite easy if you know the housegirls to get a bottle of whisky at a time like this, and Muriuki had been found snoring and drunk at the wheel of his car. They had fired him and left him there, dead drunk outside their friend's gate. Seth knew he would hear of Muriuki again soon enough.

Somebody's gardener will have spoken to somebody else's maid who will know the brother of somebody's watchman, and Muriuki will have been found again, in greatly diminished circumstances, of course. Now reduced to being just a watchman, on endless night shifts, walking about muffled in old hats and rags and with scarves around your head and big heavy coats, and no

doubt a rung'u or some other thing to lug around. Nairobi is really quite small like that, in the end.

But these days, Madam isn't talking at all, isn't saying anything except for things like "We're going to town, that Italian place." And then she doesn't say anything else, expects Seth to know what Italian place she means as she sits in the back, silenced by grief and loss and pain so big it is heavy, like another passenger, or a body in the trunk. Or she says "Home, please." and goes back inside her pain, closing the door behind her, leaving her solitary, trapped in her mourning with all the curtains closed. Her cell phone rings and remains unanswered. This is not Madam-type behaviour at all.

Seth has on more than one occasion turned his head to hear her response and been met with nothing, just her eyes which are on nothing at all. He took the wrong turn once, on purpose, just to test her, to see if she was still aware that she was in a moving car with another human being driving it: and that time too, there was nothing in her eyes.

The only one Madam seems to see at all these days is Madam's Husband. Madam has gathered all her seeing, every last bit, and pointed it all in one direction. She has started looking at Madam's Husband, really looking, as if her eyes were a surgeon's knife and he a disease, staring and staring at him in silence. Madam's husband doesn't even notice. Or he notices but he doesn't care. It is just a look, what can it do, what can it possibly understand of your life, your world, your dealings and decisions?

The shelter of the trees of the arboretum ends, and Seth drives smoothly up the hill to Riverside. At the top of the hill, at the junction of Ring Road Riverside and Riverside proper, there is a policeman lounging by the curb. The policeman is not directing traffic, he is not checking cars. He is wearing the police uniform as if it belongs to someone else, as if he had that morning woken up naked and disoriented in strange surroundings, with nothing but this set of police clothes to put on.

The peach walls of the Australian High Commission and the hedges of Chiromo campus pull Seth out of his reverie. He merges onto Waiyaki Way, pausing only to give way to a lorry full of men in green riot gear and red berets, and accelerates up to the appropriate speed, feeling the smooth pick-up of the car with satisfaction. He loves driving this car—he cannot think of being parted from it; he and this car belong together. The angular bell-tower of Consolata catches his eye for an instant; the UNHCR headquarters flashes past.

As the cars sweep up towards Westlands, another *matatu* with "Da PERFUMED garden" with the 'perfume' done in dripping green and purple font charges past on the right, cuts in front of Seth, and swerves into the far left lane. The lorry with the men in red berets is just in front of it, and the *matatu* driver swings back out onto the center lane, as if to overtake it. The lorry, at this same instant, swings out to its right also, towards the *matatu*, and the *matatu* swerves wildly away and hits the blue Pajero in the far right lane. All lanes come to a stop, as the lorry full of the men in red berets has skewed across the lanes, like a drunken crane, and halted.

As soon as the lorry has stopped, the men at the back start to disembark, swinging down from the rope at the back onto the ground, where their boots make a hollow 'thunk' sound as they land. They are all armed. Their faces are grim, and as each new man hits the ground, the air seems to harden. The driver of the Pajero has climbed out of his car and is inspecting the damage, but also glancing towards the men with a wary eye. The passengers in the *matatu* are sitting still, held to their seats as if glued there. No one makes a sound. Two of the men in the red berets go round the front to the *matatu* driver's side, and, jerking the door open, pull him out of the van. He staggers down.

The birds are still.

Salvation arrives.

A long loud honk from the back, a deep throaty trumpet of a sound. It is like releasing a fart into a hostage situation —from someone in a car far enough behind not to have seen the men in green and red, comes a repeated exasperated hooting that is joined in chorus by two or three others. Something snaps back into place, reality shimmers and recognises itself. The lorry's driver hops into the cab and, starting the engine, pulls it off to the side. Seth, or the part of him that still knows how to drive, eases into the empty space, past the confused cluster of men and cars, drives up to the roundabout, swings right, and is decanted into the immediately comforting embrace of Westlands' disarray.

Hawkers are ranging the center strip, selling an assortment of goods catering to the mysterious combinations of Nairobi's needs. Here for sale are DVDs, magazines, flags, small sculptures of cars done in twisted metal, roses in red, orange, white, and other flowers, Arsenal paraphernalia and

Manchester United t-shirts, strawberry-flavoured car air fresheners, and puppies. Seth is taken by surprise by a wave of emotion that sweeps over him, which he recognises as nostalgia for all that is right in front of his eyes. For the solid white-and-blue bulk of the Sarit Centre. For the curio sellers on the other side of the roundabout working in cartels to sell their carvings, for the old Uchumi with the faded red paint back there, where Madam used to do all her shopping before the Nakumatt Supermarkets hit town.

He glides down lower Kabete Road and, at the furniture maker's, swings smoothly into the familiar welcoming right turn. This will be the last place in Nairobi to burn. He has an official right to be here, to drive the roads in these safe and leafy enclaves of calm. There is a girl handing out leaflets for a new restaurant. Can someone still be thinking of starting a new business, isn't everyone who is able to moving their money abroad as fast as possible and arranging for visas and exit plans? Soon, only those who have nowhere else to go will be left behind.

The country has been on the move quite a lot these past few weeks, all things considered. Everybody first did the annual migration home for the holidays, then re-arranged themselves around their polling station. Then, after everything began, people also moved their lives indoors, hunkering down in living rooms and inner courtyards behind their gates, like turtles in the sun with a hawk in the sky. Circles closing in on smaller circles, compressing them, inexorably deepening the fear that lies on the floor like a thick pool of dirty oil. Everyone inside, heads down, eyes tightly closed, lips moving in prayer.

As he drives past the well-tended hedges, and self-consciously beautiful outer gardens, Seth waits for the liquid contentment that usually slides down the back of his throat at this point on the drive home to find him. It does not come. In its place is something else—a distinct and growing tension. His shoulders stiffen. Jackson is inside the gates—he is inside the protective perimeter of Madam's house.

Seth can almost hear the thing he fears. He can hear it growling in the German engine below him. Seth has seen it on CNN at Madam's house, this thing. A malevolent child, creating strangely heaped multi-car sculptures around lamp-posts and rippling bridges into skirts. He knows what it can do: it is a mad artisanal monster with a taste for blood. Heaving in a breath, Seth tries to calls on a courage that has changed address and will not answer.

Seth had looked inside the large box before he had put it in the boot. Madam's Husband had told him that morning—had whispered it into the air as if commanding ghosts—to, upon paying for them, count them when he had them in his hands, and Seth had counted. There were two hundred and thirty-five. Two hundred and thirty-five silver-sharp edges waiting in the light. The light brown wood of the panga handles had looked incongruous, innocent, as if the pale smooth planes were new to the world.

A trickle of moisture runs into Seth's eye and stings. He blinks; he had not noticed he was sweating, and he fumbles for a handkerchief and wipes his brow. When Madam's Husband called him this morning, Seth had thought it was because Madam's Husband needed Jackson to take him to his regular golf game at the Muthaiga club, and indeed, Madam's Husband had gone off with Jackson and his golf clubs much as usual, after having given Seth his instructions about the box in the boot.

Seth rounds another of the endless curves snaking into what was once forest and sees a man with an orange shirt and two large Alsatians on a chain. The tails of the dogs are wagging fondly but the relationship between the man and the dogs is not right. He does not own the dogs, Seth can tell, he is not the one they adore. He is simply exercising them. He is obviously familiar to them, and they will obey him, but only to a point.

He rubs his ear, which has started to itch, shuffles his bottom around on the leather seat and then wipes his upper lip. He reaches down to the radio knob and turning it on, begins to fiddle with the dial. He flicks through the stations, disembodied voices, snatches of song, an advertising jingle for a cooking fat and then static again. He switches the knob off and then on again.

Here is the clock at Red Hill. He is nearly there. He pauses at the intersection and listens to himself breathe. The fuel tank is full. He has five hundred shillings on him because of some change he has not yet had a chance to return to Madam. His driving license is in order, and so is his I.D. The grass outside his window is an almost painful deep bright green. There is a different clock on each of the faces of the white cube-shaped head balancing on top of a slender pole. A risk. The clock is black and white. The longer of the two hands moves. Just an edge, a twitch; Seth is barely sure he has seen it but it was pointing at 29 past just a second ago and now it is pointing at 30, straight up and down.

The car stalls, and Seth jumps. The Mercedes never stalls. It is not that kind of car. Seth's hand reaches down and turns the ignition to the 'off' switch, and waits a beat. He wipes his palms on his trouser legs. He reaches up again and grips the steering wheel position firmly in the correct 10-minutes-to-two o'clock position, turns the ignition switch on and turns the car gently, smoothly homewards. He greets the guards at the gates as always, with a friendly wave of his hand and a smile. Seth and the guards sometimes make jokes about having to walk two kilometres to the kiosk to get a pack of *mozos* when at work, when where they live there is always a kiosk a few paces away.

It is then that the thought occurs to him. He realises, as if he has just been attempting to sit down on something sharp, that some of those kiosks in those places where the guards are from are gone now, they have floated away in spires of smoke, surrounded by sparks of angry orange and leaping red flames.

Perhaps the distance between kiosks has been equalised: a long walk either way. Seth himself lives in the row behind Madam's house, in the shelter of a white-washed one-roomed haven of sanity furnished by mended bits of furniture that Madam had, for her own well-judged reasons, decided to discard. Seth sees in his mind the wooden table with one metal leg that sits in the corner of his room. The table leg that is metal is a piece of tubing that Seth has bolted on. On top of the table is a stack of car magazines and a small black Bible, shiny with use. Everything else is put away into the small drawer, or under the bed, because Seth is an orderly man who likes to keep his surfaces clean. He likes to see the tops of things looking properly dusted and wiped down, likes the symmetry of nothing but angles and corners and flat surfaces in sight.

Seth glides into the driveway and halts at the gate, letting the murmur of the big car's engine signal the guard to open the gate. The guards and household staff can distinguish the precise rich contralto of Madam's Mercedes Benz from the more gritty one of her new four wheel-drive, can tell while the car is still at the nearest kiosk from Madam's house that Jackson and the Hummer are coming back.

Sometimes they can even tell the mood required for the upcoming arrivals: certain speeds of coming round the final curve and the sound of certain well-known bumps being negotiated in a different gear from normal, can be surprisingly explicit indications of the temperature of the owners of the house.

He drives into the parking lot, and into the garage. It is very quiet after the noise of the engine is cut off abruptly by Seth with one swift wrist-motion. Seth does not know if Madam even knows about the errand on which he had been sent by Madam's Husband. The brooding passion that has engulfed Madam has her so deeply in its grip that she seems to glow like the furnace room of a coal-driven train. She is a forge in which something new is being created. Her will is roiling and massing and Seth can no longer read her signs.

When Seth opens the back door of the house and steps into the kitchen, he finds Joshua the cook chopping vegetables. The radio is switched on low, to some music radio station, but Joshua is not singing along under his breath as usual. Seth turns his head and sees Jackson seated at the kitchen table, silently reading a newspaper, his back straight and composed as always and his hands placed on the table on either side of the page. Seth steps towards him to ask him to tell Madam's Husband that he, Seth, has returned with Madam's Husband's box. It would be rude for Seth to go over Jackson's head and talk directly to Madam's Husband while Jackson is in the house. He will deliver his news to Madam's Husband in private, and in Kikuyu of course, at the appropriate time.

J oshua is still chopping vegetables. Jackson becomes aware of Seth's presence: there is a deepening of the stillness with which he holds his head. His hands move on the table, closer to the page. He lifts his eyes to look at Seth. Seth opens his mouth to speak, but Jackson stands up and turns to the corridor leading to the dining room and Madam's Husband's study. Seth follows him.

Wambui Mwangi divides her time between Canada, where she teaches political science at the University of Toronto, and Kenya, where she is project manager of GenerationKenya. She has a passion for post-colonial theory and Kenyan political history, and is a member of the Concerned Kenyan Writers.

PHOREN

Shalini Gidoomal

I'm riding the lioness in the window of my father's shop on Government Road. She's a big beast and hard to mount because my shoulder only comes up to her side. I have to stand on the elephant-foot stool, grab a fistful of short mane and kick my leg over to vault up onto her. Her fur feels scratchy on my inner thigh – not at all soft. I kick at her sides with my heels, urging her to move forward, but she's stiff and stuffed and can only wobble lightly from side to side. From her back I can lean forward and hook my finger round her bared teeth. They're smooth then softly ridged and snarl through the window at passers-by on this main Nairobi thoroughfare.

My father doesn't mind me sitting on the lioness but his brother, Uncle Ravi, is much more disapproving. He's just walked into the shop, back from price-spying on City Furrier and Devan Singh, who he says are 'competition.' I know they are more expensive than our shop and rich *mzungus* like to buy from them. Uncle Ravi – who likes to remind everybody that he is the oldest - is much smaller than my papa. Both are thinner than my Uncle Noti, who's a big fatty with a long black beard. Uncle Noti is funny, when he isn't scary. He giggles a lot and wraps his arm around whichever pretty white lady I am supposed to call Auntie. They can't really be our aunties; they change so often. All my dad's other brothers only ever had one auntie.

There are other things in the shop that I love to play with – big drums made from stretched cowskins, which make a throbbing boom when you hit them hard with the wooden knobkerries. There are lots of hats and bags and coats and rugs made out of different animals. There's even a Tommies gazelle, which makes me sad as they are small and sweet and I don't think that my papa needs to make them into things for others to buy. Once, at the Animal Orphanage, a baby Tommie had followed me around all day and let me stroke him and feed him grass. The hat on our rack could have been made from his mama.

I'm in the shop instead of school today because I have lice, and Mum is afraid they will jump onto other people's hair. She gives me two shillings to buy something for myself so I run into Ebrahim's supermarket next door. It's really modern, with a black and white tiled floor and long white shiny shelves full of new things from all over the world. I rummage through the hair clips and choose a shiny glitter pink one from a box that says 'Made in China' on the side. I'm still fiddling with my new clip as I step out of the shop and bounce right into a group of men walking outside. They've got long knotty hair almost down to their bums, and are wearing dirty grey clothes full of dust which rises out of where I bumped them. I jump back quickly and notice the tattered shoes with holes. They're clutching woven *mkeka* bundles tight under their arms and they move past, then stop outside our shop, peer into the window and come in.

My dad looks up, quickly finishes what he is doing, orders tea, and disappears into the back room with a torch and the men with their bundles. Mostly I'm not allowed back there, but today he lets me come, too. I should get lice more often. Everyone is being so nice! We don't have electric light so when Papa opens the *mkeka* bundles, he has to use a torch to examine the things the long haired men brought. I peer over to look. There's a pile of skins – leopard, lion, zebra, impala. I put my hand up over my nose really politely - they smell horrible. My dad doesn't seem to notice and inspects them all carefully in the tiny back room of the shop. He shines the torch on the head and then each paw, making sure that they aren't squashed. He lays the skin out flat and runs his hand along the coat, tutting sometimes as he strokes the hide. As one man leans forwards over me to talk to Papa, I can feel his long dreadlocks snaking onto my shoulder. I wonder if my lice are going to migrate to him. They'd get lost in that forest of hair if they decided to jump off my head. The man nods as he replies to my papa, his hair jigging.

The dreadlock man smiles very widely when my papa gives him lots of lilac hundred-shilling notes, tells him to leave the skins, and asks him to come with more. I don't know why Papa is so excited. It's not like he's buying the clean, lovely new stuff you can get next door in Ebrahim's after all.

Uncle Noti comes into the back to check on the things my papa has bought. He's in a good mood because he has a new auntie, whom he met with a white hunter friend on the terrace of the Norfolk Hotel. I know her, too; she's my friend Loretta's mum. Actually she already has her own husband, although I heard someone say that he was gay. Enid Blyton said gay meant to be happy like the Famous Five were after solving a mystery. But maybe her husband wasn't happy enough because it seems Loretta's mum much prefers to be with Uncle Noti. Last week she dropped Loretta at our house for us to play and hasn't picked her up since. She got to stay lots of nights with us. I'm jealous because I like to have sleepovers, but my mamma doesn't like us staying anywhere other than at my grandparents, Nani and Kaki. They live nearby in Westlands, on Forces Lane, in a little two storey ex-army house with red velvet sofas and a parrot called Kasuku. Their cook has thick heavy glasses that are cracked on the side and held together with cellotape. We call him Masala Man on account of his constant grinding, pounding, and chopping of spices, sitting on a stool in the garden next to the bird table.

I like going to my nani's house because she doesn't mind if we jump on the sofas, and she makes the most delicious puris for breakfast. They are hot, puffy and crispy round the edges. The best is to peel off the top of the puri bubble and eat that bit on its own before dipping the rest into tea. I like to do this slowly, and stay at the breakfast table long after everyone has left.

I especially love the Mahabharata comics that Nani bought to teach us about our religion. 'No good to only know Jesus,' she says about our divinity lessons at school, and in truth, these are much more exciting than Bible tales. My favourite story is when the monkey god Hanuman flies across the wide sea to Ceylon and breaks into Ravenna's evil kingdom to rescue Rama's wife Sita. He brought her back safely and the world was saved. Sometimes I read so long, dipping and eating, that my tummy feels like Krishna's must have done when he stole all the cow's milk from the village girls by the river and had to retire up a tree to sleep off his excesses. I had a picture in my room of a blue Krishna playing his flute under a banyan tree to entice the maidens to him. 'It was embroidered by the Chinese,' Nani told me. I thought Uncle Noti must be a bit like Krishna, if uglier, because he was good at finding maidens too.

I ask Mama if I can go to Taws and get a new comic, but she says no. She wants to take me home to use paraffin and that metal lice comb on my hair again today. I sneak into the back room to avoid her. As I kneel to get under the rickety table, there's a sharp bang-bang on the back door and I bash my back on the table leg as I jump. Uncle Noti comes into the dark room. I try to slink further under the table. He strikes a match, lights the candle stub, and unlocks the door. Another batch of men – smaller, sneakier and pale-skinned – enter, shoving the metal door hard, because it sticks when you try to open it. They are carrying bows and arrows and don't smile so much.

'Encourage them,' I hear Papa say to Uncle Noti in our language as he pokes his head round the door. 'We need them now that Tanzania has closed its border; those Tanga traders can't get skins, let alone tusks, through to Kenya right now.'

After they leave, Uncle Noti blows out the candle, says 'crazy Somalis,' and goes back into the main shop. I'm so relieved. My legs feel cramped and my bum is numb from the cold stone floor. I prefer paraffin to this. I count to 20 and then peep round the door and slide into the shop as well.

They're not supposed to hunt, these Somalis, but they do it anyway for money.

'Everyone wants to sell their skins to our shop,' said Papa. I know he pays much more than City Furriers, and he sometimes serves them tea and samosas, so the wild-haired men and the crazy Somalis (who are good at hiding their hunting from the wildlife officers) come to our place first and take the leftovers to the other shop afterwards.

I prefer the long-haired men. Papa said they are called *Mau Mau*.

'They're freedom fighters that got forgotten after Independence,' he explained. They wanted to help run Nairobi, and even Kenya, but got into an argument with the police about cutting their hair and behaving properly. The cops said they couldn't be in Nairobi because they were too scruffy, so they were given special rifles, as thank-you presents for helping the country get free from the British. They were told to hunt in the bush. They already knew how to do this because they lived in the forest for a long time and forgot how to live in a house. They didn't get hungry because they could eat the animals they were allowed to shoot, and then Papa could buy the skins to make into the stuff we sell to tourists, like the long leopard coat that Uncle Ravi got cross about yesterday when he found out that Uncle Noti gave it to Loretta's mum as a present.

'You can't be handing over such expensive items like that to your women, *yaar.*' Uncle Noti just pretended not to hear.

The *Mau Mau*s start visiting regularly. My favourite comes nearly every week. He's called General Kamiti and is very famous because he helped Kenya very much in fighting against the Britishers. He told me he killed a leopard once without any weapons, just by wrestling with it until he broke its neck. Most times, he marches into the shop and slaps his pistol down on my papa's desk as a greeting. He doesn't really have a license but nobody is going to stop him from hunting, my papa said. One time, when papa was in hospital for a small operation, he came to visit him there with five other *Mau Mau* men who carried their skins with them and laid them out on the floor of his room at the MP Shah for him to inspect. 'He likes me too much,' joked my papa when I asked why they couldn't have seen Uncle Ravi or Uncle Noti.

Even with the regular visits through the front and back door, Papa still goes chasing other skin-selling men. Often, he's the one who has to make visits to see Minister Oloitiptip about business, although he refuses to go on Monday because that's veg day and we go down to Supreme near Tom Mboya street and get takeaway *makhni dal* as a treat. 'Don't give them sweets,' insists Mama as we set out. 'God knows what oils and sugars they put into them, but it rots their teeth up.'

I reckon meat is much worse for teeth. I decide this after I go with Papa to Lavington one Friday after school to see Minister Oloitiptip. He has amazing long holes in his ears, like someone cut a whole chunk out of them. He's sitting on the floor of his house with his legs straight out in front of him so we join him there on the bristly patterned carpet. We drink Cokes and tear big chunks of meat off the bone with our teeth. Bits of it get stuck in my teeth and under my fingernails. It's oily and greasy; I sneakily try to wipe my fingers on the carpet, but lots of fur sticks to the meat oil on my fingers. Papa eats lots of it, but I fiddle with one piece.

'Have you managed to arrange your premises to your satisfaction now?' asks Mr Oloitiptip. It has taken Papa ages to get everything right after he had to quickly move stuff out of our smaller shop, Treasure Curios last month. He got a call and was told that they had to give it away. So Uncle Noti, Uncle Ravi and Papa had to quickly hire one of those *mkototeni* wooden carts and carry off as much stuff as they could before the new owner, Mr Mutua, turned up. Lots of the beaded jewellery that Minister Oloitiptip sold to Papa got left behind, but they did remove the giraffe skin buckets. And they took my lioness, propped it on the top of the cart and dragged it to Government Road, her new home in a much better window in our bigger shop.

This was just before my ninth birthday. I remember because it was around the same time that Loretta stopped spending the night. Her mama came round late one night when we were asleep and picked her up out of my room to go home. I wasn't allowed to get out of bed and could only hear the whisperings; Papa telling Mama that 'Jenny had beaten Loretta's mum over the head with a stiletto at the Sombrero Club; such a big noise; they physically threw him out; she went to hospital for stitches; Noti hiding at LP's house.' Auntie Jenny was Uncle Noti's extra-new very busty lady, who brought us Mars Bars from England. She had long front teeth that stuck out when she smiled and she called me darling a lot. I was surprised that she liked the Sombrero – it was a naked lady place. I knew that from the advertisement in the *Nation* newspaper every day. It said 'ADULTS ONLY' over the booby bit of the ladies but you could tell they weren't wearing tops anyway.

The voices came again: 'Uncle Ravi wants Noti to go to India; had enough of this behaviour; people will think we are all *junglis*; time to settle down;

we'll find him a woman. No more of these *mzungu phorenas*.'

I missed Loretta, but whenever I asked about where she was, none of the grown ups would tell me anything about her. In fact they were being really secretive about everything. When I was in the shop on the weekend, Papa said I wasn't allowed to sit on the lioness any more. 'Many customers are coming,' he said, and it would be very busy in the shop.

'In fact,' he says, stroking my hair, 'you can't come to the shop this week.' I move my head away from Papa's hand. Imagine! A whole week away! It's too much, but when I open my mouth, Mama won't let me speak, 'Just listen to your papa,' she says, and I'm not allowed to say anything! So unfair! I know that if I stamp my foot mama will get cross with me, so I just leave it, and when I get home I scratch my name onto the sisal plant with a compass. As soon as I do it I feel bad, but it's there now forever and it serves them right if they don't like it.

Each day when the school bus passes the shop there are loads of people outside. I want to shout out to them, but I just stare as we bump by. The road outside the shop is stuffed with big cars parked all over the place getting in the way of traffic. The doors to the shop are shut and occasionally I see them swing open a little bit to let one person in at a time before closing again. Everyone on the street pushes and shoves to get closer to the front. Once, I saw a hand come round the door and shove a lady back to the pavement when she tried to sneak inside out of turn.

It was a week later that the lioness disappeared from the window. There was a dusty mark where she stood, but I couldn't see properly because of all the crowds outside the shop. 'Please please can we go in,' I begged Mama, 'I really want to find out what's happened to her.' Mama said it would have to be brief, and we pushed our way to the front entrance through all the people waiting. It was really squashy, and I wanted to tell everyone to move. They didn't care that it was our shop and we never had to queue like they did. They only shifted a little so they didn't lose their place in the line.

Inside was stuffed full. Papa, Uncle Ravi and Uncle Noti were laying skin after skin on the floor and then scooping them up into bundles for people to buy. It was bursting with men and ladies shoving and grabbing things from the shelves. I could hardly move without bumping into one of them. All of them were shouting instructions, and a muted roar of noise filled the shop.

'Wrap this handbag! Do you have any more leopard skin ones?'

'I'll pay cash for the tusks. And that zebra drum. Stop pushing me! Hoi you...are you listening? Book those tusks for me now.'

'Noti, pass me the receipt book. Move that off the floor. Serve that man waiting there; show him the sables.'

'Look darling...what do you think? Perfect for Nina von Strunkel's cocktails next week?'

Papa turned, irritated, to Uncle Ravi who struggled to fold things properly and told him, 'get useful and check for thievery – anyone can put the ivory bracelets in their pockets.' Papa never talked like that to Uncle Noti, who we all knew was brainy and would shout back. I saw someone that looked like Loretta's mum pick up four handbags and put them on one side, her blonde head turning left and right as she elbowed her way through the shop.

They couldn't have fitted a single extra person in the shop or an extra word in the air without the whole place popping and falling out onto Government Road. No wonder all these people were outside. I tried to push my way to Papa, but he turned to Mama and ordered: 'Take her home, this is not the place for children right now.'

We had to leave without finding out anything about the lioness.

336

I HATE Loretta. She stopped playing dibs with me at school today. She told me her mum thinks Uncle Noti is a hustler, which means he's not nice, and neither am I, because I'm his relative. She got the other girls to gang up and they chanted 'Paki Paki brownface' at me and refused to sit next to me in class. I felt prickly hot in the back of my head, but I refused to cry, climbing up into the guava tree all break-time instead. I dream about hitting Loretta on the head with a deadly shot from my biggest marble, but I don't do it. She might nick it, and that would be even worse.

I spend more time going round to Bubli's house instead. We want to go see Saturday Night Fever, which has just opened at Kenya Cinema, but we're not allowed because it is a grown up movie, which means kissing. Normally, Papa sits next to me and puts his hands over my eyes during the naughty bits of other movies like James Bond, but this one has swearing, too, and he can't cover eyes and ears, so we don't go. Instead I mooch about at home. I haven't been allowed in the shop since I tried to find out about the lioness, and papa comes home late, sleeps, and gets up early to go back there.

'You need more rest, my love' admonishes ma, but papa shrugs and says 'deadlines,' before jumping back into the car to go into town.

I'm sure the President has taken the lioness just like he took Treasure Curios to give to his friend.

'Where's she gone?,' I asked papa, when I saw the space in the window. I felt hot in my face as I asked and could feel my big toe wiggling without my permission in my Clarks.

'To America,' he replied.

'Didn't the President want her?' I asked.

He didn't, but the man who bought her promised to look after her. She had company, too, so she wouldn't be lonely. Lots of our animal things had been sold to the American man. And English ladies and Italian people. Even Kenyans had come to buy our things, big knobbly ivory rings and bracelets, tusks and buffalo heads for their walls.

And this time we wouldn't get any more because they'd been chased away by the President's ban.

How come the President didn't want us to sell any more animal things? And why didn't papa tell me that he was really truly going to sell my lioness? I felt cheated by both of them. I would have bagged the lioness for my bedroom. And maybe a zebra hat and some leopard slippers. We could have kept the impala skin Bubli wore in the school play, Snow White, when he played the deer killed by the huntsman to give the wicked queen its heart instead of Snow White's. What could I take to show off at school now?

I couldn't tell Papa that it would be tough to compete with Loretta, who got tons of pocket money to buy records from Uncle LP's shop, and who was still being mean to me. She just brought a new Osibisa one last week with flying red and green elephants and lizards on the cover. And she had all the Boney M's, but she wouldn't let me borrow them. How would sisal baskets or wooden bracelets compare to that? Her records were *phoren*. They had to come all the way from England to Kenya.

She even had Space Dust which she brought to school. So I was extra nice and let her have one of my best marbles so she'd give me a taste. It fizzled and crackled on my tongue and tasted horrible. It wasn't worth the eight-leaf bombie I had traded at all. Loretta said I didn't like Space Dust because I was a coolie and ate too many chapatti and chillies. She didn't say coolie like it meant I had been cool and managed to touch the out-of-bounds willow tree on the playing fields, or won a dibs competition though.

When I asked Mama about coolies, she got mad and ranted. 'These two-bit colonialists think their skin colour makes them superior to everyone. Thieves! Common *mwizis*. They can't even cook food properly. Who do they think built their famous railway if it wasn't coolies? And who supplied them with goods all the way along the line? And who arranges timber? Who, hah?'

She thumped the chapatti mix with extra vigour, her knuckles leaving pockmark dips in the dough. 'We could be living in a palace if they hadn't made such a mess of India. Instead we have to lose everything fleeing to here, and they still think their white makes them better. Rubbish people.' I knew I shouldn't tell papa about what Loretta said because he always said 'the British' like he was spitting something horrible out of his mouth. And Papa didn't like Loretta's mum anyway.

I hope Uncle Noti doesn't go buy a wife like Auntie Aruna. She came from India, too, and Uncle Ravi said she was from a high-up family that was very important and prayed a lot. Auntie Aruna prayed a lot too – she wanted to be like Mother Theresa and to help the poor. At the temple she prostrated herself on the ground, knees tucked under her, head resting on the floor mats before sitting up straight, her head covered with a sari, rocking back and forth as she sung. She looked like a weeble – those ones that never fall down no matter how hard you push them. When the temple collected money for schooling for Dr Barnado's orphans she made everybody give her at least 2000 shillings so that she could win praise at the temple for getting the most donations.

'*Arey* Noti, this is less than you spend for one night with those women,' she said. 'The hospital bills from Jenny's adventure cost you more than I am asking for these struggling babies who also need books and all.'

'Hnnh! It feels like paying a bribe,' grumbled Uncle Noti, but he always handed over the money.

He doesn't come to the shop much either these days, and I know why. It's really boring in there now. All the animal things – my lioness, the furry handbags, the zebra rugs, the big drums, the necklaces, even the elephant tusks have all gone. All that was left in the shop were things like green canvas hats with Kenya printed on the front, painted batiks of Mount Kenya, beaded bits, and some wooden carvings. My papa said I could have a lovely painted bracelet as a present because the lioness was gone, but it didn't feel like it was a fair swap - which I told him.

'In that case, take whatever you like,' he said But when I looked around, there was nothing that I really wanted. Lots of shops had wooden stools and bracelets. Ours was special because we had all those other things too. I asked when another lioness was coming to the window. He told me 'the President said we would not be able to have any more animals at all.' They were for the game parks only. They were born free and were going to stay free.

We all knew that, as the President was leading the country, we had to obey. He was such an important man that he was known as *Mzee*. I thought it meant old with grey hair – like the shopkeepers in Highridge called out to the cook to entice him to buy their vegetables, but Papa said it was for respect because he was the leader of the nation. Everyone had the same pictures of him. He was upstairs and downstairs in Papa's shop. Mr. Ebrahim's supermarket next door had one. Our school had one in the Headmaster's office – I'd seen it through the windows when Bubli was being tackied for failing French verbs. Even Uncle LP had a picture of the president at his cool record shop, Assanands, although he put his low down on the wall so that he could hang guitars higher up. 'Not having people touching the guitars unless they really want to buy,' he told me once, giving me some Orbit gum – we weren't allowed Orbit at home. Along with the new pictures of *Mzee* we also had to stand up at the movies when they showed the Kenya flag and played the National Anthem -because the President said so. People did it even though he wasn't there himself to check. 'You would get beaten by *askaris* with big boots,' otherwise, whispered Bubli. Sometimes we would stand up at home in front of the TV when the flag came on even if no one was watching. I figured out the National Anthem on the piano too. It was only five notes round middle C and really easy. I was scared people would find out that I had learnt it while sitting down on a stool instead of standing, so I didn't tell my mama.

A week later, I was sure there were robbers trying to squeeze through the bars on my window. I lay there even though my heart was thumping and my hands were wet-sweaty, but then I got up to find Mama even though I was not supposed to. I sneaked down the stairs towards the sitting room where I could hear her voice. She was talking in the same cross way she did when she caught me eating flowers from the garden. Papa and Uncle Ravi were there whispering in angry quiet voices. Uncle Noti was the loudest, sitting on the edge of the sofa and waving his drink around. I could see little spits coming from his mouth as he shouted at Uncle Ravi. He was being scary.

'Don't think you can send me off like some post mail package to find some good cooking woman to bring back here. India is not even home anymore but you think I'll find this perfect girl over there? If I want my share of shillings from my labour to go to Bacchus Club or Casino on whisky with white women, that's my affair.'

Unce Ravi interrupted him; 'Noti, people are talking about the troubles you are having with your lady friends. *Arey!* Women beating each other in the street like that! See, we have children now – you must settle, too. A good Indian woman can look after you. Aruna also feels the same way.'

'Pah! To be like you! Sitting in the big office doing small money dukawallah nonsense. Your head is so slow that you can't do more than check for cheating on tea money or buying petrol. And that wife of yours! Always tapping us for cash to make her look better. This pious nonsense of hers with her head on the floor supplicating to the gods. But if she had to help her own, with no outward praising from the temple women - then she doesn't care at all.'

'Don't you talk about my wife like that. She's bringing up our children right. We have to keep our culture. And what do you do? Throwing money around town like some irresponsible *goondah* with no schooling. As oldest and head of the family I need to keep respect in this town. You go to India!'

I see Mama puts her hands to her lips to make them be quieter. Papa doesn't say anything. He's staring at Uncle Noti and then at the portrait of our family that's on the wall.

'You think your kids would be at nice schools without my input? Who thought of using *Mau Mau* hunting quotas? Who do you think made us such big ivory traders? Did you suffer in Japan to find good customers? Where's the big money coming from for the fancy house you want to build on Riverside Drive?' Uncle Noti takes a large swig from his glass.

'Take your ambitions to River Road where they belong;' he banged it down on the table.

'That's *enough*, Noti,' says Mama. Papa and Uncle Noti are staring at each other. Why doesn't papa speak?

'So you are going to go with this goatshit on this?' says Uncle Noti to papa. There's no reply from papa. 'It's best for the family,' says Uncle Ravi. Uncle Noti stands up.

I run back to my room very quickly before he sees me on the stairs. I lie very still in bed, like I do when I want the robbers, who might come through the window, to think I am dead. I hear Uncle Noti's red Alfa Romeo – the coolest car – revving out of our gate. I hear the clink of Mama's bracelets at my bedroom door. I hold my breath to be deader, but she doesn't come in.

It's a few days since I watched the fight and Uncle Noti hasn't been to the shop or to the house. Normally he likes to come and drink Black Label whisky with papa and talk about grown-up things, while Mum fries *bhajias*. He often takes off his shoes and his toenails are long and horny and really gross.

We've got a new batch of wooden giraffes that arrived to replace the real animals we used to have, I was trailing my fingers down the neck of one when the shop door swung open and shut hard. It rattled the white plastic closed sign on the door. It was another group of men, but this time they came direct from the President. They weren't friendly like General Kamiti and the dreadlocked men who sometimes gave me sweets that mama wouldn't let me eat. These guys wore suits and didn't want to go to the back room. They kept their guns on their belts and I heard '*phoren* accounts,' and 'not suitable; illegal; ad *haki* this is a verrrry serious crime.' I saw my papa smile like Auntie Aruna, with only his lips moving wide across his face. He *ka-chinged* the big metal till, took something out, and then shook hands with the biggest and fattest of the men who had many marks on his face. They stared at each other and then they left.

Papa locked up the shop quickly, hustling me out the door and into the car to go home. I knew I couldn't ask him about the suit-men - like I didn't ask about where Uncle Noti had gone. 'Do you think Hanuman could go across the ocean to America to rescue the lioness?' I said instead to make him smile. He didn't reply. At home I watched cartoons, then *Mambo Leo*, which says the Somalis and Ethiopians in the countries next door are fighting badly. Mama sent me to bed after that, so she could talk with Papa. I hate it when they do that.

Papa didn't' go to work today and instead spent lots of time on the phone in his study. I'm not allowed to interrupt so I went outside to the sandpit in the garden because I know I could hear him through the window from there.

'The bloody bastard's sent a letter to every MP with details of the accounts,' said Papa. 'Every one. Information on UK, Canada, all all. Even given amounts in each account. We're finished. I've already had someone call me for meetings to discuss the letters. It's too much *chai* to try to find. Trying to get Rupa to help, but its too widespread. Noti's run to England, took off with Jenny.'

I know this is bad. I sit in the sand, dig, sit, dig again. I know nobody wants to explain. Later that afternoon Papa comes to look at the broken seat of the go-cart. I wanted to explain that it wasn't my fault and was telling him how 'Bubli, twisted down the hill....' but I didn't get to finish what I was saying because there was a long loud honk at the gate and two suit-men drove into the driveway. They shouted horribly at my papa before taking his nice car away, the blue Mercedes with seats that smelt like the best skins used to make handbags at the shop. They tore out his Ganesh hanging from the mirror and threw it out onto the driveway. They were scarier than Uncle Noti in his worst mood, bringing their faces very close to Papa's. Loretta did that to me once and it was horrible. I moved far back when she did this, but Papa kept trying to be nice to them. I hid by the swings so he couldn't send me back into the house, and had to bite hard on my lip to not cry. I was so happy when they drove off.

I didn't have to go to school the next day because after the suit-men left, Papa said we're going on a surprise holiday as everyone was a bit tired after the busy time at the shop. It was a really great adventure because we were not going to Mombasa, but on a big plane to England! Not a supersonic pointy nose new Concord like the one that had just flown at record speed from London to New York, but still, a big jumbo from the new Kenya Airways. We were flying to a *phoren* land where I could buy my own Mars Bars and all the latest records – even the ones that never came to Assanand's. And I knew from school that we would arrive just before the Queen would start her jubilating celebration of reigning for 25 years, I even knew she was here at Treetops when she found out about becoming queen.

'Can we go visit Buckingham Palace?' I ask Mama. She's not listening, and is focused on throwing some of my things into a suitcase. 'I want to take that pink bikini,' I say, but she snaps back that I won't need it and then softens. 'Just let me finish this *beta*. No, you can't take that toy, its too big. We must hurry to catch the plane.'

We collect Bubli, Uncle Ravi, Auntie Aruna and squish their big suitcases in Mama's green 504. We drive past the shop on the way to the airport. There is a big CLOSED sign on the door since it is the first time we had ever all gone on holiday together. Normally, Papa, Uncle Ravi or Uncle Noti has to stay to mind the shop. Somebody has put wooden boards in the window where my lioness used to stand roaring at everybody with me on her back. Mama's mouth goes all fluttery and she looks like she is going to cry, but Papa fixes her with a stern look. Auntie Aruna keeps pressing and twisting her hands together, and all the wrinkles on her forehead are showing.

On the way to the airport, some elephants wandered across the road in front of our car and we had to wait for them all to cross. Bubli counted 30 but I'm sure it was 31. The grown-ups got very impatient like Mama did earlier when I said I wanted to call Loretta to gloat about going away. 'No,' said mama, 'this is a secret surprise. We're not telling any friends about leaving. Now jump in the car quickly.' So I didn't say goodbye to anybody.

But I console myself that they can drool over my *phoren* things when I come back.

Shalini Gidoomal is a freelance journalist, writer, businesswoman and inveterate traveller, born, and currently living in Nairobi. She has worked for various UK and international magazines and newspapers, including The Independent, News of the World, Today, FHM, GQ *and* Architectural Digest. *Her short stories and non-fiction have been published in* The Obituary Tango, Jungfrau *and* Kwani 04. *She is a member of the Concerned Kenyan Writers group.*

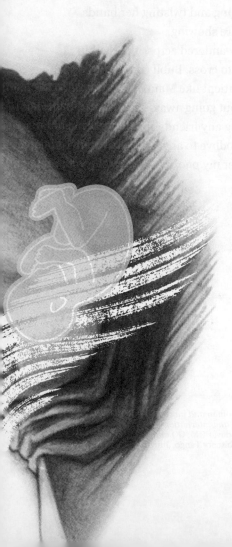

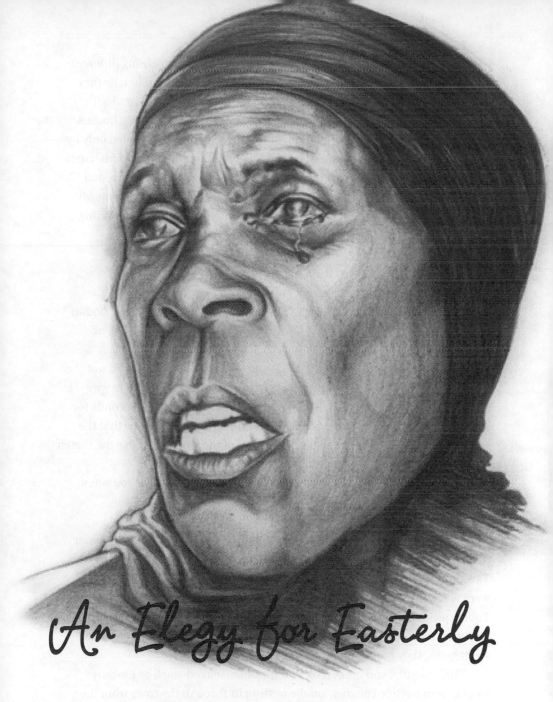

An Elegy for Easterly

Petina Gappah

I

It was the children who first noticed that there was something different about the woman they called Martha Mupengo. They followed her, as they often did, past the houses in Easterly Farm, houses of pole and mud with thick black plastic sheeting for walls and clear plastic for windows, houses that erupted without city permission, unnumbered houses identified only by reference to the names of their occupants. They followed her past *Mai*James' house, *Mai*Toby's house, past the house occupied by Josephat's wife, and Josephat when he was on leave from the mine, past the house of the newly arrived couple that no one really knew, all the way past the people waiting with plastic buckets to take water from Easterly's only tap.

'Where are you going, Martha Mupengo?' they sang.

She turned and showed them her teeth.

'May I have 20 cents,' she said, and lifted up her dress.

Giddy with delight, the children pointed at her nakedness. '*Hee, haana bhurugwa*,' they screeched. '*Hee*, Martha has no panties on, she has no panties on.'

However many times Martha Mupengo lifted her dress, they did not tire of it. As the dress fell back, it occurred to the children that there was something a little different, a little slow about her. It took a few seconds for Tobias, the sharp-eyed leader of Easterly's under-eights, to notice that the something different was the slight protrusion of the stomach above the thatch of dark hair.

'*Haa*, Martha Mupengo is swollen,' he shouted. 'What have you eaten, Martha Mupengo?'

The children took up the chorus. 'What have you eaten, Martha Mupengo?' they shouted as they followed her to her house in the far corner of Easterly. Superstition prevented them from entering. Tobias' chief rival Tawanda, a boy with four missing teeth and eyes as big as Tobias' ears were wide, threw a stick through the open doorway. Not to be outdone, Tobias picked up an empty baked beans can. He struck a metal rod against it, but even this clanging did not bring Martha out. After a few more failed stratagems, they moved on.

Their mouths and lungs took in the smoke-soaked smell of Easterly: smoke from outside cooking, smoke wafting in through the trees from the roadside where women roasted maize in the rainy season, smoke from burning grass three fields away, cigarette smoke. They kicked the empty

346

can to each other until hunger and a sudden quarrel propelled Tobias to his family's house.

His mother *Mai*Toby sat at her sewing machine. Around her were swirls of fabric, sky blue, magnolia, buttermilk and bolts of white stuffing for the duvets she made to sell. The small generator powering the sewing machine sent diesel fumes into the room. Tobias raised his voice above the machine.

'I am hungry.'

'I have not yet cooked; go and play.'

He sat in the doorway. He knew that attention was always given those who bore the news. Casting about for such newness, he remembered Martha. 'Martha's stomach is swollen,' he said.

'Mmmm?'

'Martha, she is ever so swollen.'

'*Ho nhai*?'

He indicated with his arms and said again, 'Her stomach is this big.'

'*Hoo*,' his mother said without looking up. One half of her mind was on the work before her, and the other half was on another matter: should she, right this minute, put elaborate candlewick on this duvet, or should she use that time to walk all the way to *Mai*James' to make a call to follow up on that 10 million she was owed? *Mai*James operated a phone shop from her house. She walked her customers to a hillock at the end of the farm and stood next to them as they telephoned. On the hillock, *Mai*James opened the two mobiles she had and inserted one SIM card after the other to see which would get the best reception. Her phone was convenient, but there was this: *Mai*James was the source of most of the gossip at Easterly.

II

In her home, Martha slept.

Her name and memory, past and dreams, were lost in the foggy corners of her mind. She lived in the house and slept on the mattress on which a man called Titus Zunguza had killed first his woman and then himself. The cries of Titus Zunguza's woman were loud in the night. Help would have come, for the people of Easterly lived to avoid the police. But by the time Godwills Mabhena, who lived next to *Mai*James, had crossed the distance to Titus Zunguza's house and roused a sufficient number of neighbours to enter, it was too late. And when the police did come, it was the clear fact of the murder-suicide that kept the long arm of the law from reaching into every house.

Six months after the deaths, when blood still showed on the mattress, Martha claimed the house simply by moving in. As the lone place of horror at Easterly, the house was left untouched; even the children acted out the terror of the murderous night from a distance.

They called her Martha because *Mai*James said that was exactly how her husband's niece, Martha, had looked in the last days when her illness had spread to her brain. 'That is how she looked,' *Mai*James said. 'Just like that, nothing in the face, just a smile and nothing more.'

It was the children who called her Mupengo, Mudunyaz, and other variations on lunacy. The name Martha Mupengo stuck more than the others, becoming as much a part of her as the dresses from flamboyantly coloured material, bright with exotic flowers, poppies and roses and bluebells – dresses that had belonged to Titus Zunguza's woman and that hung on Martha's thin frame.

She was not one of the early arrivals at Easterly.

She did not come with those who arrived after the government cleaned up the townships to make Harare pristine for the three-day visit of the Queen of England. All the women who walk alone at night are prostitutes, the government said. Lock them up, the Queen is coming. There are illegal structures in the townships they said. Clean them up. The townships are too full of people, they said, gather them up and put them in the places the Queen will not see; in Porta Farm, in Hatcliffe, in Dzivaresekwa Extension, in Easterly. Allow them temporary structures and promise them real walls and doors, windows and toilets.

And so they hid away their poverty, put on plastic smiles and planted new flowers in the streets.

Long after the memories of the Queen's visit had faded and the broken arms of the arrested women were healed, Easterly Farm took root. The first wave was followed by a second and by another, and yet another. Martha did not come with the first wave, nor with the next, nor with the one after that. She just appeared, as though from nowhere.

She did not speak beyond her request for 20 cents.

Tobias, Tawanda and the children thought this just another sign of madness; she was asking for something they could not give. Senses, they thought, we have five senses and not 20, until Tobias's father *Ba*Toby, the only adult who took the trouble to explain anything, told them that cents were an old type of money, coins of different colours. In the days before a loaf of bread cost half a million dollars, he said, one hundred cents made one dollar. He took down an old tin and said as he opened it, 'We used the coins as recently as 2000.'

'Eight years ago, I remember,' said an older child. 'The five cent-coin had a rabbit, the 10-cent a baobab tree. The twenty had ... had ... umm, *I* know ... Beit Bridge.'

'Birchenough Bridge,' said *Ba*Toby. 'Beitbridge is one word, and it is a town.'

'The 50 had the setting sun ...'

'Rising sun,' said *Ba*Toby.

'And the dollar coin had the Zimbabwe Ruins,' the child continued.

'Well done, good effort,' said *Ba*Toby. He spoke in the hearty tones of Mr. Barwa, his history teacher from Form Three. He, too, would have liked to teach the wonders of Uthman-dan-Fodio's Caliphate of Sokoto and Tshaka's horseshoe battle formation, but providence in the shape of the premature arrival of Tobias had deposited him, grease under his nails, at the corner of Kaguvi Street and High Road, where he repaired broken-down cars for a living.

As he showed them the coins, he remembered a joke he had heard that day. He repeated it to the children. 'Before the President was elected, the Zimbabwe Ruins were a prehistoric monument in Masvingo province. Now, the Zimbabwe Ruins extend to the whole country.' The children looked at him blankly before running off to play, leaving him to laugh with his whole body shaking.

The children understood that Martha's memory was frozen in a time before they could remember, the time of once upon a time, of good times that their parents had known, of days when it was normal to have more than leftovers for breakfast, a time of filtered memories. 'We danced to records at Christmas,' *Ba*Toby was heard to say. 'We had reason to dance then; we had our Christmas bonuses.'

Like Martha's madness, the Christmas records and bonuses were added to the play of Easterly Farm. And for the children of Easterly, it was Christmas at least once a week.

III

In the mornings, the men and women of Easterly washed off their sleep smells in buckets of water that had to be heated in the winter. They dressed in shirts and skirts ironed straight with coal irons. In their smart clothes, thumbing lifts at the side of the road, they looked like anyone else, from anywhere else.

The formal workers of Easterly Farm were few: the country had become a nation of traders. They were blessed to have four countries bordering them: to the north, Zambia, formerly one-Zambia-one-nation-one-robot-one-petrol-station, Zambia of the joke currency had become the place to go for scarce commodities; to the east, Mozambique, their almost colony, *kudanana kwevanhu veMozambiki neZimbabwe*, reliant on their solidarity pacts and friendship treaties, on their soldiers guarding the Beira Corridor; this Mozambique was now the place from which to withdraw the foreign money not available in their own country; to the west, Botswana, how they had laughed at Botswana with no building taller than 13 storeys, the same Botswana that now said it was so full of them that it was erecting a fence along the border to electrify their dreams of three meals a day; and, to the south, cupping Africa in her hands of plenty, Ndaza, *ku*South, Joni, Jubheki, Wenera, South Africa.

They had become a nation of traders.

So it was that in the mornings the women of the markets rose early and caught the mouth of the rooster. In Mbare Musika they loaded boxes of leaf vegetables, tomatoes and onions, sacks of potatoes, yellow bursts of spotted bananas. They took omnibuses to Mufakose, to Kuwadzana and Glen Norah to stand in stalls and coax customers.

'One million for two, five million for six, only half a million.'

'Nice bananas, nice tomatoes, buy some nice bananas.'

They sang out their wares as they walked the streets.

'*Mbambaira, muriwo, ma*tomato, onion, *ma*banana, *ma*orange.'

The men and boys went to Siyaso, the smoke-laced secondhand market where the expectation of profit defied the experience of breaking even. In this section, hubcaps, bolts, nuts, adapters, spanners. Over there, an entire floor given over to the mysterious bits, spiked and heavy, rusted and box-shaped, that give life to appliances. In the next, sink separators, plugs, cellphone chargers. Under the bridge, cobblers making *manyatera* sandals out of old tyres. The shoes were made to measure; 'Just put your foot here, *blaz*,' the sole of the shoe sketched out and cut out around the foot, a hammering of strips of old tire onto the sole, and lo, 15-minute footwear. In Siyaso it was not unknown for a man whose car had been relieved of its radio or hubcaps to buy them back from the man into whose hands they had fallen. At a discount.

On the other side of Mbare, among the zhing zhong products from China, the shiny clothes spelling out cheerful poverty, the glittery tank tops and body tops imported in striped carrier bags from Dubai, among the Gucchii bags and Prada shoes, among the Louise Viton bags, the boys of Mupedzanhamo competed to get the best customers.

'Sister, you look so smart. With this on you, you will be smarter still.'

'Leave my sister be, she was looking this way, this way sister.'

'Sister, sister, this way.'

'This way, sister.'

'This way.'

'Sister.'

'My *si.*'

They spent the day away from Easterly Farm, in the city, in the markets, in Siyaso. They stood at street corners selling belts with steel buckles, brightly coloured Afro-combs studded with mirrors, individual cigarettes smoked over a corner newspaper, boiled eggs with pinches of salt in brown paper. They passed on whispered rumours about the President's health.

'He tumbled off the stairs of a plane in Malaysia.'

'Yah, that is what happens to people who suffer from foot and mouth, people who talk too much and travel too much.'

At the end of the day, they packed up their wares and they returned to Easterly Farm, smelling of heat and dust, to be greeted again by Martha Mupengo.

'May I have 20 cents,' she said, and lifted up her dress.

IV

Josephat's wife was the first of the adults to recognise Martha's condition. It was five years since Josephat's wife had married Josephat. She had tasted the sound of her new identity on her tongue and liked it so much that she called herself nothing else. 'This is Josephat's wife,' she said when she spoke into the telephone on the hillock above the Farm. 'Hello, hello. It's Josephat's wife. Josephat's *wife.*'

'It is like she is the first woman in the entire world to be married,' *Mai*James said to *Mai*Toby.

'*Vatsva vetsambo,*' said *Mai*Toby. 'Give her another couple of years of marriage and she will be smiling on the other side of her face.'

On that day, Josephat's wife was walking slowly back into Easterly, careful not to dislodge the thick wad of cotton the nurses had placed between her legs. Like air seeping out of the wheels of a bus on the rocky road to Magunje, the joy was seeping out of the marriage. *Kusvodza*, they called it at the hospital, which put her in mind of *kusvedza*, slipping, sliding, and that is what was happening, the babies slipped and slid out in a mess of blood and flesh. She had moved to Easterly Farm to protect the unborn, fleeing from Mutoko where Josephat had brought her as a bride. After three miscarriages, she believed the tales of witchcraft that were whispered about Josephat's aunts on his father's side.

'They are eating my children,' she declared when Josephat found her at his two-room house at Hartley Mine near Chegutu. She stayed only six months. After another miscarriage, she remembered the whispers about the foreman's wife, and her friend Rebecca who kept the bottle-store.

'They are eating my children,' she said and moved to her aunt's house in Mbare. There she remained until the family was evicted and set up home in Easterly Farm. After another miscarriage, she said to her aunt, 'You are eating my children.'

Her aunt did not take this well. She had, after all, sympathised with Josephat's wife, even telling her of other people who might be eating her children. In the fight that followed, Josephat's wife lost a tooth and all the buttons of her dress. Fate prevented the further loss of buttons and teeth by killing the younger brother of the aunt's husband. By throwing the dead brother's widow and her young family out of their house in Chitungwiza, the aunt and her husband acquired a new house, and Josephat's wife was left in Easterly.

In the evenings, she read from her Bible, her lips moving as she read the promises for the faithful. 'Is there any among you that is sick? Let him call for the elders of the Church; and let them pray over him, anointing him with oil in the name of the Lord. And the prayer of faith shall save the sick.'

From church to church she flitted, worshipping in township backrooms while drunken revellers roared outside, mosquitoes gorging on her blood in the open fields as she prayed among the white-clad, visiting prophets with shaven heads and hooked staffs who put their hands on her head and on her breasts. At the Sacred Church of the Anointed Lamb, at the Temple of God's Deliverance, at the Church of our Saviour of Glad Tidings, she cried out her need in the language of tongues. She chased a child as her fellow penitents chased salvation, chased a path out of penury, chased away the unbearable heaviness of loneliness, sought some kind of redemption. And if the Lord remained deaf, that was because she had not asked hard enough, prayed hard enough, she thought.

She was walking past *Mai*Toby's house on the way to her own when she remembered that *MaiToby* had told her about a new church whose congregation prayed in the field near Sherwood Golf Course in Sentosa. 'You can't miss them,' *Mai*Toby had said. 'You go along Quendon until you reach the Tokwe flats. They worship under a tree on which hangs a big square flag; it has a white cross on a red background.'

It meant taking three commuter omnibuses, Josephat's wife thought. First, the omnibus to Mabvuku, then one to town. She would have to walk for 15 minutes or so from Fourth Street to Leopold Takawira, take an omnibus to Avondale and walk for another 45 minutes to Sentosa.

'I will rise at five,' she thought, 'and catch the mouth of the rooster.'

She remembered that she had not been able to reach her husband at the mine to tell him of yet another miscarriage. The trajectory of that thought directed her feet towards *Mai*James' house. It was then that she saw Martha. The woman did not need to lift her dress to reveal the full contours of pregnancy. The sight reached that part of Josephat's wife's spirit that still remained to be crushed. She ran past Martha, they brushed shoulders, Martha staggered a little, but Josephat's wife moved on.

'May I have 20 cents,' Martha called out after her.

That night, Josephat's wife ate only her tears.

V

In her dreams, Josephat's wife turned to follow the sound of a crying child. At Hartley Mine, her husband Josephat eased himself out of the foreman's wife's friend, Rebecca, who kept the bottle store. He turned his mind to the increasing joylessness of his marriage bed. Before, his wife had opened all of herself to him, had taken all of him in, rising, rising, rising to meet him, before falling, falling down with him.

Now it was only after prayers for a child that she lay back, her eye only on the outcome. 'It is a matter of course that we will have children,' Josephat had thought when they married. 'Boys, naturally. Two boys, and maybe a girl.'

He no longer cared what came. All he wanted was to stop the pain. He eased himself out of Rebecca, lay back, and thought of his wife in Easterly.

VI

The winter of the birth of Martha's child was a winter of broken promises. The government promised that prices would go down and salaries up. Instead, the opposite happened. The opposition promised that there would be protests. Instead they bickered over who should hold three of the top six positions of leadership. From the skies fell *zvimvuramabwe*, hailstones of frozen heat that melted on the laughing tongues of Easterly's children. The children jabbed fingers at the corpses of the frogs petrified in the stream near the farm. The water tap burst.

*Mai*James and *Ba*Toby argued over whether this winter was colder than the one in the last year of the war. *Mai*James spoke for the winter of the war, *Ba*Toby for the present winter. 'You were no higher than Toby *uyu*,' *Mai*James said with no rancour. 'What can you possibly remember about that?'

It was the government that settled the matter.

'Our satellite images indicate that a warm front is expected from the Eastern Highlands. The warm weather is expected to hold, so pack away those heaters and jerseys. And a very good night to you from your friendly meteorologist, Stan Mukasa. You are listening to *nhepfenyuro yenyu*, Radio Zimbabwe. Over to Nathaniel Moyo now, with *You and Your Farm*.'

This meant that *Ba*Toby was right. If the government said inflation would go down, it was sure to rise. If they said there was a bumper harvest, starvation would follow. 'If the government says the sky is blue, we should all

The winter of the birth of Martha's child was a winter of broken promises.

look up to check,' said *BaToby*.

That winter brought the threat of more evictions. There had been talk of evictions before, there was nothing new there. They brushed it aside and put more illegal firewood on their fires. Godwills Mabhena who lived next to *Mai*James burnt his best trousers.

VII

By the middle of that winter, all of Easterly knew that Martha was expecting a child. The men made ribald comments about where she could have found a man to do the deed. The women worked to convince themselves that it was a matter external to Easterly, to themselves, to their men. 'You know how she disappears for days on end sometimes,' said *Mai*Toby. 'And you know how wild some of those street kids are.'

'Street kids? Some of them are men.'

'My point exactly.'

'Should someone not do something, I don't know, call someone, maybe the police?' asked the female half of the couple whom nobody really knew.

'Yes, you are very right,' said *Mai*James. 'Someone should do something.'

'That woman acts like we are in the suburbs,' *Mai*James later said to *Mai*Toby. 'Police? Easterly? *Ho-do*!' They clapped hands together as they laughed.

'*Haiwa*, even if you call them, would they come? It took what, two days for them to come that time when Titus Zunguza ...'

'*Ndizvo*, they will not come if *we* have a problem, what about for Martha?'

'And even if they did, what then?'

The female half of the couple that no one really knew remembered that her brother's wife attended the same church as a woman who worked in social welfare. 'You mean Maggie,' her brother's wife said. 'Maggie moved *ku*South with her husband long back. I am sure by now her husband drives a really good car, *mbishi chaiyo*.'

She got the number of the social department from the directory. But the number she dialled was out of service, and after three more attempts, she gave it up. 'There is time enough to do something,' she thought.

And when the children ran around Martha and laughed, 'Go and play somewhere else,' *Mai*Toby scolded them. 'Did your mothers not teach you to respect your elders? And as for you, *wemazinzeve*,' she turned to Tobias. 'Come and wash yourself.'

The winter of Martha's baby was the winter of Josephat's leave from the mine.

It was the last winter of all.

VIII

On the night that Martha gave birth, Josephat's wife walked to Easterly from a praying field near Mabvuku. She did not notice the residents gathered in clusters around their homes. Only when she walked past Martha's house did the sounds of Easterly reach her. Was that a moan, she wondered. Yes, that sounded like a cry of pain. Without thinking, she walked-ran into Martha's house. By the light of the moon falling through the plastic sheeting, she saw Martha, naked on her mattress, the head of her baby between her legs.

'I'll get help,' Josephat's wife said. 'I'll get help.'

She made for the door. Another moan stopped her and she turned back. She knelt by the mattress and looked between Martha's legs. '20 cents,' Martha said and fainted.

Josephat's wife dug into the still woman and grabbed a shoulder. Her hand slipped. She cried tears of frustration. Again, she dug, she pulled, she eased the baby out. Martha's blood flowed onto the mattress. 'Tie the cord,' Josephat's wife said out loud and tied it.

She looked around for something with which to cut the cord. There was nothing, and the baby almost slipped from her hands. Through a film of tears she chewed on Martha's flesh, closing her mind to the taste of blood, she chewed and tugged on the cord until the baby was free. She wiped the blood from her mouth with the back of her hand. The baby cried, she held it to her chest, and felt an answering rise in her breasts. She sobbed out laughter. Her heart loud in her chest, she took up the first thing she saw, a poppy-covered dress, and wrapped the baby in it.

In her house she heated water and wiped the baby clean. She dressed it in the clothes of the children who had slipped from her. She put the baby to breast and he sucked on air until both fell asleep. This was the vision that met Josephat when he returned after midnight. 'Whose child is that?'

'God has given me this child,' she said.

In the half-light Josephat saw his wife's face and his stomach turned to water. 'I will go to the police,' he said. 'You cannot snatch a child and expect me to do nothing.'

His wife clutched the baby closer. "This is God's will. We cannot let Martha look after it. How can we let her look after a child?'

'What are you talking about, who is Martha?'

'Martha Martha, I left her in her house, she gave birth to it. She can't look after it, this is God's ...'

Josephat blundered out of the room. A great fear seized him. He counted, calculated and found it was just as he thought.

Ten months before he had arrived home and found his wife not there. 'She has gone to an all night prayer-session,' a neighbour said. A wave of anger and repulsion washed over him. He had only this and the next night before he was to go back.

'A wasted journey,' he thought.

He had gone to the beer garden in Mabvuku. The smell of his wife was in the blankets when he returned, but she wasn't home. The hunger for a woman came over him. He left his house to urinate and relieved himself against the wall through the pain of his erection. A movement to the right caught his eye. He saw the shape of a woman. His mind turned immediately to thoughts of sorcery. He lit a cigarette and in the flare of the match saw the mad woman. 'May I have 20 cents,' she said, and lifted her up dress.

The need for a woman hit him again. He almost staggered beneath its force. He followed the woman to her house, and in the corner he grappled her to the ground, forced himself on her, let himself go, and in that moment came to himself. 'Forgive me,' he said, 'forgive me.'

He did not look at her until she said, 'May I have 20 cents.' He looked at her smiling face with horror; he fell over his trousers and backwards into the door. He pulled up his trousers as he ran and did not stop running until he reached his house. 'It is not me,' he said again and again. 'This is not me.'

His hand shook out a cigarette to light. There was a smell of burning filter, he had lit the wrong end. He bargained with God, he bargained with the spirits on both his mother's and his father's sides. He bargained with himself. He would touch no woman other than his wife. He would not leave her, even if she never bore him a child. And even as he later gave in to Rebecca, to Juliet and the others, he told himself that these others meant nothing at all.

357

IX

Josephat found Martha lying on the floor on her back. He raised her left arm, it fell back. In a second he considered all possibilities. He covered her body with a blanket, and left the house. Snatches of conversation reached his ears from the group gathered around *BaToby*. For the first time he realised that Easterly was still up, unusually so; it was well after midnight and yet here were people gathered around in knots in the moonlight. He moved close, he had to know, had anyone seen, what had they seen?

The Babel of voices was interlaced with incredulity and fear.

'They were at Union Avenue today, they took all the wares.'

'They just threw everything in the back of the lorries.'

'Didn't care what they broke. Just threw everything.'

'In Mufakose it was the same, they destroyed everything.'

'Siyaso is gone, Mupedzanhamo too.'

'Union Avenue flea market.'

'*Kwese neku*Africa Unity, it is all cleared.'

'Even *kuma*surburbs, they attacked Chisipite market.'

'My cousin-brother said they will come for the houses next.'

'They would not dare.'

'*Hanzi* there are bulldozers at Porta Farm as we speak.'

'If they can destroy Siyaso ...'

'But they can't destroy Siyaso.'

'That is not possible,' said *Ba*Toby, 'I will not believe it.'

'I was there,' Godwills Mabhena said. 'I was there.'

'You men, the only thing you know is to talk and talk,' *Mai*James said. 'Where are you when action is required? Where were you when they took down Siyaso? *Nyararazvako*.' The last word of comfort was directed to the crying child on her hip. His mother was one of three women arrested in Mufakose, two for attempting to take their clothes off in protest, the third, the child's mother, for clinging to her box of produce even as a truncheon came down, again, again, on her bleeding knuckles. The child sniffled into *Mai*James's bosom.

'I will not believe it,' *Ba*Toby said again.

X

In his house Josephat took down a navy blue suitcase and threw clothes into it. His wife held the baby in a tender lock and crooned a lullaby that

Josephat's own mother had sung to him.

'*Your child will not be consoled, sister.*'

'We are leaving,' he said.

'*She cries for her mother, gone away.*'

'We have to pack and leave.'

'*Gone away, to Chidyamupunga.*'

'The bulldozers are coming.'

'*Chidyamupunga, cucumbers are rotting.*'

'We have to leave now.'

'*Cucumbers are rotting beyond Mungezi.*'

'Ellen, please.'

She looked up at him. He swallowed. Her smile in the half-light put him in mind of Martha. 'We have to leave,' he said . He picked up an armful of baby clothes. He held them in his hands for a moment, then stuffed them into the suitcase and closed it.

'It is time to go,' he said. As they walked, to Josephat's mind came the words of his mother's lullaby.

'*Cucumbers are rotting beyond Mungezi.*
Beyond Mungezi there is a big white knife,
A big white knife to cut good meat,
To cut good meat dried on a dry bare rock ...'

They stole out of Easterly Farm and into the dawn.

When the morning rose over Easterly, not even the children noticed Martha's absence. They were running away from the bulldozers. It was only when Josephat and his wife had almost reached Chegutu that the bulldozers, having razed the entire line of houses from *Mai*James to *Ba*Toby, having crushed beneath them the house from which Josephat and his wife had fled, and having razed that of the new couple that no one really knew, finally lumbered towards Martha's house in the corner and exposed her body, stiff in death, her child's afterbirth wedged between her legs.

Petina Gappah is a Zimbabwean writer. She lives in Geneva where she works as a lawyer. She loves Kenya.

The War Hero
Akiyo Michael Kasaija

This is so much destruction
I lie in some blind turmoil
Groaning at the tatters that was-
my latest collection of verse
the viscera of earth
spluttered and gaping
groaning and laughing-
silly war, who will live to tell it all
when you kill me-
I know what its like
the war trench in my mind is fresh-
cannot save me-can it?
From missiles that assault me.

You can assemble me to run
like an elite machine
In a cushion of theories
I can coast along endlessly
making a melody to every of your muse;
this is no school for me
standing here desperate to rot
sludges of broken ego
sauntering …waving in the midday sun
Idly sketching your next thought
building what they can call you,
you could be anything my pen wishes
If you let me-
What is this politics of referendums,
and of Kampala's streets?
That give me tranquil in the hours I wander
on streets with hidden souls
Buildings-
Moonlight-
This is Pilkington Road
unhurrying in its ascent
to meet Nile Avenue,
the shadows craftily beckoning
to some quick pleasure,
the few lights of Kampala
blazing in a lighted chord
a vehicle scuttling out of some shadow
to blast its way along the blank road.
A madman strutting on the pavement
Singing
I could live here forever
If you let me-
This is some destruction
And I lie in some blind turmoil
I cannot fight you anymore
When you decide you are a General
This is not my kind of war
Give me my pencil please-
-wf -

Fie ye great men!

Akiyo Michael Kasaija

Great man
You wrought your wield
   To sue the wretched from this world
    Damn!
   To cull them with sufferings
     That benefits you
     That pity, great man, breaks our hearts.
      Break my rapier tip
   For my venom boils hot
Ready to strike someone.
   The wretched people
     Make me draw tears,
       To invoke such passions in me
         You great men also ire me a lot.

   Why soldier?
       Why do you think but of death
     Screw you soldier!
   You stole my home
Damn you soldier, damn you!
zombie of the great men
Can't you think clearly on your own?
See what you do to us, soldier.
Can't you take a little pity soldier?
The great men with cataracts in their eyes,
Soldier,
You are my hope, soldier
Love is the dire need of the wretched earth.

                              – wf –

Akiyo Michael Kasaija is a Ugandan poet.

361

Gold
Idil Abshir

Cultures like liquid gold
Beauty which continually unfolds
This is my Africa
Our light was robbed and we continue to shine
But reflectors, cameras and Photoshop manage to block that out.
Our pain is treated like a disease with no origin
I yearn to yell that the only thing in our world which was ever one-sided was
Immaculate Conception
Within and without our dealings are riddled with deception
Treatment in customs feels like quarantine for contagious infection!

According to Bono DNA is the main reason to step up and help
GAP agrees
In place of strength and compassion is a separation of 6 degrees
How will any of us ever feel free?
You can sew up our outside but our inside still bleeds
You can't put a Band-Aid on a broken heart
We have to build trust and re-grow our missing parts.

I am afraid our liquid gold will dry
Our cultures will die
And our children will be born with golden glitter on their faces never knowing why.

Idil Abshir is a young Somali woman who was born and raised in Kenya. She is currently studying Writing at The New School University.

DIE NASTY
Kitu Sewer

Die nasty ita die viasty
Criminals hawakuji cheap
Tip of the iceberg

Hajaribu kufit nafasi
Yangu wasikufeed mabaki
Mix makali naka alvaro
Orango ni ka manu diba
Ngo kwa saxophone
Switch vaco usioys kuwa
Markable life yangu yote
Ni parable
Hit kwa mangoro zenu
U hadi zangaro

Paul Mboya, aka **'Kitu Sewer,'** *is a Nairobi-based artist, musician and poet. The name Kitu Sewer refers to the environment he grew up in, near the Dandora dumpsite.*

WATU PEOPLE'S DILEMMA
Kitu Sewer

Top layer za ma mest player
Umangwa na ma back bencher
Speak of the devil na anatokea
Talk of the mayor na alitokomea na chain
The moreunawapunng
Uzia mzigo the more heavier
The more tunaumia akli the more crazier
Kati ya nyama na mboga gain healthier
Hewa safi ni suffocater
Kati ya God na dawa
Za kulevya nani saviour
Kulingana na report ya Steadman wangapi ni ma walking dead man

Watu hawataki ma
Statue za kina dedan tunawajua
Wanataka statues poa ya
Kuishi wamadha na watoi
Waache kuteta
Kwako ni gain clever
Ni kupee fish urudi tena
Au ndoano uji save forever

God's Blessings

Ada Udechukwu

Mama's invitation for a thanksgiving service at GOD'S BLESSINGS UNLIMITED, the Pentecostal church she attended, arrived well in advance, and neither I nor Osita could figure a way of declining without hurting his mother's feelings. So, on this appointed Sunday, we picked her up and left our four year old daughter Adamma in the care of Mama's housegirl.

Out on the expressway, with Enugu several miles behind us, our Peugeot picked up speed, easily overtaking the few vehicles we chanced upon. And as we drove south, I gazed at the lush vegetation flashing past on both sides of the road—dust-coated elephant grass on the fringes and stunted cashew trees and farmlands of cassava plants further off. From time to time, the car was buffeted by strong winds, and then clouds of dust rose from the road's unpaved laterite shoulder, to add yet another coat of red to the bushy grass growing along the roadside.

The atmosphere in the car was stifling. I couldn't decide what was worse: the heat or Mama's presence behind me; together, they made for an almost unbearable situation. But I didn't dare roll my window down further than its allotted crack because Mama complained the wind disturbed her and the dust aggravated her catarrh.

Mama kept up a constant chatter in the back seat, her voice sharp with irritation, and her knees digging into the back of my seat as she moved around. She went through her usual litany: *Osita ought to return home to the village more regularly and attend to his obligations as head of the Okoye family; the new house in the family compound needed to be completed; ten thousand naira was needed urgently by the -m-nna for Papa Emeka's funeral...* While Mama spoke, both Osita and I sat in silence, only exchanging exasperated looks whenever she leaned into the space between our seats, to emphasize a particular point.

An hour into the journey, Mama's arm skimmed past my head. She pointed out our exit. Osita merged onto a feeder road and, under Mama's guidance, drove a short distance to a roadside market where she instructed him to pull up beside a mound of yams. The shriveled tubers didn't look promising, and when cooked were sure to be dry and fibrous, for it was early May and the harvest of new yams still some months away. Nevertheless, Mama disembarked and began bargaining for yams. While Osita left to open the trunk so the animals could get some air, I watched Mama's exchange with the yam sellers through my side mirror. She picked over the yams in different mounds, selecting tubers, returning them, and taking up others before finally settling on two tubers.

Osita put Mama's yams on the floor behind his seat and left to close the trunk. A hoarse bleat sounded from the back of the car where he struggled with Mama's ram, trying to force it down. The chickens responded with a ruckus of flapping wings, squawking and scratching the floor of the trunk.

Finally, Osita got the animals quieted and secured in their respective corners and we drove away, continuing down the road.

About ten minutes later, we entered a small village and Mama directed Osita to a narrow dirt road. From all sides, branches reached out and scratched the car, forcing Osita to swing the steering abruptly as he avoided them and navigated the uneven terrain. Some way down, he hesitated in front of a large eroded pothole in the middle of the road; Mama assured him it was passable. Shifting gears and inching into the depression, Osita winced as the car's chassis hit the earth, grating against the soil, until we got back on level ground. At the end of the road, we burst out into a clearing.

Ahead of us, a low gate swung on its hinges. We entered a compound ringed by a flimsy wall of raffia mats. Three zinc lean-tos were ranged round a central unpainted building where a group of people were assembled. Within minutes of our entrance, a loud cry went up and several people dressed in flowing white robes and caps—identical to the ones Mama, Osita, and I wore—ran toward us, descending on the car like a flock of cattle egrets. Mama rolled down her window, calling out greetings.

Osita brought the car to a stop in a grassy lot. The three of us got out and joined Mama's fellow supplicants for a trek to the church. Our procession moved slowly: bare feet solemnly treading the earth and white gowns billowing in the wind. Without realizing it, I stepped on Mama's heel. She eyed me and sucked her teeth in disgust. Wordlessly, I moved back and kept pace with Osita. While we walked together, I picked and cradled stones with my toes, counting eight before my feet hit the paved floor of the church entrance. I hobbled in with the last tiny pebble tucked between the first two toes of my right foot, pleased at my even score.

'Praise God, Sistas, Broda,' a man greeted, beckoning us forward.

We passed through an arch of plaited palm fronds and stood in a small foyer. 'Blessings, Brother Okoro,' Mama said, one palm flattened against her breast.

Osita repeated the greeting.

Mama poked her elbow into my side.

'Blessings,' I murmured under my breath.

Mama's elbow dug into me again.

'B-les-sings, Bro-ther O-ko-ro.' I dragged the syllables, my voice pitched high and my fingers drumming against my chest.

Brother Okoro shook his head, eyed me, and then moved to attend to

367

the person behind. My eyes locked with Mama's. I held her gaze and turned away only when Osita tugged at my hand.

Mama stepped ahead of us and we followed her to a row of benches in the middle of the hall. Squeezed between her and Osita, I perched on the edge of my seat, holding my breath against the nauseating mix of sweat and incense in the air. For what seemed like an interminable length of time, I sat fidgeting in my seat and listening to unfamiliar hymns.

An hour passed. The singing stopped and a low chanting filled the hall. People around us swayed in their seats; some stood in rapture, waving their hands in the air, grasping at holiness visible only to them. Mama pulled me to my feet. She chanted along with the rest of the congregation; I rose and sat, bowed and kneeled, taking my cue from her. Osita followed suit.

A bell rang. Hushed whispers filled the air. Mama leaned across to Osita and whispered, 'Pastor Olode.'

The congregation rose and faced the aisle. A man stood there, dressed in a white robe embroidered with bright red and gold threads; behind him, two women rattled beaded gourds. Pastor Olode made his way down the aisle walking in step to the rhythm knocked out by the women. Row after row, he reached out and laid hands on the bowed heads thrust to him. Midway down, a woman he anointed wailed 'Jesus,' and fell back clutching her chest.

Pastor Olode stood at our row. Mama stepped forward. She held her palms up, knelt, and then grasped the hem of Pastor Olode's robe, placing it to her lips. I sneaked a look at Osita, but he was engrossed in the scene. A few seconds later, the Pastor's stocky frame faced the next row, and Mama was beside me again. Only now, she pressed both hands against her heaving breast.

Tambourines shook, an electronic keyboard whined, and the lead singer broke into a solo, welcoming Pastor Olode to the altar. He smiled, executed a few dance steps, and signaled for quiet. The music faded and four men lined up in pairs on opposite sides of a red carpet, facing each other with their arms extended and linked. Pastor strode through the men and walked up to a raised dais where he took his seat on a velvet upholstered throne-like chair.

Mama got up, and Osita and I followed her to the back of the church to collect her offering. I picked up the yams; Mama grasped the chickens by their legs, one in each hand; and Osita took hold of the ram's raffia leash. In single file, we made our way back down the aisle accompanied by a gospel tune. At the bottom of the dais, two warders relieved us of our gifts and we were directed to ascend and kneel before Pastor Olode.

'Sister Eunice, Brother Osita and wife, we thank God for your life.' Pastor spread his arms over us.

A loud 'Amen' burst forth from the congregation.

Mama got up and faced them. She waved her arms from side to side and called out, 'Praise the Lord!'

'Alleluia,' the congregation replied. Osita chorused along with them, winking at me when he caught me looking at him. I smiled and linked my arm through his, enjoying the conspiracy we shared. I knew that being here meant nothing to either of us. Mama's conversion was a private joke between us and our attendance at this thanksgiving service was simply to humor her.

A chord broke from the electric keyboard and Mama's falsetto filled the hall. *'Higher, higher Jesus, lift me Jesus higher,'* she sang, pitching her body forward and stabbing her index finger at the ceiling. Soon, other voices joined in and the congregation swayed as one to the rhythm of the music.

Osita drew me to him, one arm resting lightly on my waist. I moved in tandem.

Mama held her hands up for quiet. 'Brothers and Sisters in Christ, our God is mighty. If not for his power and almighty grace, I would not be standing here today. You see my son, Engineer Osita Okoye...' Mama pointed at Osita, paused to wipe her dry brow, and continued, 'the Lord entered him that fateful day and took the steering from his hand as we entered the valley of the shadow of death so that we...'

'We feared no evil!' The congregation chorused.

'On the expressway, vehicles passed us fiam-fiam.' Mama skimmed one palm against the other to illustrate how fast the cars traveled.

For the rest of Mama's hour-long testimony about the armed robbery attack she and Osita eluded weeks ago, she stopped at appropriate intervals to utter phrases like 'praise the Lord,' 'allelu-alleluia,' and 'cleansed by the blood of Jesus.' At the end, she mentioned how bullets bounced off the car the moment Osita drove into the robber's ambush because of the protection Pastor provided.

I pictured the two stickers adorned with God's Blessings' logos plastered on the front and back windshields of Mama's car, and the small bottle of holy water she kept on the dashboard, and marveled at her naiveté. But the congregation rose and applauded. Some shook their heads in wonder; others exclaimed, 'Chineke! Na wah oh! - d-egwu!'

Mama turned and beckoned to Osita and me. We joined her and the congregation cheered. I bowed my head, mortified that these people believed I might be one of them. The three of us walked back to Pastor Olode and knelt before him. Pastor spread his arms out, embracing the air above our heads, and saying, 'Let us pray, Brothers and Sisters in Christ.' Then he launched into a lengthy prayer, thanking God for everything: the church, the congregation, Mama, the whole Okoye family, and finally, for allowing him the privilege of leading God's sheep to the Promised Land. While Pastor Olode prayed, Mama clasped her hands tightly in front of her, her eyes pinched shut, and her lips pursed. At certain points in the prayer, she rubbed her palms and sucked her breath in, savoring Pastor's words. I sneaked a look at my watch: it was 2.00PM; we'd been in church for over three hours.

After the last of a series of Amens, Pastor Olode clasped his palms round our heads—Mama first, me next, and Osita last—murmuring blessings. When Pastor was through, we rose to our feet and he pulled Osita aside. They stood a little ways from me: Pastor's fleshy lips a fraction from Osita's ear, and Osita deferentially tilting his head to receive whatever it was Pastor offered. I strained to catch the conversation, but heard only fragments. None of which made any sense

Pastor Olode clapped three times. He linked hands with Osita and raised their intertwined arms. 'Praise God, Brother Osita is now a child of God!'

The congregation responded with whistles and cheers. Osita grinned. Mama jumped forward and ululated. Her sweat-beaded face shone as she danced around Pastor and Osita. Mama circled them twice; arms raised, and waist swinging left and right, she kept repeating, 'Thank you, Lord.'

Pastor reached for me. I backed away from his outstretched palm. He smiled and said, 'In good time, my sister: God's time.'

At home, later in evening, Osita and I joked, making fun of Mama's testimony and his part in the drama. Osita mimicked Pastor Olode's guttural voice, asking if I accepted Christ as my personal savior and we burst out laughing.

But, in the days following Mama's thanksgiving service, while I struggled against her persistent invitations to prayer meetings—begging off with the excuse of my pregnancy, she filled Osita's head with her superstitious religiosity.

T wo weeks later, Osita begged me to accompany Mama to see Pastor

Olode. Somehow, Mama convinced him that a healing consultation was vital to the safe delivery of the baby we expected. So I agreed to Osita's request, telling myself no harm could come of it, and that nothing bad could come of few extra prayers. We were both anxious about this birth.

Mama and I left for God's Blessings that afternoon. I was surprised by the transformation there. Grass covered the once denuded grounds of the compound; shrubs and flowering plants lined a stone flagged walkway to the main building; and identical pre-fabricated bungalows now stood in place of the zinc structures I remembered from my earlier visit. In the parking lot, a collection of BMWs, Mercedes, and other glamorous cars lined up in neat squares.

Inside the church, we were greeted by a warder who led us to Pastor Olode's office. There, Mama outlined my case, telling Pastor about our misfortune: two miscarriages in the three years since the birth of my first and only child. As she spoke, Pastor's bloodshot eyes darted over my body and rested for an uncomfortably long time on my middle section.

Pastor Olode placed a palm on my stomach; his fingers crept upward and grazed my breast.

My skin tingled warningly and I drew away.

'The work of Satan, my Sister.' Pastor smiled and turned to Mama.

Mama stared dazedly as if the Holy Ghost were before her while Pastor Olode proceeded to explain how a particularly potent demon dwelt in my womb. She wrung her hands and appealed to him to help her. Neither she nor Pastor spoke with me. After a while, the two of them embraced. Pastor calmed Mama with requests that she leave the matter in God's hands. Then the two of them fell to their knees and dragged me down. Pastor Olode prayed for us, his words slurred with exaggerated emotion. At the end, we rose and Pastor told Mama that he was the only man who could save me because no doctor could battle Satan.

Pastor waved Mama away from me. She stepped back and flattened herself against a wall. Chalking a circle around me and marking four crosses at points north, south, west, and east, he walked along the perimeter and scattered water at me, calling out, 'Father, forgive her, unworthy vessel.' Then he entered the circle, knocked two sticks over my head, dropped them, and made the sign of the cross.

The front of my dress was soaked, the outline of my nipples and navel clear, and I saw he was aroused.

I dipped my hands in a basin and stirred the soapy suds, ignoring the provocation, forcing myself to keep calm. "When was this decided?"

Pastor Olode presented Mama with a bottle of murky yellow liquid: the medicine required to prepare my body so I might receive God's protection and bounty.

Later, at home, Osita listened intently while Mama relayed Pastor's diagnosis. That night he brought me a small cup that stank of urine. I looked at him with disgust.

'Just take it, will you. If I have to force you, I will.' Osita pushed the cup to my lips.

His voice held unmistakable menace and, suddenly, I saw the excuses I'd lulled myself with for what they were: fear. Osita's eyes frightened me; my hand rose to take the cup, my lips parted, and I sipped. While I gagged and swallowed, Osita stood over me and made a hasty sign of the cross.

From then on, he regularly spoke to me of his new faith, mouthing platitudes about true subjugation to God, and how all misfortune evaporated if a man was born again. He immersed himself in church activities, not only going to Sunday service, but also attending bible classes and mid-week services. Some weekends, after vigils that kept him at church overnight, I barely recognized the feverish unkempt body standing before me and speaking about Pastor Olode's miracles: the new cars that filled Brother Innocent's garages, the visa to America Sister Amaka secured.

Some days later, things changed for the worse after Pastor introduced Osita to certain influential Brothers at God's Blessings. With their help, Osita began securing key contracts for his engineering firm. And now, God's Blessings consumed Osita, as it did Mama. He bombarded me daily with misinterpreted Bible passages and stories about the miracles performed by Pastor Olode. If I questioned the veracity of his statements, he asked whether I wanted to deny him his just reward.

Soon, God's Blessings encroached on the most intimate spaces of our lives as Osita sank deeper into irrational behavior. He fasted and prayed according to Pastor Olode's stipulations. He decorated our flat with tawdry religious posters; candles and incense stood at strategic points in a bid to ward off the demons Pastor warned about. And worst of all, Osita invited his new Brothers-and-Sisters-in-Christ—people I didn't know—to visit regularly. They never left without some gift of food or money. And sometimes, at the weekends, they stayed overnight for vigils. At such times, I endured restless nights filled with the sound of indecipherable prayers and chanting and woke to find sleeping bodies littering the parlor.

After the fourth of these all night vigils, Osita told me of a vision Pastor Olode relayed at Sunday service concerning a break in communication: the Lord decreed riches for Osita to claim, but an unbeliever stood in the way. Incredulously, I listened to Osita threaten me if I continued to keep him from partaking of Pastor's prophesies. I couldn't understand why he didn't see what a charlatan Pastor Olode was, but there was no reasoning with him.

I looked from behind a curtain pulled against the parlor window, fingering its plush red velvet and watching Osita leave with Adamma. She skipped around him, cutting into his strides toward the black Pathfinder he'd brought home a week before. At the car, the two of them waved at the kitchen window, missing me by a room. For a second, I allowed myself to hope Osita might come back. That's all it would take; it wouldn't matter that at breakfast he shouted at me in front of Adamma, again.

Osita dropped his arm and helped Adamma into her seat. He secured her seat belt, got behind the wheel, slammed his door, and drove off. The grind of tires sent up a cloud of red dust and when it cleared reckless marks lined the unpaved driveway. He'd be late coming home, taking Adamma out from school early to attend mid-week Supplication Service with Pastor Olode before returning home.

Drawing aside the curtain, I breathed in the scent of dampened earth sent up from showers somewhere in the distance. An ominous blue-black swathe blotted the overcast sky. Thunder sounded and lightning streaked across in a jagged spear. Within minutes, a heavy wind set the frangipani trees along the drive shaking like frenzied dervishes. Rain drops fell in thuds, pock-marking the laterite. Diagonal lashes followed and soon, muddy red rivulets coursed over the drive. I shut the louvered windows against the downpour and laughed softly. Osita should be here to see *this* miraculous cleansing.

Breakfast stood uneaten on the table: glasses of orange juices, twin bowls of cold guinea corn porridge, and plates of coagulated eggs. Like mute sentinels, they mocked me and I recalled Osita's hateful words spewed earlier in the morning when he harangued me about my lack of faith and told me I had only my stubborn self to blame if anything happened to the baby in my womb. It seemed that Pastor's awful potion—which I took every morning— was not enough. Pastor required one final ceremony.

Each time he brought it up, I told Osita I wasn't going anywhere near Pastor Olode. I was well past the crucial months now and my regular antenatal visits and checkups with my gynecologist Dr. Onuora showed that everything was fine. Still, we weren't taking chances: I was to undergo a caesarean for this birth and the doctor decided that some time in the week preceding my due date, the baby would be delivered. I knew this child would live, with or without Pastor Olode's intervention. Secretly though, I still worried a little about the baby—unable to put aside the memory of my miscarriages. I stared into the flickering flame of the tea light and pictured Osita holding our son at his naming ceremony. *Ositadimma*. I whispered the name, thinking of its meaning and what it prophesied...*if things begin to be good from today...* Osita would come to his senses once our son was born. He had to.

The flame in front of me sunk into its pool of melted wax and snuffed out. My gaze shifted uneasily from the ceramic warmer in which it stood, and I looked at the teapot, its chipped spout bearing the mark of Osita's first religious retreat the weekend before.

The morning of that Friday, Osita nonchalantly informed me Pastor mandated two days of prayer and fasting for all the new converts—Osita, Brother Obi, Sister Ifeyinwa, Sister Caro, Brother Ako, and his wife, Sister Margaret. They were to test their faith by spending time in isolation at the church's prayer house. How convenient I thought, this matching number of brothers and sisters. But I kept my suspicions to myself, knowing it was hopeless to try and talk Osita out of going. Then, on Sunday morning, as Osita joined me for breakfast, the self-righteous smirk of accomplishment on his face confirmed my fears. Once again, he delivered yet another message from Pastor Olode instructing that I prayerfully consider the divisive wedge my lack of support drove between my husband and myself.

I sat quietly while Osita spoke, oblivious of the food in his mouth. He embellished Pastor's message, telling me I should know the time had come for me to understand that he, Osita, must have a partner—a true believer to share in what the Lord prepared for him. I watched a moist bread crumb quiver on his lip. Pastor's words goaded me and I picked up the teapot, pouring its contents into Osita's already full cup. An amber waterfall fell into the saucer and slid in a thin stream to the edge of the table. Osita cursed, grabbed the teapot from my hands, and threw it on the floor. After that, he never spoke to me again about what went on at church, but I couldn't forget, knowing as I did, that plenty of Sisters would do anything Pastor Olode asked of them; Brothers, too.

I roused myself, smiling ruefully at the sudden image of a wild orgy that surfaced in my mind.

For the rest of the morning and early afternoon, I moved about the flat, listlessly attending to chores. I ventured into Adamma's bedroom at regular intervals. Hers was the only room in our home Osita had not tampered with and I felt safe there, able, if only momentarily, to lose myself and forget the events of the past several weeks.

Hours later, standing at the stove and staring into a congealed mass of soup that I'd warmed twice already, the compound gate swung back and Osita drove in. I started water boiling for garri and looked out the kitchen window. Adamma got out of the car clutching two small bananas in one hand and a plastic bag of groundnuts in the other. She dashed to the flat, calling out, 'Mummy, I went to the club.'

I met her at the front door and squeezed her body against mine.

'Sorry we're late. We stopped for a treat.' Osita looked over Adamma's head and into the flat at some distant point beyond me.

His lie exasperated me and without speaking, I turned away.

In the kitchen, the kettle whistled and I hastened to it. I poured hot water into a bowl and sifted two cups of garri over it. Transfixed by the swollen cassava grains, I stood for a moment, wanting to cry out, to succumb to the hopelessness I felt at the simple rhythms of my tasks. Low puttering sounds came from the soup pot on the stove and I stabbed at the sticky okro with a spoon. With the serving bowls in hand, I arched my back against the swing door and pivoted into the dining room.

A sharp pain in my pelvis caused me to stop. And although it passed quickly—with the baby's limbs rippling the front of my dress in a wave of small knobs—I hesitated.

'Everyday, everyday, garri, everyday,' Adamma sang, dancing around me.

'Be quiet Adamma, it is time to bless.' Osita pulled out her chair and pointed to it.

Adamma looked from me to her father. I nodded and she sat and bowed her head. I did the same. Osita prayed his usual ten minutes and we ate in silence. After the meal, I left with Adamma to settle her down for siesta.

When I returned to the dinning room, Osita was still sitting at the table. I cleared the dishes and went into the kitchen. Osita followed me and stood, leaning against the door while I stacked the dirty dishes on the kitchen table and filled the washing basins with water.

'Añuli, Mama is bringing a house girl to live with us tomorrow.' He kicked the table leg.

I dipped my hands in a basin and stirred the soapy suds, ignoring the provocation, forcing myself to keep calm. 'When was this decided?'

'What does it matter? You are in no condition to be doing housework and I don't see why I should either. Besides, you'll need help when the baby comes. Anyway, the arrangements have already been made.'

'Osita, please, Adamma.' I placed a finger to my lips, then turned away and sponged off a plate, saying, 'Anyway, my mother will be here as soon as the baby is born, you know that.'

Osita stepped up behind me and my body tensed.

'Look at me, Añuli, and show respect.' He gripped my shoulder and turned me around. 'For how long will your mother be here? What happens when she leaves? Mama says you cannot expect me to waste my time fetching water, cooking, and doing housework for you when I have more pressing duties.'

'Mama says, Mama says. I am tired of hearing about your mother.'

Osita's arm swung out. He brought his hand down, looking at it as if it didn't belong to him.

I woke late. My limbs felt heavy, my ankles swollen. Bands of sunlight shimmered against the bedroom walls. A film of sweat covered my forehead and I wiped it. My nightdress clung to me in patches where perspiration soaked through and I lifted it, fanning myself. I knew I needed to get dressed and be ready for Osita when he came to take me to the hospital, but I wasn't able to summon the energy. During the last few days, it had become increasingly difficult for me to do the simplest things for myself. I couldn't understand it.

With some effort, I sat up and smoothed the rumpled sheets around my legs. I meticulously picked at each wrinkle, attempting to straighten the tangled bedcovers, but as soon as one had been attended to, another appeared.

Outside, rain drops spattered against the window sill and landed on the leaves of the croton shrubs with a soft *slurp-slurp* sound. I turned to the window behind me and peered through its louvered blades, following lines of glittering raindrops as they fell from the asbestos roofing, exploded on the cement pavement below, and settled into worn grooves scooped by rainy seasons past. Twin puddles wavered in my eyes as they, too, filled.

The rain broke off and I continued to sit there, twisted toward the window, gazing at the leaves on the trees. Soon, a dissonant melody interrupted my reverie. From the parlor, the voice of our new house girl Ngozi swelled with her latest gospel favorite: 'Jesus is my savior. I will-u-follow him.' As she sang, dull thuds from the furniture she dragged around accompanied the shrill fervor of her words.

Without warning, my bowels churned. I slipped into a pair of rubber slippers and walked stiffly to the connecting bathroom while my stomach emitted a prolonged growl. There, I sat on the toilet for a time, my eyes shut as I strained to relieve myself. The void in front of me filled: *Mama and Osita whispering...Pastor Olode scattering water at me....* I shivered and opened my eyes.

Back in bed, still feeling nauseous, I lay down. Black spots blinded my vision for seconds at a time. I placed my palm on my stomach. When last had I felt my baby? Yesterday? I couldn't remember and my heart beat quickened. Why wasn't the baby moving?

The compound gate opened and I looked out. Osita was home early.

My carryall stood in a corner, packed with everything I needed. Weeks ago, Adamma helped me fold the tiny undershirts and cotton nappies. When she handed me the baby powder, I squeezed some onto my hand and rubbed it on her cheeks. The two of us giggled. I missed the sound of her.

Osita argued with someone in the corridor. I called out to him, but there was no response. Instead, the bedroom door opened and Mama entered with a woman.

'Oya, Sister Mgbeke, hurry up.' Mama pushed the woman toward me.

'Sista, take am easy. Softly, softly, now. Put your leg for ground,' Sister Mgbeke said as she advanced.

Mama stepped up to the bed and pinned my legs down. The two of them dragged me to the edge and Sister Mgbeke eased her right arm under my thighs. I resisted feebly, my strength draining under their hands, but certain that whatever it took I would not let them take me. Then, in one deft move, Sister Mgbeke gripped her arm tightly around my waist and pulled me off the bed, sending us both into a faltering dive. She stepped quickly back on one foot, momentarily trusting the weight of our two bodies to the pulsating muscles threading her lower leg before letting me slide to the floor.

'Chineke, Aunty, wetin we go do now? You must-to help me, I no fit carry am like baby,' Sister Mgbeke appealed to Mama.

A door slammed. Voices rose in the hallway. People hung in the doorway, looking in at us. Two women stepped out from the crowd, came up to the bed, and propped me between them.

'The Lord has made a great miracle today. Let us welcome our sister into the bosom of the Lord!' Pastor Olode appeared at the bedroom door, shaking a yellow raffia tasseled staff in my direction.

I understood, then. Fear rooted me and I tried to give voice to the words in my head. 'Is...I...help me,' words lurched from my mouth as everything spread and I bore down. My legs buckled and I fell to the floor.

Faces crowded around me, arms pulled me forward. Negotiations took place as voices suggested I be seated, and others insisted I kneel before Pastor.

Dark forms rose and took shape in the room where I lay. A door, walls, chair. I saw that my arm was connected to a drip. Gingerly, I touched the flattened dome of my belly. Then I flexed my feet, willing my toes to move. It took a while.

I lifted the curtain behind me and twisted to one side. A haze of burnished orange-gold spread over the compound and the clinic's buildings and grounds glowed strangely. In the sky, magenta-tinted slivers streaked the deepening twilight.

The door opened. Osita stood there, framed by a halo of light from the corridor bulb. He held his arms out to me and walked forward. At the bed, he bent over me and said, 'Witch, killer of my children.'

In that moment, I saw nothing. Then Osita pushed a basin under my face, thrusting it in every direction I turned, until I couldn't escape the small body, lying there with its umbilical cord twisted round its neck.

Ada Udechukwu is a writer and an artist. She has published short stories in The Atlantic Monthly, Callaloo, *and* PMS: Poem.Memoir.Story. *Her drawings, paintings and textiles have been exhibited in galleries in Nigeria and the United States.*

NDILEKA!

Kgaogelo Lekota

'Nomsa'

I cannot believe it, you know, I mean this just does not happen on these types of occasions. Today must be Christmas or I might just be dreaming, I think. I think to myself what about I move my hand a little bit. It shivers and I start to think about chicken livers. The sort that is tossed into red wine and cooked in some sort of a way. Still thinking my eyes roam around and I find a beautiful flower to look at absentmindedly. *It is a flower*, wow what a revelation, I believe; and I don't know what to call it. Maybe it has one of those Latin names like *lugubriouslytis beautyfulacko*. But I just don't know at all.

"What are you thinking about?"

I am quiet stunned, gob smacked that's more like it. A fumble of words follow and all of a suddenness my awareness is scarred. It doesn't want to admit it, the awareness that is. It keeps telling me to tell her that I am actually you see, thinking about chicken livers and flowers.

"You know I mean, sort of uhm... you are beautiful."

"You are so sweet"

My heart, as they say it in great romance novels like Mills & Boons to be precise, skips a beat.

"Ahhh look at that, he's blushing. You are so cute when you do that"; just as it, the heart, prepares for another attempt she finishes the sentence with, "my friend."

Eish I am disgusted, flabbergasted you name it. I almost say to her I did not bring you all the way here from one of those Dunwell flats to the fishpond for you to tell me that I'm your friend. But my blushing gets the better of me and my mouth betrays me and with a perpetual intermittent cute smile I say, "the pleasure is all yours."

I look at her once again and I can't help myself but admire her money eyes. She smiles at me and I blurb it out, "Ndileka, you're rich."

"What did you say?"

"I mean yours, eish your eyes are like Shuttleworth, the works I promise you. They are worth billions."

"You don't stop talking rubbish wena neh. 'Nomsa' you haven't changed at all."

"Jahman, hows tings," he greets.

"Aya, biig tings r bout to b gwan king," I respond. Anyways, my moment of glory is ruined. He must just go to Mens Res and watch DSTV or something, play with himself even. Hopefully he will get it. But then again he drives his brothers black RUN-X and most importantly he can afford Debonaires pizzas five times a lecture week. This is a man that pays for meals at the dining hall, books all three per day and sometimes eats none of the meals and still he doesn't complain. Money smells good, he smells good therefore it's hard for the girls to not notice.

He sits down slowly and deliberately as if he is sitting on eggs. I need a gun, somebody somewhere lend me a gun! Clearly he did not get my hint but patience killed no cat.

"Jahman r u gwan b hittin da Babylon H-two-O?" My last attempt, hopefully this will divert his attention.

This short, fat, dark, privileged, previously disadvantaged façade of a man declines. You know it's a disadvantage being a continuously disadvantaged peoples. I look at my Ndileka and I see that she is oblivious to my struggle. I look at Fat-joe on the other hand and I see the inevitable. He is going to make a move, I can see it. What he doesn't know is that a dying horse kicks like it is dead. I prepare my intellectual weaponry, lets go it's time for war.

"Eh ntwana what you think of the transformation discourse hie mo Wits?" I'm thinking, here's my opportunity. "Don't you think the skeletonised issue here is the cantankerous dichotomy it represents? Or maybe it is the deep soporific chasms it forms aptly at the conjecture that deconstructs this whole deductive philosophy acrobatically generally also."

"Yah, cats like you should think about that, you know what I'm saying G. Don't get me wrong Jahman. I'm deep. I'm conscious. That is I'm consciously into chicks see," he guffaws, caw-caw-caw.

In a split second I think geez man that's a mouthful. Ndileka laughs too. I've lost. With no rebbutal I have no choice. I join in too. Maybe it pays to be an idiot, after all. Idiots get all the chicks, intellectuals have the PIG(the Post-Graduate drinking hole). Eish Ndiks, eish Ndiks my heart, my heart pours tsunamis. Tsunamis that wash, wash your smile making its whites whiter and its blues super blue. Eish your surf super blue smile where did you get it? That's what I am going to say to her. *Phela* she is my woman of platinum, gold and honey. My night in shining corrugated iron. Ndileka my baby powder, the fire in my mind is jealous of you. My queen of milk of magnesia; oh my Durban star no rose grows for you in Soweto but alas in Rosebank specifically named after you. I bow in your shadow and sweat, gosh you are so hot.

A pinch...

"Ouch!" I'm jolted and she smiles at me.

"Listen sweety"

God she didn't say that with a smile on her face *nogal*.

"I need to visit the loo, will I find you here?"

"Of course I'm not going anywhere", I say.

Ndileka

I need a breadth of fresh hair. Men! I don't know why they have to do this. I look at him and he's always smiling like the motion of a seagull swooping over the Atlantic. He takes me on my wings, this shy thing. Well then again I would say he gives me that sweet tasting chocolate feeling when my mind is somewhere else. Oh I like him; I mean the brother has it in his smile. Oh I like him, but why do men take such a long time to say what's on their minds. I mean especially the ones you happen to like.

Take for instance this guy that I like. We were sitting perfectly talking about nothing that matters. We weren't being deep at all but in a way we were. It's amazing how something that is so simple can turn out to be so complex and something that is complex turns out to be so simple. I should have said vice versa there. That would have been simple enough to master. So there he was, being sweet and all. Smiling and sounding like a mid morning breeze maybe. Sweeping my roots high up into the air. His eyes showing that flair that fires his passion constantly, I don't know how he does it. His every movement, his gestures; it is almost as if he was in a trance, stuttering, you know when your eyes are shut except the not, the light hits your retina but your brain refuses to register it, it happens like a movie that you are watching but you hear nothing like one of Pastor Morris's sermons on a hot Sunday afternoon when you think about nothing at all, basically it's as if you are sleeping with your eyes open, you are drinking without pouring the liquids down your throat, you are smiling but your face is in anger mode, you are walking but your feet

HE TAKES ME ON MY WINGS, THIS SHY THING.

are rooted at one spot, you are laughing but your mouth is not responding, sounds like a bad dream when I think about it but that doesn't matter, what matters is that time seems to drag out and you forget that you are supposed to be concentrating on a beautiful soul that is trying to pour it's heart out to you; sometimes I wonder what goes on, in men's minds.

You know, Pastor Morris once said that he feels quite sad when he sees couples fighting, breaking up, divorcing and what-not, I mean have you ever wondered how sacred a sacred marriage is? Why are we constantly seeking partners? Why God put us here on earth to love people? For one I am conscious about saying yes to a guy I don't even know. Even those that I do know, you know. Men are always thinking about sex. 'This one and that one is tight and if ever, I get her I am the man', type of thing. Don't dare say I am wrong. You know that I am right. One day, he comes along and says, '"hi!'

He says that you are looking quite suave, like Venus before the sun rises, just before the red, orange and pink coalesce into a natural blue of the waking sky. He continues to say that you bring all things natural, bright and jubilant to his artificial day. One guy said that to me by the way, not in so many words though, the way he smiled at me did the trick, my black brother. One who says plenty but speaks nothing. He seems to be that exception in life, to all the rules that govern your heart. That ticket to your first night out, your first date, your first kiss. By the way you've had plenty smooches but he makes things new. He seems to know that you are screaming inside for restoration. So he entertains you. Speaks his own language to the tune of your soul. Plucks the strings of your guitar without touching it. He is diversely happy in your hidden joy. Sometimes you wonder if it was ever meant to be. One minute you are happy and the next you take a wrong turn and you are sad. Maybe that's what Pastor Morris meant. Love can be a dangerous business or game, you know. You never know. I don't even know if I should ask you for advice. I mean what would you do? Sometimes I just want to fall from a tall building somewhere in Braamfontein or on campus, just because... I don't know really. Just because I want to, I suppose. It's organic, you know, falling for someone. It feels good but is it worth it? It's all, emotional isn't it? I don't know why I am thinking about all this. It's like a deep, yet cold yet simple feeling. It caves in when the good times roll, when there is joy and jubilation, when the sun shines twenty four hours a day, when the bird sings without chirping to ones soul. The question is will that ever happen? Will one ever get to that point where one feels that I love and I am being loved? Will that time ever come?

Maybe it's chronic, something that you need to live with, and something that you need to accept. But why am I falling in love when I don't want to? I really don't want to. I have seen them all, especially in my family. Some get pregnant because they want to keep their men. The less said about them the better. It's about the feeling I suppose. The feeling that you get when all you can think about is him. What he is going to say when he sees you, how you are going to act when he does say something and you act like you are not interested. Later you kick yourself, you know, I mean here is this guy that you've wanted always and that opportunity flies by, gone with the wind. Maybe you might as well call yourself Scarlet 'O Hara and go with the wind.

'N omsa'

This is difficult, 'Of course I'm not going anywhere', why did I say that? I could go with her, you know. But then I would need to invent a need to go to toilet also. Then again the prospect of drunkard's left-overs on the toilet floorslike vomit and not forgetting the number two aroma just to impress Ndiks, hm nah it's a bit embarrassing. Besides sitting here and admiring the pond can buy me time. I remember the first time I came here...

"Ndileka, I can't let a hot chick like you walk to the Matrix alone. Besides I think you need a drink to cool off. Hot chicks need a coke or something to be cool sometimes. Get it, *hayi sonnie* I'm going to release an album called, hot chicks like Ndileka *baya baleka* mix tape."

Without a word, they go. I suppose she cannot resist. I'm broke he's not. I take her to the fish pond for a date. He begins at the Matrix and then they might end up at a Mugg & Bean for a cup of coffee in the northern suburbs. Revolting isn't it? Disgusting. A cup of coffee. Millions are starving out there and people are buying cups of coffee. Maybe I'm stretching it a bit but you get my point don't you?

I check my watch and its seven *op die kop*. She doesn't like to miss 'Generations'. It is quite possible that she would give up everything including her own bones for that soapy. But you know, I have to do it. Tell her that I am mindless without her. My heart pumps water without the red stuff when I don't hear her voice. Ndileka I hope you can hear me as you take a dump. I wonder how it smells though but I think I loved you before I was born. I think we are meant to be.

There's a slight breeze now. Ndileka is not making her way back. Maybe she's dumping mountains up in there, excuse my Chinese, I mean it can't possibly take a normal human being this long to empty their intestines. This makes me feel uncomfortable and speaking of which, my butt feels as wooden as the benches I'm sitting on. Maybe I should check out what the fish are up to. Eish my butt feels like a washing plank and my back hurts. Bad omen; bad backs, women and planks equals disaster I tell you.

I walk over to the fishpond. The fish are dancing, playing games otherwise they're just darting about. Some may be even asking out women fish down there. Like hey, (what's a babe in Fishese?) anyway like hey *mtwana* your big bad eyes make my gills to breathe oxygen. Then maybe the female fish says to the male; you are too orange for my liking and you eat too much, besides between you and a shark I'd rather be eaten by a shark.

I wonder if they actually get thirsty. Then they would have to drink water they piss and fart in but then again they must be thinking the same about us. I mean we breathe air that we piss and fart in, that sort of thing. You know what I mean? But that's not the least of my worries right now. How am I going to tell her?

My plan must have been too rigid. I don't know what else could go wrong. Not considering outside factors like Sipho can be a major downfall. He is clearly interested and I really don't know what to do about him. All the solutions I can come up with are illegal. Besides they need money which I don't have. The fish won't give me a solution unless one of them is poisonous. Feed him poisonous fish, that's it.

I check the contents of my bag. In it there's a yellow rose that was supposed to smooth my way into Ndileka's heart. I bought it at Campus Square earlier today, might as well feed it to the fish. You know but what must a guy do? I mean it happens to me all the time. You buy gifts. You pick flowers on flower beds that are not your own and leave them, the flowers, at their doorsteps. Any time they need you are up and about just for them. then it just so happens that Steve Lekoelea is on campus in his RAV 4 or S3 parked at Sunnyside and the girl you're trying to impress looses her mind. Oh my god she says, she goes nuts and leaves you in her room and you think God, what must I do? I'm there everyday and he pitches once in every three months and the girl goes crazy. She even asks you to go fetch a fruit pack for her. That's because she won't be coming back for supper. You do it diligently. Breakfast the next day you look for her in the dining hall because you want to give her, her fruit pack. You think agh shame she is probably hungry, she's not in her room, so yoghurt and an apple would give her a perfect start to the day. You don't dare call her because you know what she might be doing. You don't even think about that. So you send her an SMS:

HAV UR FRUITPAK WHER R U?

Your fingers tremble but you manage to send it. MESSAGE SENT, your phone blinks and makes you see that envelope that disappears into a post box. Balance check: YOU HAVE R0.01 IN YOUR ACCOUNT. Two hours later she replies:

PLS CALL ME

Damn, the last two rands, in your pockets, suddenly feels heavily unremovable. Phone call or two loose ciggies. Fourteen times four seconds worth of airtime at a public phone or two highs. Against your better judgement you call. Voice mail, 'leave a message', you leave it. You've got fifty cents left but just as you put the phone down, it vanishes, your last fifty gone to the public fone vendor.. Life sucks doesn't it?

"I'm da shiznit son. You better recognize playa. That girl of yours", a long pause and repetitive nodding of the head, sweet-Jesus that punk is back!

"is comin to the movies with me son. Goin for a French shower be right back aight. You should come, come to big papa for some lessons not those fish, they wont teach you ish. *Yesses* that's a rhyme. *Ah mara di bra van jou, o dese ma bra!* I should give you lessons *ntwana*. Oh by the way, if she asks you, don't come. Three's a company and a shagless night for me, you dig?"

I shrug. Defeat.

"Sure boss. She's all yours", I bellow in a low baritone. I'm not irie... Jah is not on my side.

"A tip from the master chief. All you need is money not lurv, you dig? I'm gonna get laid, I'm gonna get laid", he carries on like a four year old with his first ice cream, titillating his friends who don't have it. Sipho then saunters away with a grotesque, Quasimodo-walk.

"Me don need dat *kak* talk from Babylon trash like you, you overstand! You... you... downpresser you! Bumma clad you! you, you batty boy you!"

I stand up with the intent to do grievous bodily harm and a firm attempt to commit murder as well. But I'm subdued by soft touch from nowhere. I hear some voice, a distant whisper through my anger. It is as if it says 'forgive him father for he knows not what he knows not what he is knowing'.

"Leave him, I'm not going anywhere, I'm here now. There's no need to fight." Is it my queen? Is it you? him Selasie I the first, is great.

The silence begins. It is long. Drags out the word elastically itself. The stars come out silently vanishing and appearing in this golden moment, momentarily. Dreamily, the flowers breezily slow down motion like a simile, happily. Goosebumps conquer my skin wearily. They defy the coolness of night intermittently. Well the fish, they're another story, that happens without taking place, maybe it is quite corny; that I am here, she is here and she is...agh I must tell her. Tell her now. Now is the time. the time to tell her... pause...silence...heartbeat...one...two...three.

"Ndileka I, I, esih uhm you know?"

"Know what?"

Damn she knows. Must I whip out the rose now? No wait! It's not perfect yet.

"Eish if you only knew how much I hate Sipho..."

"I know", she fidgets.

Bad sign for me, I'm not going to do this but it looks like she's expecting something. You know, for me to say something profound and romantic. Damn I don't know why I mentioned Sipho. I messed it up. It's now or never.

"Listen Ndileka I've been moaning, eish I meant meaning to say..eish"

"Shh don't say anymore, you'll torture yourself", she leans over until her breath moves my eardrums and she sings me a whispered song.

Kgaogelo Lekota is a visual artist, poet, and writer of many stories and plays. He currently works as an administrative officer at the Wits Writing Centre at the University of the Witwatersand, in Johannesburg.

PARABLE
OF THE LION'S
HEAD

Samdi Lazarus Musu

From the ceilings, the cupboards, the barns, the holes in the ground, rats were scurrying out of town, away from all human habitation. Cats should be seen making no effort to catch any of them. One could hear dogs howling all over the town under the cover of darkness.

Help! Help! Help!!! The whole town reverberated with cries for help almost at once. The time? A second past midnight, December 31, 1999 – a day those who believe the world would end this century have long waited for. A man had been transformed into a two-ton elephant, his bed had collapsed under his weight, leaving his screaming wife in total confusion amidst the wreckage. In another house, a newly married couple who had slept in a tight embrace after hours of love-making woke up to a rude shock; the woman had been transformed into a big python and the almost choked her man to death in her new vice-like embrace.

By daybreak the next day, all families worldwide had one or two members who had turned into animals. Those living near the sea ran and jumped into it. But alas! They couldn't escape, many of them became fish, others became part-fish, part-human: they developed appendages like gills and fins, their bodies became slimy and in place of lungs they now had swim bladders, and gills in place of cheeks. Others became part-woman and part-frog. One of the world's fashion models became a human frog; her head, face, eyes and mouth were those of a frog and she had a pair of frog's legs to match. She now hopped around, preferring wet shady places like river banks, where she stuck out her long sticky tongue to catch all kinds of insects for food.

What had happened was quite normal. This was a spiral, and humanity had just stepped into the past. We were starting all over again at a lower rung of our evolutionary ladder just to re-learn things we had forgotten.

Somehow humanity adapted to this great change much faster than expected, and all animals, irrespective of whether they had once been human or not, could now talk and humans could understand them clearly. Since everybody is used to having at least one member of his or her family be an animal, nothing seemed strange anymore. One could see a snake kissing a woman passionately and winding itself around her, a dog riding a bicycle on a major highway, canaries broadcasting programmes on the World Service, donkeys conducting songs at choirs, baboons driving buses in which the passengers were a mixture of people and animals.

Meal times were now very interesting. Women whose husbands were now snakes brought home rats and rabbits after intense negotiations with other rats and rabbits in the open market. One could also find humans on sale as food for lions, tigers and hyenas, who took humans for their food every day in a trade by barter. No animal was more important than another; a perfect understanding between two-legged creatures such as humans and birds and various four-legged creatures was now in place.

Not even the United Nations Secretary General was spared; he too had been transformed into a two-horned rhino. His wife now took him to graze in a food plain near his new home in the Amazon jungles. He had become an avid grass-eater and a wallower too; he delighted in immersing himself in mud and stagnant water during the hotter parts of the day to lower his body temperature while thinking about solutions to the numerous crises the world over. His wife kept an eye on him all day long as he grazed or wallowed to protect him from people who would shoot him and use his horns for an aphrodisiac.

Studying animals and chatting with them was now a favourite pastime. The perspective of humans who were now animals had undergone a profound change. They were now giving other humans good advice. Even animal aggression was now another kind of lesson to humans. Birds, after scolding and flapping in an angry prelude to battle, would settle their differences by turning furiously to nest building. When puppies were scrapping, if one was triumphant and tried to carry his victory to the point of damaging the other, the mother immediately cuffed him into neutrality, teaching him to respect the defeat of his brother. Warlords from different countries now spent time learning these valuable lessons. This seemed to have had a sobering effect on them, making most of them vow from then on that rather than kill their opponents as was usually the case, they would engage in dialogue.

Sometimes world leaders would gather and try to predict the reactions of different animals to different situations. The animals almost always put them to shame. Yesterday, a lion killed a zebra. They gathered, watching and debating; some said the lion was going to eat everything and if anything remained, the lion would bury it; that it wouldn't let other animals have a taste. Others said if the lion ate to its fill and anything remained, the hyena would drag it to its cave and eat up everything alone. But something happened that shocked all the humans watching. The lion ate to its fill and didn't even look at what remained, just turned and left. Next came the hyena; it ate up the zebra's testicles, picked a few big bones here and there while the scavengers (vultures) were jumping excitedly but didn't come near. Next came the jackal and his cousin, the fox, and after a loud laugh they both settled on the animals intestines while the vultures waited patiently.

A former statesman went to one of the vultures and asked how it could just stand and watch all other animals consume the best parts of the dead zebra. The vulture laughed first and then replied:

'Oh, we all have choices. The last scraps of meat are easier to swallow. I have no teeth to tear large chunks of flesh, and I am not even bothered about that. I eat just what I need'.

The statesman looked at the vulture and shook his head. 'But you need to hide some for yourself and your family when your belly is full', he said.

'No, I don't need to hide what is not mine; that is theft. The moment I started that behaviour all other animals would adopt it. Even the lion when next he kills another zebra would refuse all of us taking our share. That is human behavior, not ours. We animals don't behave like that! We do things with clearly defined motives. We are not greedy, we don't kill for fun. We kill only when we are provoked or when we need to eat what we have killed. You humans are worse than us. You should be put in zoos for us to look at you. Anyway, many of you are already doing that to yourselves. You build houses with high walls complete with electrified barbed wire, not against us but against your fellow humans. Isn't it a shame that one of you can single-handedly steal what is meant for a million people? Can you consume all you have stolen in your lifetime?'

The statesman remembered the money meant for the disaster relief fund that he had embezzled, on account of which 5000 people died in a refugee camp. He refused to answer the vulture's questions. He walked away, leaving it to savour the last piece of the zebra's entrails.

Meanwhile, in spite of the fact that more than half of humanity were now animals, this did not prevent the emergence of a strong dictatorship in one African nation; perhaps because of that everyone in that country became an animal. Not even a single human being remained there, unlike the other nations. The dictator himself became a lion while his victims (his people) became sheep, goats, or cows, except for several journalists and writers who became parrots. The dictator started his reign of terror by first eating all the parrots. After eating all the parrots, the lion-dictator was afflicted with a terrible hunger. He started eating his friends amongst the other animals – the cows, sheep and goats.

The animals took to organizing themselves and devising methods to protect themselves, but even that didn't help them. Their leaders had betrayed them; they, too, were now eating fellow cows, sheep and goats. No one could trust the other. They found each other's meat delicious the moment they tasted the blood of their kind. The predator teamed up with the 'predatee' to wreak havoc on the rest of the animals until none remained. The lion now turned to the leaders and said:

'Select amongst yourelves who I should eat when next I am hungry.'

This request came as a shock, but there was nothing they could do. They then caught a cow and sacrificed it that day, the next day a sheep, then a goat. But the lion's hunger became more severe with each animal sacrificed until it had eaten all the animals except a young sheep which had refused to cooperate with the other animals in anything involving the lion.

He had taken it upon himself to protect himself, moving out only at night to graze and then going to the bottom of the water fall to drink cool water before dawn, effectively dodging the lion. The lion had for long known about the existence of this sheep but did not know how to deceive it and finally eat it up like all the others. It had never seen the sheep in the daytime before to know exactly where he hid.

It rained heavily one night, making it difficult for the sheep to come out and graze at midnight as usual, so he waited till dawn for the rain to abate. The sheep started grazing at dawn, the grass was lush, green and very tasty; it kept eating without lifting its head, not even noticing the sunrise until all was bright. It then went down to the foot of the waterfall to drink as usual. At the top of the waterfall the lion had come for a drink too.

He looked down, saw the sheep and roared:

'Hey, young sheep, you are polluting this waterfall with bits of grass from your dirty mouth.'

'But... but.. Sir, you are drinking from the source up there, and I am down here drinking. I should be accusing you of polluting the water for me down here, not you accusing me up there'.

The lion was outraged. He had to change his accusation to something more plausible if he were to succeed in deceiving the sheep until it swallowed the bait and got eaten.

'You insulted me two years ago and refused to apologise,' the lion roared.

'But I am only eight months. I am not even up to one year in age. Look at my teeth sir, I can count them for you,' the sheep pleaded.

'Then it must be your elder brother, a white sheep with black spots around its ears like you,' the lion roared desperately. He was getting impatient.

'My mother died during my birth, I am an only child,' the sheep said

The lion fell silent and went into a deep meditation for a few moments before finally coming up with a new strategy. It had occurred to the lion that to control someone's perception of reality is the greatest power an individual can exert over another. He smiled and continued:

'I am pleased to hear that you are an only child, and a clever one, I must confess! You are the only sheep capable of reconciling all lions and sheep both dead and alive, so that all lions will stop eating all sheep the world over.'

The sheep felt that was going to be a great contribution. He felt he was on the threshold of doing something really great.

'How can that be achieved, sir?' the sheep asked in a rejuvenated tone.

'Oh, that is simple,' the lion replied. 'All you need to do is just say to me: 'I accept the guilt of all insults heaped by all sheep worldwide on lions in the past, now and in the future, and I'm ready to shake hands with my brother the lion in total reconciliation."

'Is that all you want me to say and do?'

'Oh yes, that's all,' replied the lion

The sheep felt this was just an innocent and simple apology costing nothing.

'I am guilty,' the sheep admitted, 'and I accept all the guilt of my ancestors worldwide.'

'Wonderful! Come forward, my friend and let's seal it through a handshake that will forever change the course of history; you are indeed a clever sheep, come forward please,' the lion purred.

The sheep climbed up the hill to meet the lion; when the lion saw the sheep coming, it started clapping its hands and singing praise songs!

'You courageous sheep, you great king of sheep, this handshake will confirm your greatness.'

The proud sheep came close and extended its forelimb for the historic handshake; almost instantly the smile on the lion's face disappeared.

One has a way of knowing he or she has come face to face with death at times. At that point, you just let go and allow nature to return you to your eternal roots; so it was for the sheep. He was too frightened even to bleat loudly, but had to, when the lion severed its limb from the rest of its body with a deep bite. The second bite separated the sheep's head from its neck. The lion then went to that same water source it had accused the sheep of polluting to wash its bloody mouth.

Something happened after this last meal; the lion's hunger increased a hundred-fold. It roared from dusk to dawn until it finally turned on itself. It started on its leg by first eating the fore limbs; the moment it tasted its own blood the hunger increased a million-fold and it devoured its own entrails and all; leaving only its head.

Not only the victims of dictatorship are in danger, but the dictator himself knows he can fall any day, any time, anywhere.

Samdi Lazarus Musa *is a Nigerian writer. He dedicates this story to Ken Saro Wiwa.*

Africa Centre for Open Governance

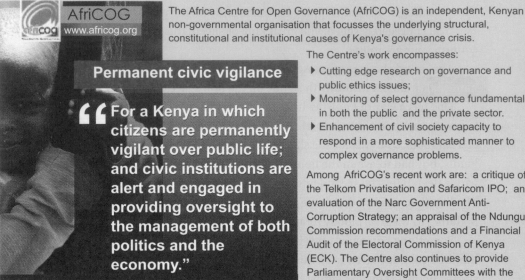

AfriCOG
www.africog.org

The Africa Centre for Open Governance (AfriCOG) is an independent, Kenyan non-governmental organisation that focusses the underlying structural, constitutional and institutional causes of Kenya's governance crisis.

Permanent civic vigilance

" **For a Kenya in which citizens are permanently vigilant over public life; and civic institutions are alert and engaged in providing oversight to the management of both politics and the economy.**"

Sheema Court, Kasuku Road,
(Off Lenana Road, next to CVS Plaza)
P.O Box 18157-00100, Nairobi, Kenya.
Tel: +254 20 2723031; 0737 463166; Fax: 2714675
admin@africog.org

The Centre's work encompasses:

▸ Cutting edge research on governance and public ethics issues;
▸ Monitoring of select governance fundamentals in both the public and the private sector.
▸ Enhancement of civil society capacity to respond in a more sophisticated manner to complex governance problems.

Among AfriCOG's recent work are: a critique of the Telkom Privatisation and Safaricom IPO; an evaluation of the Narc Government Anti-Corruption Strategy; an appraisal of the Ndungu Commission recommendations and a Financial Audit of the Electoral Commission of Kenya (ECK). The Centre also continues to provide Parliamentary Oversight Committees with the background research on various topical issues. Additionally, the Centre facilitates Kenyans for Peace with Truth & Justice (KPTJ) and the Movement for Political Accountability (MOPA).

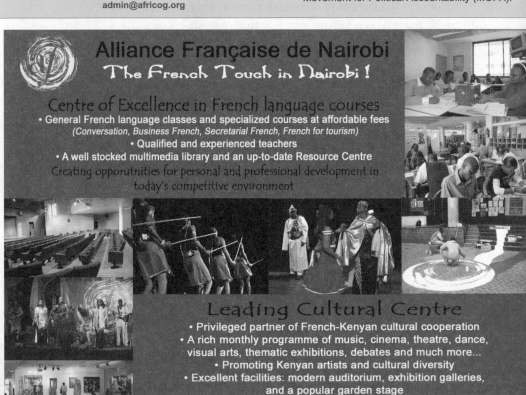

Alliance Française de Nairobi
The French Touch in Nairobi !

Centre of Excellence in French language courses
• General French language classes and specialized courses at affordable fees
(Conversation, Business French, Secretarial French, French for tourism)
• Qualified and experienced teachers
• A well stocked multimedia library and an up-to-date Resource Centre
Creating opporutnities for personal and professional development in today's competitive environment

Leading Cultural Centre
• Privileged partner of French-Kenyan cultural cooperation
• A rich monthly programme of music, cinema, theatre, dance, visual arts, thematic exhibitions, debates and much more...
• Promoting Kenyan artists and cultural diversity
• Excellent facilities: modern auditorium, exhibition galleries, and a popular garden stage

Loita/Monrovia streets, P.O Box 45475, 00100 Nairobi, Kenya
Tel: +254 20 34 00 54/79, Fax: +254 20 31 52 07
Email: info@alliancefrnairobi.org

24 Nairobi, the first exploration of the sense and sensibility of place by a mixed generation, multi-cultural group of creative professionals who call Nairobi home.

They are travelling the fault lines in a city of blends. Through the project, the team shall dig into the place that is the city.

Gritty, realistic imaginative and stimulating outcome is expected framed against a time formula that reveals the city's distinct character: Dawn. Day. Dusk. Night.

Taking a look at the myriad angles through journeys of writers, photographers, technical artists and others who will take Nairobi apart with their imagination.

24 Nairobi is a collection of photos and writings that will be exhibited at the Nairobi Museum to show, on the 24nairobi.com website to share and in a coffeetable book to keep.

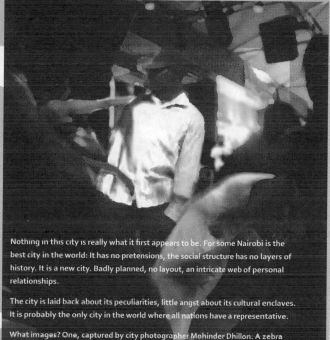

Nothing in this city is really what it first appears to be. For some Nairobi is the best city in the world: It has no pretensions, the social structure has no layers of history. It is a new city. Badly planned, no layout, an intricate web of personal relationships.

The city is laid back about its peculiarities, little angst about its cultural enclaves. It is probably the only city in the world where all nations have a representative.

What images? One, captured by city photographer Mohinder Dhillon. A zebra crossing a zebra crossing in Nairobi.

It is a city with secrets, surprise and unexpectedness.

WRITE FOR KWANI

Submission Guidelines

Kwani Trust is dedicated to collecting and promoting the work of African writers, known and unknown, and encourages submissions. Our editorial panel normally has two reading periods each year. If you would like to contribute, please follow the guidelines below:

- We prefer email submissions. Please attach your work as a word document (*.doc) or in Rich Text Format (*.rtf) instead of pasting it into the body of the email.
- Use double spacing and Times New Roman font, size 12 on a plain white background (no colour please).
- The document should be paginated and have left and right margins of at least 1" (one inch).
- We do not consider unsolicited photography or art.

While the content of our journal is generally reflective of the Kenyan cultural scene, we do accept, at the discretion of the editors, stories from non-Kenyan spaces that fit our profile. We prefer to work with unpublished material, but are willing to publish exceptional pieces that have not yet been published in Kenya.

We request first time Kenyan rights from our writers, as well as one time web rights. If we do publish your work, the work may be published elsewhere one month after publication in Kwani?.

Please note that due to the large volume of work received, we are unable to respond to all submissions individually.

If submitting your work via email, send it to submissions@kwani.org.

If you are unable to send your work via email, you may deliver it to our offices at:
2nd Floor, Savla Plaza
Mogotio Road, Westlands
Nairobi

Postal submissions can also be sent to:
Submissions Editor
Kwani Trust
P.O. Box 2895
Nairobi
00100

www.kwani.org

YASUYOSHI CHIBA

64

64

68

71

125

130

143

143

143

143

143

176

177

182

183

183

192

193

202

203

240

58

206-207

240

184-185

210

246

224

213

247

295

219

293

295

239

294

294

TOM OTIENO

49

63

235

54

167-168

291

57

225

OTHER KWANI TRUST TITLES

Kwani? 01 (ISBN: 9966-9836-0-0)
Kwani? 02 (ISBN: 9966-9836-2-7)
Kwani? 03 (ISBN: 9966-9836-4-3)
Kwani? 04 (ISBN: 9966-9836-6-X)
Kwani? 05, Part 1 (ISBN: 9966-7182-1-4)

Kwani? Series
Chimamanda Adichie -*Half Of a Yellow Sun* (ISBN: 9966-9836-8-6)
Chimamanda Adichie -*Purple Hibiscus* (ISBN: 9966-9836-9-4)
Joseph Muthee -*Kizuizini* (ISBN: 9966-9836-7-8)
Billy Kahora-*The True Story of David Munyakei* (ISBN: 9966-7008-9-7)

Kwanini? Series
Binyavanga Wainaina -*Discovering Home* (ISBN: 9966-7008-4-6)
Binyavanga Wainaina -*Beyond River Yei* (ISBN: 9966-7008-7-0)
Binyavanga Wainaina -*How To Write About Africa* (ISBN: 9966-7008-2-X)
Yvonne Adhiambo Owour -*Weight of Whispers* (ISBN: 9966-7008-3-8)
Chimamanda Adichie -*You In America* (ISBN: 9966-7008-0-3)
Wambui Mwangi -*Internally Misplaced* (ISBN: 9966-7008-8-9)
Mzee Ondego -*The Life of Mzee Ondego* (ISBN: 9966-7182-0-6)
CKW -*Kwanini Special Edition* (ISBN: 9966-7008-1-1)
Parselelo Kantai -*The Cock Thief* (ISBN: 9966-7008-6-2)
Richard Onyango -*The Life and Times of Richard Onyango* (ISBN: 9966-7008-5-4)

SPEND LESS TIME IN QUEUES

✉
12AB345 Confirmed.
KShs. 4500 sent to
Safaricom Postpaid
for Account
0722123456

You can now pay your
Postpaid bill via M-PESA.

The Better Option.

M-PESA **YOUR**ADVANTAGE
SAFARICOM PERSONAL POSTPAID

Safaricom